A REASON TO HOPE

Books by the same author

about Christianity

GOD'S CROSS IN OUR WORLD
THE LAST THINGS NOW
RELIGION AND CHANGE
WHAT IS REAL IN CHRISTIANITY?
GOOD NEWS IN ACTS
JESUS FOR MODERN MAN
A KEY TO THE OLD TESTAMENT
WHAT ANGLICANS BELIEVE

about the life of the Church

NOT ANGELS BUT ANGLICANS
THIS CHURCH OF ENGLAND
MOVEMENTS INTO TOMORROW
A HISTORY OF THE KING'S SCHOOL, CANTERBURY
F. J. SHIRLEY, AN EXTRAORDINARY HEADMASTER
IAN RAMSEY, BISHOP OF DURHAM
ST. MARGARET'S, WESTMINSTER
THE BRITISH CHURCHES TURN TO THE FUTURE
LEADERS OF THE CHURCH OF ENGLAND, 1828-1978

A REASON TO HOPE

David L. Edwards

COLLINS
1978

Published by Collins
London · Glasgow
Cleveland · New York · Toronto
Sydney · Auckland · Johannesburg

The quotation from *Religion in Four Dimensions* by
Walter Kaufman on p. 62 is reprinted with permission of the
publisher, Reader's Digest Press. © 1976 in all countries
of the International Copyright Union by
Walter Kaufman.
The quotation from *Meditation and Piety in the Far East*
by K. L. Reichelt on p. 63 is reprinted with permission of
the publisher, Harper & Row.

First published in Great Britain 1978

UK ISBN 0 00 215582 6

© David L. Edwards 1978

First published in the USA 1978
Library of Congress Catalog Card Number 78-56996
USA ISBN 0-529-05620-8

Made and printed in Great Britain by
William Collins Sons & Co Ltd Glasgow

*To Billy and Pierre Collins
Christian publishers
and the friends of many authors*

CONTENTS

Preface ... 9

Part One

A WINDOW OPEN

1 An Englishman Notices a Revolution ... 13
2 A Religious Response ... 22

Part Two

NOT A FLUKE BUT A PURPOSE

1 Our Failure of Nerve ... 31
2 A Strange Universe ... 33
3 A Home for Life ... 40
4 Science and Religion ... 55
5 A View of the Creation ... 65
6 A Choice for This Generation ... 75

Part Three

NOT DOOM BUT LIBERATION

1 Are We Doomed? ... 83
2 A Hope ... 91
3 Zero Growth? ... 104
4 The Self-Preservation of the Rich ... 111
5 The Self-Liberation of the Poor ... 130
6 Man's Decision ... 140

Part Four

NOT MARXISM BUT EUROPE

1 Conserving Socialism ... 149
2 The Appeal of Marxism ... 156

3	The Reality of Marxism	162
4	A Marxist Britain?	169
5	What Europe Means	175
6	What Europe Offers	183

Part Five

NOT DOGMA BUT RESPONSE

1	A Response to Life	191
2	The God above Idols	200
3	The Christ above Doctrine	208
4	The Church above Decline	218
5	The Rock above Nations	232
6	New Acts of God	243
	Index	247

PREFACE

At present, is hope reasonable? Is the future at all attractive? I have written this book for those who, like me, ask such questions not only about their private wishes but also about humanity's prospects.

Writing about the present and the near future is not so easy as it sounds. In comparison, writing history is child's play. So is writing about Utopia or (more fashionable nowadays) the long-range doom forecast. But I enjoy reading books which put together the puzzle of the age in which I have to live, and the supply of such books suggests that many fellow-readers share my interest. The point is, of course, that the detailed information which pours in one's direction from television, radio, newspapers, magazines and technical publications can easily leave one in a state of well-informed confusion or electronic indigestion. One learns immediately about a disaster on the other side of the world. The mood of the moment is as audible as the music of the week. But there is still a place for books which discuss the trends behind the news, called biblically the 'signs of the times'. It is the function of such books to say not something new but something true – and if the author fails in that very difficult enterprise, at least the reader may be irritated into thinking out what is the truth of the situation.

In the first part of the book I say something about why I have come to think that human life is not as pointless or as doomed as many of my contemporaries believe. If that opening seems egocentric, be assured that this is not an autobiography and I am scarcely mentioned in the book's other parts, which are really essays on some of the fears which haunt my generation.

I attempt to explore the alleged lack of meaning in the universe disclosed by science, and the next section is about the alleged hopelessness of the tasks facing both the rich and the poorer nations in our time. These, I think, are the great fears which have made so many of my generation lose their nerve.

Then I try to consider Marxism, writing as one who believes that the United States of Europe is for his country the only long-term alternative to Marxism. Finally I offer a chapter about religion, although the perspective from which I have viewed other subjects has been Christian. I do not think that there is a single, simple Christian view of our time. Indeed, I do not think that there is a single, simple Christianity in our time. What I do think is that, amid much confusion, religion matters in our time and religion is being changed like almost everything else in our time – an age which is so confusing because so creative. I believe in the God who at the present moment is acting on his usual magnificent scale. In the last analysis that is why I think that there is still in our time a reason to hope.

I am indebted to many whose books and talk have helped me, and in the course of my argument I make some suggestions for further reading; but I have not burdened this non-technical book with footnotes or a bibliography and I hope I may be forgiven for acknowledging only three debts here. One is to the *Church Times*, which under Bernard Palmer's editorship has made me think by asking for one or two articles on new books or current affairs each week. I am indebted to Westminster Abbey, which over seven and a half years gave me some leisure in which to read, with the politics of Britain on my doorstep. And although they are not to blame for my opinions, I am very grateful to the two Speakers of the House of Commons whom I served as Chaplain: Lord Selwyn-Lloyd and the Right Honourable George Thomas, M.P.

Quotations from the Bible are from the Good News Bible, published by the Bible Societies and William Collins in 1976.

The Deanery,
Norwich   D.L.E.

Part One
A WINDOW OPEN

1   An Englishman Notices a Revolution

Every view of where we are and what we have to hope for is personal. So I offer a brief explanation of how my view comes out of my life.

My father, like many other Englishmen, made his life in Egypt when that country was virtually a part of the British Empire. Born in 1929, I was sent to English schools chosen for their imperial connections. The first specialized in preparing boys for the Royal Navy, for at that stage I had a fantasy about myself as an admiral, another Nelson. My second school awarded a scholarship to sons of English civil servants in the colonies. It was the King's School, Canterbury.

One part of me took to all this. I actually wrote a history of the King's School – the oldest in England, since education has been conducted around Canterbury Cathedral since the seventh century. When he died I wrote a biography of my headmaster, F. J. Shirley, a great character of whom I was very fond. Having begun to enjoy England I raised no objection when I had to spend a couple of years in the British Army. Since then I have worked in one famous and established English place after another – in two of the most beautiful of the Oxford colleges; at the London church of St Martin-in-the-Fields; at King's College, Cambridge; and at Westminster Abbey. It has been my life to be a priest of the Church of England. And I treasure the memory's resulting pile of stones.

The breakwater at Port Said, stretching far into the Mediterranean. When I knew it, it was dominated by the statue of de Lesseps who had built the Suez Canal, as it turned out for Disraeli to buy for Queen Victoria. At night the quayside was floodlit as chains of labourers went up the gangways carrying the coal on to the ships which had already called at Gibraltar and Malta, to fuel them for their further voyages to India or Singapore or Australia. Near my colonial home in Cairo, the Sphinx.

The nave of Canterbury Cathedral: a forest of stone which

Chaucer's pilgrims must have watched being built. Above it Bell Harry Tower, one of the most assured (if also one of the last) constructions of the English Middle Ages. The Black Prince's Chapel down in the crypt, so much more lovely than his character.

Oxford: the cloisters of Magdalen College where I spent three years, close to the deer park and Addison's Walk by the river. The High: Macaulay said that it was an Englishman's worst fear to see a foreign army marching down that street. All Souls College: the candlelit table which introduced me to the worlds of politics and economics, the great library where some other young Fellows had been known to play cricket, the great lawn over which I sometimes walked after dinner with what Edward Gibbon called 'the brisk intemperance of youth'.

London's centre, Trafalgar Square: the stone lions, the living pigeons, the cascading fountains, the many demonstrations. And St Martin's church, elegantly classical. Its most famous vicar, Dick Sheppard, called it 'God's drawing room'. Into it – as I knew it, and since – would go many seeking the price of a cup of tea, or an escape from an addiction, or simply friendship in their loneliness. The vicar under whom I served, Austen Williams, has been for twenty-one years the heart of a great welcome, particularly to the young and the coloured; and over the years I have not forgotten his preaching of his vision.

A very different church, King's College Chapel: the top-hatted choristers processing to Evensong across the river and past the daffodils in the Cambridge Backs; the windows like radiant jewels when lit up from inside by the lamps for television; the day-long queues for the carol services; that miraculous vault which had to be cleaned because of the effects of candle smoke (in the 1960s!); the new arrangement of the East end to enable Rubens' *Adoration of the Magi* to be installed over the altar.

Westminster Abbey: the great church linked with the nation's story since 1065, the great congregation glowing with pleasure at a royal occasion, the pride around a new memorial in Poets' Corner, the international invasion of some three and a half million visitors a year, the silence early in the morning or at night. St Margaret's, the ancient parish church of Westminster which I have served as Rector: a church echoing like the Abbey itself with the history of nine centuries. The fourteenth-century Crypt Chapel down the steps from William II's Westminster Hall. The chamber of the House of Commons, which I have entered in the Speaker's procession exactly as Big Ben struck 2.30, dressed in silver-buckled shoes, a black silk cassock, white gloves and a tricorn hat, to read prayers which (changing the names of the Royal Family) have been recited on every parliamentary day since the reign of Charles II.

I am also grateful for the people. It is less easy to write about them because most of them are still alive, but I should be false to my experience if I did not write just a few words. The greatest privilege of a priest's life is that he has a more ready access than most men into other people's lives, often at turning points – and there is an education there not to be found in books. The people who have confided their worries in me, or who have come to be married, or who have brought their babies to be christened, or who have turned to me when dying or bereaved, are people to whom I offer thanks. And the Members of Parliament who have given me their friendship have cured me of the easy cynicism about politicians. Had I stayed in Oxford as a Fellow of All Souls, or in Cambridge as a Fellow of King's, I should have become more learned, since both colleges are delightfully adjacent to great university libraries; but my nature is such that without the people I have served in London I should not have been wiser.

I suppose that I might have treated any of the places where it has been my good fortune to live as an ivory tower high above trouble. But even an ivory tower has a window – and looking out of my window, I have not been able to avoid noticing one of history's most changeful half-centuries.

Although born right into it, I have seen the end of imperialism. Since my father went out to Egypt in 1912 to be an inspector of schools, and since what he did to create an educational system there was only a fragment of the good side of imperialism, I cannot be among those who reject the whole complex fact of the British Empire as one single crime against humanity. But like most of my fellow-countrymen I finally saw that the Empire had gone in 1956, when Port Said and part of the Suez Canal were briefly re-occupied by the British Army. The fact that the Army had to be pulled out because of the world's indignation brought home to me the much bigger fact that the English and the other whites simply had to bow before the new anti-colonial storm.

I learned more when the British Council of Churches asked me to be chairman of its agency for world development, Christian Aid. That appointment, for seven years from 1971, made me listen to the spokesmen of the three thousand million human beings who lived in the 'less developed' or (to put it bluntly) in the poorer nations. Among them a thousand million are inadequately fed, and according to the World Bank about five hundred million live in 'absolute poverty'. Most of our discussions in Christian Aid have been about the practical problems involved in raising and spending nearly five million pounds a year. But in every case the opinions of the people on the spot have been taken seriously, and one of the opinions which most people hold in today's world is that the whole world-system is stinkingly unjust. Accordingly we have sponsored a large educational programme within Britain. For example, jointly with Oxfam we launched and sustained the campaigning monthly magazine, *New Internationalist*.

At the same time I have seen a collapse of self-confidence in the society around me. There has been widespread guilt about European civilization after 1914 and again after 1939. There has been continuing guilt about this society's relationship with the poor and coloured majority of mankind. It is said that when white men first appeared in Africa or Asia they were thought to be lepers. I have lived into a period when whites often seem to be moral lepers – and when many of the most intelligent among them do believe that their society is being justly punished for its misdeeds in Auschwitz, Hiroshima, Algeria or Vietnam. Inevitably Christianity has been denounced as the white man's religion. But is it?

Before I was ordained I hesitated, with something like agony of spirit, before committing myself to a life as a spokesman of religion, and as things have turned out I have experienced the decline of the Christian Church rather vividly. While I was a part-time curate at St Martin-in-the-Fields my main work was as a publisher of theology. I was Editor and Managing Director of the SCM Press, which before I arrived had grown from an obscure existence as the publications department of the Student Christian Movement into a modest fame as one of the world's leading houses for theology.

While at the SCM Press I published a good deal of controversially radical theology which attempted to restate Christianity in answer to the challenges of secular unbelief. In 1963 I brought out *Honest to God*, the paperback by Dr John Robinson, then Bishop of Woolwich, which quickly reached a world-wide sale of a million copies. I also published British editions of more considerable works from Germany or America – Rudolf Bultmann's 'demythologizing' theology from Germany, for example, or from America Paul van Buren's effort to extract *The Secular Meaning of the Gospel*, or Harvey Cox's welcome to the triumphs of *The Secular City*. As I now look back, I am sure that the ferment of thought which such books stirred up was valuable, indeed long overdue, and I do not wish to retract a word from the long essay of welcome, 'A New Stirring in English Christianity', which I contributed to *The Honest to God Debate*. But I am glad that I never thought that any of the authors whom I served and encouraged in the 1960s had said the last word. Theologically what happened then was that the challenges of the modern scientific world were faced again as they had been in the 1920s and early thirties. (The interval was a period under the shadow of Adolf Hitler; against him the Churches and theologians mobilized a spiritual resistance which, very understandably, was conservative in spirit.) These have been extremely harsh challenges, and it has not been easy for Christians to be sure of the right response. I was more saddened than surprised when my very able successor as Editor of the SCM Press, John Bowden, wrote a book full of gloom about the condition of the Church (*Voices in the Wilderness*, 1977).

When I went to Cambridge for four years as Dean of King's

College (1966-70), I was further exposed to a secular age. The devout King Henry VI's attempt to impress the college which he founded (along with Eton) by building an immense chapel of frozen beauty as a bastion of orthodoxy and royalism became the subject of sonnets by William Wordsworth and many other awed tributes. For all I know, King Henry's formula worked for a time in what was left of the Middle Ages. But I can testify that later it became counter-productive.

In the eighteenth century King's College had living in it a clergyman who was also an austere saint, Charles Simeon the Evangelical preacher; for many years he was cold-shouldered by his hard-drinking colleagues. In the twentieth century the college, while still firmly linked with Eton and lesser public schools, became well known for a more delicate kind of civilization expressed in much agnosticism and some homosexuality. It was a home-from-home for the Bloomsbury set of intellectuals and aesthetes. When I was Dean of King's the college's character had changed again. So far from being snobbish, the image was now aggressively of the Left. So far from being conspicuously homosexual, this was one of the first Cambridge men's colleges to admit girls as students. But these changes had not put King's any more firmly on the side of religious belief or bourgeois morality.

On the whole the members of this college, young or old, did not seem to know quite what to make of the chapel bequeathed to them by history, or of the priests who presumably conducted rites within it; although most of them were friendly enough and some of them went to church. I made a few minor changes to make sure that participation in religious activities would be entirely voluntary. I even modernized some of those activities. But for the most part I could only survey the scene. Not only was the chapel one of the world's architectural masterpieces; its choir was usually reckoned to be the best in England. It would have been vandalism to have changed much. So as I said goodnight to people at the door after a service, they might compliment me on the singing and its context by saying: 'Quite out of this world!' Then I would leave the chapel to watch what I could see of the world.

Although the young among whom I lived were an elite, many of them were troubled in their consciences about the poverty of most of their contemporaries in the world and wanted to show it. Over their deliberately tatty jeans their T-shirts sometimes displayed the bearded face of Che Guevara – for when they shot him down in October 1967 the Bolivian Army kindly gave a hero to a whole student generation. In 1968 reports of exciting demonstrations, including some violence, reached Cambridge; for a few days in May there seemed to be another French Revolution, led by students. Our revolutionaries could not stand idly by. One memorable night the graceful Senate House next to King's College Chapel was occupied by students in revolt. Creeping in, I listened to speeches urging the destruction of all the gates, railings and spikes which identified the ancient university with private property.

Of course this Cambridge scene of privileged revolution had its comic elements, but I do not mean to suggest that I was laughing all the time. A recent Dean of King's had been found one morning dead in the Great Court. Almost certainly he had thrown himself off the chapel roof. To be a symbol of the Establishment, of Christendom, in a society which rejected the past in a very intelligent and articulate fashion was no laughing matter. Anyway, even if I had not been in a somewhat exposed position myself I should not have wished to laugh at the causes which attracted the young. They were serious and creative causes, including the liberation of the mind from ignorance, prejudice and superstition through the natural and social sciences. Indeed, under the stimulus of a questioning university I wrote my two biggest books – a general survey of *Religion and Change* contributed to a series of 'Twentieth Century Studies', and a collection of portraits of *Leaders of the Church of England* in the period since 1828, leading up to the questions how and why the Church's revival in the Victorian Age had petered out. Not long after leaving Cambridge I wrote a shorter book whose title sums up what I was thinking all the time: *What is Real in Christianity?*

More recently I have had the experience of holding together a small company of Christians who meet for worship in Westminster's Parliament Square. The traffic of the square can be heard inside the ancient church and the tourists invade it. Across St Margaret Street the House of Commons debates, and in that street many demonstrators make their anger felt. What has St Margaret's, Westminster, to do with that turbulent world? It used to be famous for its fashionable weddings but nowadays there are far fewer of these – and fewer people in the regular congregation Sunday by Sunday. I have sometimes asked myself whether regular churchgoing will survive. In the age of television many a cinema manager must have asked himself a similar question.

Of course I wish that I had been able to cope more adequately with this changing world. It is largely my own fault – as I can see by looking at the autobiographies of my predecessors as Dean of King's and Sub-Dean of Westminster: Alec Vidler's *Scenes from a Clerical Life* (1977) and Max Warren's *Crowded Canvas* (1974). But I know that men and movements more worthy than I am to carry the name Christian have been as disturbed as I have been. When in 1973 I wrote *The British Churches Turn to the Future* as a report about the national Church Leaders' Conference in Birmingham I quoted the comment on that problem-burdened gathering by Michael Ramsey, then Archbishop of Canterbury: 'glimmers of faith in the midst of frustration and despair'. I think of the Student Christian Movement. For a time I served as its General Secretary for Great Britain and Ireland, and in gratitude for many friendships I wrote a short history of its work since the 1870s: *Movements into Tomorrow*. But I have watched the SCM ceasing to be a fairly large and comprehensive movement with branches in almost all the universities and colleges in Britain and with a very lively international spread (the World Student Christian Federation). Instead it has become a small, very radical, body, clear about the need for the transformation of society but not so clear about what Christians have to contribute to the tomorrow.

Or I think of the World Council of Churches, one of the most important and promising developments in twentieth-century Christianity. An Oxford contemporary of mine, David Jenkins, spent some years on the staff of the WCC and wrote an eloquent book after the experience: *The Contradiction of Christianity* (1976). He concluded that the biggest contradiction of Christianity was the behaviour of Christians, particularly white ones. In my own more sheltered life I have seen enough to agree with him and to be grateful to the WCC for doing something about it. I went to the WCC's big Church and Society Conference in Geneva in 1966 and to its Assembly in Uppsala two years later, and I contributed a chapter on 'Signs of Radicalism' to *The Ecumenical Advance*, the official history of WCC from 1948 to 1968. But I have watched the WCC making more impact in politics than in religion. Its most dramatic work in recent years has been its 'Program to Combat Racism'; it has never considered launching a 'Program to Combat Atheism'. It has been a voice for the voiceless poor – but it has been less firm and bold about the main topics of the New Testament. And because the religious thought of the WCC has declined in quality over the years, its social thought has not maintained the level achieved in (for example) the studies around the theme of 'Christ the Hope of the World' in the early 1950s.

I very much welcomed the decision of the British Council of Churches in 1973 to organize an extensive programme of study and discussion with the theme 'Britain Today and Tomorrow'. I played a small part in the programme myself, and learned a lot. But when I read the reports of these groups restating the British Churches' message to their society, I saw that the thesis running through all the material was that the Churches ought to identify with the poor. It is the message of the WCC, and obviously it is a message derived from the Gospel and the tradition of the Christian saints. But I have asked myself: can nothing else now worth saying be derived from the Gospel, is not our complex society entitled to rather more complex guidance, is not our Godless society in need of a rather more profound religion? I offered a criticism of the BCC project in two long articles in the *Church Times* (4 and 11 November 1977), and need write no more about it here. What I am trying to offer in this book is something more constructive than criticism.

2 A Religious Response

For myself I can only say that, although no holy man, I am glad that I became and have remained a Christian and a priest. Religious experience – or such of it as I have known – has been the greatest joy given to me with life. I am keeping a rather fuller discussion of religion for the last chapter of this book. Here I offer only one definition of religion, which comes from an American scholar well known for his sociological analysis of Muslim life in Indonesia and Morocco (*Islam Observed*, 1969). I quote it because it stresses that religion is a vision of life around a centre. In his essay contributed to *The Religious Situation* 1968 (edited by Donald Cutler), Clifford Geertz said that religion is fundamentally an answer to the threat of chaos. Positively it is

'(1) A system of symbols which acts to
(2) establish powerful, pervasive and long-lasting moods and motivations in men by
(3) formulating conceptions of a general order of existence and
(4) clothing these conceptions with such an aura of factuality that
(5) the moods and motivations seem uniquely realistic.'

To that general sociological description I add the briefest of accounts of some results of believing a religious 'system of symbols' to be realistic. Religion, I have found, is calming and disciplining the self until the 'self' of selfishness is replaced by a quieter, humbler and cleaner person. That, I have learned, is what meditation is about in its first stages. But the other stages in prayer are more important. Religion is the assurance that life is not ultimately pointless, the world not ultimately tragic, because the world's life and (for what it matters) my own are ultimately under the control of God. And God, the Source and Ground of all that exists or is possible, is at least what I mean when I use the words 'good' and 'loving'. So, in the last analysis, religion is delighted adoration.

For myself, that is true. And for others? Is the decline in churchgoing all that need be said about the religious situation? Ought the Churches to settle down into being minor supporters of progressive secular trends?

At the end of Samuel Beckett's *Waiting for Godot* there is a stage direction which says as much as anything else in that haunting play. Eventually they have agreed that since 'Godot' will not come they will give up waiting, and that ends their talk. Then comes the final direction: *They do not move.* And that seems to me a true description of our time.

In many countries people would say: of course a really convincing religion is worth waiting for. People are sure that they need religion and that they need it strong. More than anything else they have, it is what consoles them when there is not enough food; it is what holds together the family, the village and the tribe: it is what gives dignity and beauty to their whole way of life. The only convincing substitute for it seems to be not 'Hollywood' – it is curious that the name is still given, even when television has driven most of the studios out of business, to the Western style of materialism – but Marxism, a mixture of theoretical atheism with the enthusiasm of a practical religion. Yet the influence of Marxism in the contemporary world is only one reminder of the need to renew religion even in those countries where it retains its ancient prominence. Everywhere modernization challenges the old religious laws and creeds. The book I have mentioned by Clifford Geertz ends with a picture of a young Muslim flying to America with the Koran in one hand and a whisky in the other.

Russia, Japan and the rich nations of the West, are of course far more materialistic and secular than India or Africa. But when I wrote *Religion and Change* I found no reason to think that the religious attitude was going to disappear in any of these countries, and I have found no reason since then. The best sociological analysis – summed up in (for example) Michael Hill's *A Sociology of Religion* (1973) – suggests that as a social phenomenon religion is not dead. On the question of whether God is dead, even the sociologists are uncertain. I have listened to much heart-searching about the values of these rich societies and I have read some of it in my contemporaries' books. Many of the current questions seem to be basically religious. Do we sincerely want to be rich? Do we really think that big is beautiful, that technical efficiency is the supreme goal, or that endless economic growth would be desirable? If we still count 'being human' as a value more important than an abundance of possessions, what do we reckon about the spirit of man? And the extent of the interest in more explicitly religious questions is shown by the popularity of religious programmes on television and radio. In Britain over a thousand religious books have been published each year since the mid-1950s.

In Oxford in the early 1950s I sensed the intellectual appeal of a calm, cool, clear insight into old questions. Those questions had, it seemed, become insoluble because people in the past had allowed themselves to become agitated, emotionally involved and rhetorically obscure. My cleverest friends among my Oxford contemporaries were pupils of a number of brilliant philosophers. The trend was all towards detachment and clarification, and the preference was for everyday common sense which could be analysed and still found to be down-to-earth or 'empirical'. For example, I learned from Gilbert Ryle's *The Concept of Mind* (1949) that the mind which featured in so many splendid-sounding sentences of the old-style metaphysical philosophies ought to be analysed sceptically, and when so analysed would be found to be a mere figure of speech. The mind, I learned, was no imprisoned spirit superior to the body, and no 'ghost in the machine'. It simply was a way of talking about people – people thinking by using their brains, on the only material they could think about: the experience reaching them through their physical senses.

For a time I was very impressed by this tough philosophy. As I have tried to use my own brain I have asked myself what the grand slogans of politics and economics really mean and what the words 'spirit' and 'God' mean, in actual experience. I have tried to think out what I am doing when I use religious language, and although I am no philosopher I wrote a memoir of Professor (later Bishop) Ian Ramsey, one of the most helpful of those British theologians who have responded to the new linguistic analysis. But I have come to see that the philosophy which impressed me in the 1950s was narrow and arid. The philosophers had fallen into the habit of laughing at the big questions and going to sleep during the big answers.

I have observed that the human mind or spirit (if I may be permitted to use such terms) insists on feeding on questions which are not trivial. These questions always contain an element of mystery in them, evoking a deeply personal response and therefore an element of splendour and enthusiasm in the answers. I have watched the big questions coming back into prominence as young people all over the West have become interested in Buddhist meditation, say, or psychic phenomena, or the psychedelic drug-trip, or Marxist utopianism, or mythological worlds such as those chronicled in the bestselling books of J. R. R. Tolkien. While the 'mind' may still be suspect, 'soul' is popular when connected with music. Africa's music, usually coming via America, is now loved in a country such as Britain because it comes from the life of a people still warm and uninhibited. It speaks of the deep togetherness of a natural community and of the deep joy of a black religion which (both in America and in Africa) can be deepened further by conversion to Christianity. That music is for me one more reminder of my own people's religious famine, which leaves the imagination and the heart frantically searching for food.

But if religion dares to speak, what can it say nowadays?

There appears to be a widespread return among religiously-minded people to their holy scriptures. I know that this is a feature of Jewish life despite the conspicuous secularization. In 1976 Muslim devotion to the Koran was the most striking feature of the great Festival of Islam which the governments of several Islamic countries mounted in London. I am told that many Hindus and Buddhists are also studying their scriptures with a renewed seriousness. Certainly in the Church of England, which I know best, the strongest movement in recent years has been the Bible-based Evangelical movement. I hope that I can appreciate these tendencies because I have found my own love for the Christian Bible growing. When I was being trained for the priesthood I was too preoccupied with the fundamental question of whether Christianity was true to pay a proper attention to the complexity of biblical studies. But when I became a preacher I had to study the Bible in order to teach it and while I was a publisher it was my task to produce the books of most of the leading biblical scholars. As I have had more time in the 1970s, I have written my own simple studies: *A Key to the Old Testament*, *Jesus for Modern Man* and *Good News in Acts*. Here is a world which I greatly enjoy exploring and mapping.

Yet I have never forgotten how strange the world of the Bible can seem to a society such as Britain today, shaped by science and industry. So I have gone on asking the very awkward questions which must arise for any honest modern reader of ancient religious literature. When I quote the Bible – and I intend to quote the Bible in this book – I always hope that any hearers or readers I may have are not under the illusion that I regard it as a magic or infallible book from which 'proof texts' can be extracted.

Being myself a child of the age of science, I have often asked what science allows to be said about religion. And therefore I have asked myself whether, by being born as a man, I have been thrown into a universe which is from first to last a fluke with no purpose at all. Although no scientist, I could not avoid feeling the force of the argument in (for example) the brilliant book of 1972 on *Chance and Necessity* by the French biochemist, Jacques Monod. Is evolution exclusively the result of chance and necessity when combined? *Chance*: because evolution depends on random mutations of genes, in an environment which depends on the chance combinations of physical elements. *Necessity*: because, while most changes in genes are disastrous, a very few happen to equip an organism to survive longer. *Necessity*: because individuals like stars, thus formed by a fluke, live and die under iron laws of physics and chemistry. According to this view, a game of chance is what we enter when we are born on to a speck of matter in a flash of time; and it is a game which we all have to leave with nothing to show for our time in it. Is that the whole truth about the human situation?

Being a man and a father alive in the last quarter of the twentieth century, I have often asked myself what chance nature allows man to survive. I have pondered Loren Eiseley's verdict on man in *The Firmament of Time* (1966). 'It is with the coming of man that a vast hole seems to open in nature, a vast black whirlpool spinning faster and faster, consuming flesh, stones, soil, minerals, sucking down the lightning, wrenching power from the atom, until the ancient sounds of nature are drowned in the cacophany of something which is no longer nature, something instead which is loose and knocking at the world's heart, something demonic and no longer planned – escaped, it may be – spewed out of nature, contending in a final giant's game against its master.' On this analysis, the game of man against nature cannot be won. Man, who has forgotten how to co-operate with the rest of nature, is now too deeply stupid to learn. Man, who has arrogantly thought it his right and even his duty to conquer nature, has succeeded only in poisoning it. And man is about to be made to drink the poison. Is that all that can be said about the future?

Being a citizen of a country which stands at the end of a great achievement and at the beginning of a great uncertainty, I have seriously asked myself whether the answer is not some kind of Marxism. Is that the baptism necessary to purge white guilt, the communion needed by those who have lost faith in the bourgeois ideology? As the centenary of Karl Marx's death and burial in London in 1883 approaches, a third of mankind lives under Communist governments and many of the rest are under Socialist governments which are often believed, by friends and foes alike, to be halfway to Marxism. As I have contemplated Marx's grave in Highgate Cemetery I have wondered whether the future will spring from that soil rather than from the famous churches where I have served. I have asked: if there is today an alternative to Marxism, what is it?

Part Two

NOT A FLUKE
BUT A PURPOSE

1 Our Failure of Nerve

Are we in a world which has meaning? Two magnificent series of lectures delivered on BBC television and subsequently published, Kenneth Clark's *Civilization* (1970) and Jacob Bronowski's more scientific *The Ascent of Man* (1973), both ended in gloom.

Lord Clark said: 'The incomprehensibility of our new cosmos seems to me, ultimately, to be the reason for the chaos of our modern art.' It also seemed to be the reason for the chaos of morals. He explained: 'I hold a number of beliefs that have been repudiated by the liveliest intellects of our time'. He listed these beliefs. They were the belief that 'order is better than chaos, creation better than destruction'; the beliefs in gentleness, forgiveness, knowledge, sympathy, courtesy; the belief that 'we are part of a great whole' so that 'all living things are our brothers and sisters'; and the belief in the 'God-given genius of certain individuals'. He lamented: 'It is lack of confidence that kills a civilization. We can destroy ourselves by cynicism and disillusion, just as effectively as by bombs . . . One may be optimistic, but one can't exactly be joyful about the prospect ahead of us.'

Dr Bronowski ended *The Ascent of Man* 'infinitely saddened to find myself suddenly surrounded by a sense of terrible loss of nerve, a retreat from knowledge into – into what? Into Zen Buddhism; into falsely profound questions about, Are we not really just animals at bottom; into extra-sensory perception and mystery. They do not lie along the line of what we are now able to know if we devote ourselves to it: an understanding of man himself. We are nature's unique experiment to make the rational intelligence prove itself sounder than the reflex. Knowledge is our destiny.' But Bronowski did not underestimate the difficulties. 'When I was a young man,' he recalled at an earlier point in his lecture, 'we all thought that mastery came from man's domination of his physical environment. Now we have learned that real mastery comes from understanding and moulding the living environment'. And he recognized that so far the greatest scientists have felt incompetent before the problems of man in society. In his lectures he referred more than once to Einstein's refusal of the Presidency of Israel. In the magazine *Encounter* (July 1971) he suggested that, since the corruption of science and society by each other had been so disastrous, the time had come for scientists to unite in rejecting all government grants and contracts unless a government were to be prepared to make a single annual grant to be distributed by the scientists at their own discretion.

This is indeed the central paradox of our science-based civilization. The tools of communication and production become more sophisticated each year, and the progress extends to knowledge and eloquence about man's cultural and scientific achievement. The Clark and Bronowski programmes, shown world-wide, were outstanding but not unique examples of what now can be done. But it all seems to end up with an 'incomprehensible' cosmos and with the doom of civilization.

It was easy to understand why the most admired writers of the time between the two world wars, and of the Second World War's aftermath, expounded as their favourite themes the lostness, loneliness, purposelessness, finitude, guilt, despair and nausea of modern man. It seemed the function of art to toll the bell over the wasteland and to announce closing time in the gardens. European civilization was then being gassed in the trenches, unemployed in the mean streets, or obliteration-bombed; and people who had practised the piano or become skilled with a test tube had to learn the use of the bayonet, or the quieter ruthlessness of resistance to an occupying army, or killing by pushing the button. America itself could not remain isolated from slumps or wars or *angst*. But as prosperity has come back, producing the highest material living standards in history, Bronowski's 'terrible loss of nerve' seems to have become widespread and permanent. It is caused by something more profound than today's news. Evidently, one cause is the dismay created by science itself. For science seems to say that King Lear was not mad but sane to tear off his clothes, joining the Fool in the night under the storm: 'Is man no more than this? . . . such a poor, bare, forked animal as thou art.'

In this climate of opinion Bronowski was surely right to add that it is no real answer to retreat from knowledge into the irrational. Our civilization is now so dependent on science that its future is bound up with science's. Reliable knowledge is now so largely scientific that the mind and the conscience will not permanently rest content in any denial or evasion of what science demonstrates. The only question worth asking is whether science does demand that we face an incomprehensible cosmos and the failure of man. I attempt to answer this question not because I am a scientist but because I am convinced that everyone in a science-based society who is capable of doing so ought to know and accept the scientific view of the world. For a number of years it was my duty (and pleasure) to attend Evensong in Westminster Abbey. That meant passing the graves of a number of those whose genius has been the glory of British science: Isaac Newton, William Herschel, the German pioneer of modern astronomy in Britain, Charles Darwin, Ernest Rutherford . . . The little journey necessary before one can reach the act of worship in the Abbey has seemed to me a tiny drama of the way that many of us must go. In our society, for thinking people, the road to religion must pass through science.

2 A Strange Universe

Among virtually all scientists there is now agreement that the development of the most complex forms of life from the simplest physical beginning is one continuous process. It is nonsense to speak of 'life' or 'mind' or 'spirit' being present before they do appear, but we need not reduce 'life' or 'mind' or 'spirit' to the realities of older and less complex forms of existence. It is nonsense to say that 'life' or 'mind' or 'spirit' interrupted the natural process by appearing from outside it, but it is also nonsense to deny the novelty of what happens when 'life' or 'mind' or 'spirit' does appear within this process.

We have always to think of one physical process which sustains 'life' or 'mind' or 'spirit'. And it is a process where no final division exists between 'matter' and 'energy'. On the grave of that dualism is written Einstein's formula of 1905, $E=mc^2$. Energy equals mass multiplied by the square of the speed of light.

There is also widespread agreement that the creation we know began when all matter-energy was concentrated in one fireball. This was between ten and twenty (and probably about thirteen) thousand million years ago. At the zero moment behind which science cannot explore, this fireball had, it seems, a radius of some five hundred million miles. Its density was so great that we cannot conceive it; and in his *The First Three Minutes* (1977), Steven Weinberg informs us that 'at about one hundredth of a second, the earliest time of which we can speak with every confidence, the temperature of the universe was about a hundred thousand million degrees centigrade'. Those first few minutes must have determined the fundamental constitution and history of our universe for its entire history. It is astonishing that the history was not immediately over.

It was at the Cavendish Laboratory in Cambridge that protons and neutrons were first proved to exist (by Rutherford in 1919 and Chadwick in 1932). Subsequent research has greatly complicated the picture. Over a hundred other kinds of elementary particles are now known, but it is impossible to measure simultaneously to a high precision both the position of a particle and the speed at which it moves. It is also impossible to predict with complete accuracy how it will move (the uncertainty principle enunciated by Heisenberg in 1927).

Scientists cannot even be certain that the particle always is a particle. When it collides with another it can be treated as a particle, but it is usually in motion, when it is best understood as a wave. For such reasons many scientists are now convinced that it is in principle impossible for man to unlock the last secrets of matter-energy. What scientists can already tell us is, however, marvellous enough. Radioactivity causes isolated neutrons to decay into electrons and protons (with negative and positive electric charges respectively). Our own century has revealed the existence of the mesons (which hold neutrons and protons like a glue composed of nuclear force) and the neutrinos (without mass or energy); while 'antimatter' excites the researches of physicists as it does the imaginations of science fiction writers. Neutrons and protons together make up an atomic nucleus, which is then encircled by one electron or more in an area which can be ten thousand times larger than the nucleus.

The expansion of the universe is generally thought to have begun when the really elementary particles in the primeval fireball were transformed into the first atoms of hydrogen, each containing one neutron, one proton and one electron. An alternative to the so-called 'big bang' has been suggested: the universe may have contained much the same number of atoms throughout infinite time, in a 'steady state'. According to this theory, as stars recede from each other and die new hydrogen atoms appear due to 'continuous creation'. Sir Fred Hoyle once advocated the theory – and is still pursuing the fascinating speculation that the last big bang may not have been the beginning of the matter which now constitutes our universe. Is it possible that other universes before this one expanded and contracted rather like elastic? But most astronomers now believe that the 'black body' radiation known since 1965 to exist in the universe cannot be explained without the big bang whose waves we still feel.

The history of the universe since those first few minutes has been recovered in outline. Even the very distant and fantastically energetic quasars (quasi-stellar objects) are being fitted into that history; their light, blue when it reaches us, was first recognized in 1963. All the stars in the sky were formed by the effects of gravitation when the primordial gas of hydrogen atoms had ceased to be entirely uniform. As the gas contracted some of it formed helium; an atom of helium contains two neutrons, two protons and two electrons. Red hot masses of hydrogen and helium then attracted more gas and dust. So a star was born. As the inward collapse of hydrogen and helium continued, atom crushing atom, nuclear fission was set up within the star and the hundred (or so) chemical elements heavier than helium were formed. Sometimes elements were ejected from the star into space as gas, dust, iron-dust, water, ice or rock, contracting in space to form planets or comets. Sometimes the star would become so dense that it first imploded by gravitational collapse and then exploded as a supernova; such explosions within our galaxy were observed on the Earth in 1054, 1572 and 1604. It might then join the interstellar gas and dust to form new stars.

In his *Astronomy and Cosmology: A Modern Course* (1975) Sir Fred Hoyle remarked how 'the whole history of science shows that each generation finds the universe to be stranger than the preceding generation ever conceived it to be'. Ever since the development of the giant telescopes in the 1920s and of radio astronomy in the 1960s, astronomers have been steadily pushing out the universe's known frontiers. Only about three thousand stars are visible to the naked eye on this planet but at present the usual estimate is that light, which travels at 186,283 miles per second, would take some hundred thousand years to cross our galaxy, the Milky Way, and at least thirty thousand million years to cross the universe. It is also generally agreed that the universe is constantly expanding with explosions of staggering violence. At a distance from the Earth of five thousand million light years, a cluster of galaxies has been observed travelling at a speed half the speed of light. This universe, Hoyle reckons, contains at least a thousand million million million stars together with their planets. But we cannot yet observe this universe much more than twenty thousand million light years away and it is in principle impossible to observe the edges of the universe as they are at the moment of the observation. So far from the astronomy of the 1960s and 1970s supporting the general picture (popular in the 1930s) of the universe already running down like a clock, astronomers now show us that the whole universe is evolving and that its expansion is open-ended. It is also possible to imagine that there may be other universes in existence. For all we know, our universe may be a pinprick in the space there is – and perhaps we ought to be worrying about universes colliding.

It is, however, certain that in the very long run what goes up must come down. Individual planets, stars and galaxies within this expanding universe do die, and many astronomers predict that at some future date the whole universe will begin contracting, burning up the galaxies by radiation. In sixty to a hundred thousand million years' time, it is suggested, the history of this universe will be over. Already stars which were at one time luminous and massive are known to have so contracted that they have become 'black holes', or the smaller 'black dwarfs', so dense that they no longer emit light. Probably the elementary particles of this universe will be reunited as one fireball again – and that will be the end of the universe we know. But possibly when they have reached that density and heat the particles will then begin another expansion. There may be many universes to come, raised from death.

At any rate, what we already see shows throughout this universe the inexorable operation of the physical laws which cause birth and death. Although these 'laws' are of course not entirely like those written in the statute book and enforced by the police, for most practical purposes they are regular enough. It is even possible that there are regularities which we cannot yet understand in what seems to us the uncertain behaviour of the subatomic particles. Einstein, for one, thought that 'God does not play dice'.

The Earth came from the Sun. Probably it was flung some 93 million miles into space from a disc formed around the Sun's equator by that star's rotation – although the gas and dust may have been scattered too thinly to justify the word 'disc'. The radioactivity of the decay of thorium and uranium into lead is one of the phenomena that have enabled scientists to date the formation of the Earth to some 4,500 million years ago. At least eight other planets and many smaller satellites accompanied the Earth on this journey from home, but together with the Sun they all continue to circle around the centre of the Milky Way at a speed of about 45,000 miles an hour in an orbit which takes some two hundred million years.

Thousands of tons of new material are added to the Earth each year as meteorites crash down, but far more important for the Earth's inhabitants has been the history of the original material – forming the highly dense and mostly liquid iron and nickel core of this planet, then the turbulent mantle, and finally the thin, rich crust. Water was sweated out, held by gravity, and then poured down on the rock in many millions of years of rain; today the sea covers some seven-tenths of the Earth's surface. Perhaps a thousand million years ago the Moon was captured by the Earth as a satellite and in that humble capacity began to cleanse the Earth with immense tides. When the early rain-beaten rocks had decayed to form sand, gradually this sand was enriched by innumerable dead organisms – and so the humus was made. About 2,500 million years ago the more developed plants in this soil first used photosynthesis, capturing energy from the Sun for their own growth, and breathed out oxygen – which today constitutes almost a quarter of the Earth's atmosphere, some seventeen thousand feet up into space. Soil and oxygen are our planet's assets, more precious than jewels; and perhaps there was a pointer to our planet's future in the fact that these assets came from life that breathed and died, enriching others while being itself ephemeral.

What we see as the Sun when we look up from the Earth is fantastically hot corona, throwing off energy which reaches the Earth as light or heat. The Sun also throws off a great magnetic wind of about four million tons of particles produced each second to cross a thousand miles in a second. But that is only the surface of a star so massive that the mass of the Earth is only .0003 per cent. The energy released in the Sun's interior comes from the conversion of 564 million tons of hydrogen into 560 million tons of helium in a second. That nuclear process is about a million times stronger than the energy which comes from the chemical process we call burning. The process has been going on for some five thousand million years, and it is thought that there is enough hydrogen left to last for another five (or it may be fifteen) thousand million years.

Fortunately for us, before this ferocious energy reaches the Sun's surface it is tamed by being absorbed, re-emitted and scattered by the atoms of helium. As it nears the surface it is transported by convection, but not at a steady rate. We can observe sunspots and massive prominences flaring up frequently, thanks to magnetic activity. The most intense emissions of energy from the Sun reach the Earth as ultraviolet and X-rays. Every year we learn again our dependence on the Sun by our experience of the seasons as the tilt of the Earth's axis and the shape of the Earth's orbit change. And every so often the Earth is plunged into a new Ice Age – it may be by a small change in this orbit, or in the speed of our planet's rotation, or in the positions of the other planets, or in the sunspot activity which slightly varies the Sun's output of energy.

No wonder that so many inhabitants of the Earth have worshipped the Sun! But the Sun, too, belongs to a universe of change; it must have a birth and a death. It seems to have been formed, from the explosion of a much larger star which in its turn had probably had ancestors. Since the oldest stars in our galaxy were probably formed some ten thousand million years ago there has been plenty of time. It seems that the mass of heavy atoms making the material familiar to us on the Earth was a legacy to the Sun from its father. Perhaps before it entered the Milky Way this material had already been thrown many times from star to star.

The Sun does not seem large enough to end its life by exploding like its father as a supernova, thus begetting new stars. Instead most astronomers expect the dying Sun to implode. When its supplies of hydrogen for conversion into helium have run out, it will sink into the old age of a faintly luminous 'white dwarf' not much bigger than the present Earth, consisting almost entirely of iron. Ultimately it will cease to be luminous. Pulsars composed entirely of neutrons and invisible to eyes or ordinary telescopes can be observed by radio astronomy (and were, in 1968). 'Black holes' cannot be observed directly but they are large enough to be observed (as one was in 1971), swallowing material by gravitation. But the Sun, being smaller, seems destined to end even more modestly as a 'black dwarf'. Presumably a black dwarf continues to occupy space and to swallow some material, but not in such a way that man's present instruments can observe it.

The Earth's inhabitants will, however, not be here to mourn the death of the great star to which they owe their existence. As gravitational energy is released on a colossal scale by its gradual contraction into dwarfhood, the Sun is likely to become very much more luminous and about fifty times fatter in a temporary career as a 'red giant'. Scientists predict that within three or four thousand million years, when the Sun enters this phase of its decline the Earth will be roasted, its oceans will boil, and all life on it will die. Then one day gravitation will cause the Earth to be swallowed up into the Sun. The star which is our father will be left to become a dwarf in privacy.

3 A Home for Life

In one way the Earth has outshone the Sun. It has given birth to life.

It is mathematically probable that life exists elsewhere. Indeed Sir Fred Hoyle has estimated that there are in the universe so many planets that there are 'a hundred million million million potential sites for life'. There is no reason why any life elsewhere should have taken the same path as life on our own planet. Life on the Earth may be the richest in this universe, or the poorest, or about average. At present, however, all that has to be left to science fiction, for life is simply not known to us outside the Earth. What we do know entitles this lovely, fragile planet to a place very close to the centre of our grateful love. In his *Chance and Necessity* Jacques Monod reflected on the 'biosphere' – this planet's covering with life – and wrote: 'Life appeared on earth: what, *before the event*, were the chances that this would occur? The present structure of the biosphere certainly does not exclude the possibility that the decisive event occurred only once. Which would mean that its *a priori* probability was virtually zero.' This may be more realistic than Hoyle's intoxicating speculation – but who knows?

After recent astronomy and probes into space, we begin to see the full wonder of the life-supporting Earth. It is thought that only about three per cent of the Sun is neither hydrogen nor helium. Yet the rotation of the disc which formed around the Sun, and its growing heat, meant that in time congealed masses of the richer elements were thrown off to form Mercury, Venus, the Earth and Mars. Then the Sun's increasing radiation swept away almost all of the hydrogen and helium remaining in its neighbourhood, so that only the richness was left. In contrast, the more distant Jupiter, a planet more than one thousand three hundred times more voluminous than the Earth, is still composed almost entirely of the two humblest elements. Uranus and Neptune, more distant still, seem to be composed mainly of water, ammonia and carbon dioxide, the hydrogen and helium having evaporated towards the periphery of the Solar system.

So the Moon and the planets close to the Earth share its own good fortune in their basic material. But they are not nearly so fortunate in other vital ways. We now know that had the Earth been much smaller, its gravitational power would not have been strong enough to hold so many of the rich gases and chemical compounds thrown up from its centre; it would have been as lifeless as the Moon, which cannot even keep an atmosphere. If the Earth's material had been less dense, and its atmospheric pressure less, it would have been as unfriendly to life as the red, icy, windswept Mars has turned out to be. Thick yellow clouds of poisonous carbon dioxide have covered Venus with an atmospheric pressure a hundred times heavier than the Earth's, absorbing almost all the heat leaving the planet and the energy streaming to it from the Sun. The explanation may be that the Earth produces less sulphuric acid, or simply that its orbit around the Sun is slightly different. Yet Venus is the Earth's nearest neighbour and has almost the same diameter. If the Earth had been nearer the Sun, it would have been as hellishly hot as Mercury, another planet which seems to be closely similar to the Earth in physical composition; just as, had it been much more distant, it would have been as inhospitable as Saturn with its great rings of ice.

The inherent properties of atoms have brought many of them together to form molecules. Simple molecules of methane, ammonia and water are made by the combination of hydrogen with carbon, nitrogen and oxygen respectively. Giant molecules combined have made matter as we commonly touch and see it. The awakening of matter into life depends on the molecules called amino acids. These life-giving acids seem to be fairly widely scattered in the universe; they have been found in meteorites. They contain carbon, hydrogen, oxygen, nitrogen and sometimes sulphur. They build up the proteins. In one group proteins are the chief components of hair, finger-nails, muscles, nerves, tendons and skin. In another group (the globular proteins) we find the catalysts which speed up the developments essential to life (the enzymes), the controls which ensure the smooth running of the living system (the hormones), and the armies which can be mobilized to do battle against invading diseases (the antibodies). But the twenty different amino acids which when strung together in their hundreds or thousands make molecules of protein do not produce life by themselves.

To make life, they have to be combined with nucleic acids. These consist of carbon, hydrogen, oxygen, nitrogen and phosphorus, and are particularly complex: a single molecule of a nucleic acid may contain up to a quarter of a million atoms. The nucleic acids essential to life are DNA (deoxyribose nucleic acid) and RNA (ribose nucleic acid). The structure of DNA, the now famous double helix, was discovered in 1953. It contains the genes which are the secrets of all growth in life – the genes control a cell's physical development like programmes which make tiny computers work. Because they have the same kinds of chemical chains that bind the atoms in molecules of water or sugar – chains which are marvellously repaired when damaged – genes are held together throughout the cell's lifetime. All the continuity of life lies in their stable combination; and all life's variety lies in the differences between their combinations. We are startled by how few genes are needed to provide the variety which exists between the species and between countless individuals. But often in nature variety is created by changing the patterns rather than by gathering a great assortment of basic materials; thus out of four letters, over two hundred thousand nine-letter words can be made.

So the question of how life began on the Earth involves the question how amino acids developed and were united with nucleic acids. That question cannot be answered with certainty. We do not even know how often life emerged on the Earth. Probably every living being on this planet is the fruit of a single chemical event – although it is also possible that life emerged many times. What we do know is that a great deal of energy was present on the Earth at the time to assist the vital union. Ultraviolet rays beat down from the Sun before the ozone layer was formed as a shield high in the atmosphere. Electrical discharges brought lightning close to the Earth's surface. Meteorites energetically bombarded the Earth. Water almost certainly played an essential part in the actual origins of life, as in many mythologies. Water could carry the necessary chemical elements and assure them of easy movement. Water could expose them to the energies of the Earth and the Sun while also sheltering them from destruction; and water could make up much of the living body (almost sixty per cent of the average human body is water). Since the suggestions made by Uparin and Haldane in the 1920s were partially substantiated by laboratory experiments in the 1950s, scientists have thought in terms of a 'hot thin soup' where amino and nucleic acids were united. An ideal setting for this would have been a dried up lagoon where the acids could have been exposed to the correct heat from the Sun, drying up the water molecules which separated them, and then carried away in their new state by incoming water.

It is clear that the heat – not too hot and not too weak – needed to unite the amino and nucleic acids took some getting, but once this marriage had taken place a single cell could be born, probably the parent of all life. We are told by the eminent geneticist Salvador Lauria that 'there is no room to doubt that all organisms that are now known have stemmed from a single successful cell lineage'. This birth of life took place some 3,500 million years ago. The smallest living organism now known is the mycoplasma in the soil, one tenth of one millionth of a metre across. It is a thousand times larger than its first ancestor, the hydrogen atom.

A cell lives when it metabolizes; it uses energy to extract chemical elements from the environment in order to build proteins, nucleic acids, carbohydrates and fats, and it discards what is surplus by respiration, producing more energy. Plants do it by a synthesis which transforms molecules of the inorganic world into compounds building life. Animals do it by feeding on plants or other living matter. Beyond this a cell must somehow reproduce itself. Science – as summed up in (for example) J. Z. Young's *Introduction to the Study of Man* (1971) – is now able to tell us much about how these marvels are performed.

A living cell consists of ordinary chemical elements brought together in a system under the control of the DNA in its nucleus – and brought together in such a way that this system tends to maintain itself by the continual expenditure of energy (homeostasis). This energy keeps the various materials in place, renews them from the surroundings and expands the cell in wellfed prosperity. So the cell by itself can be a complete living system – and some single cells are a million times larger than the mycoplasma. But more important to us is the fact that most cells when they reach a certain prosperity and size divide (mitosis). The DNA is able to ensure that these two new cells have the same instructions as the original one. Because the chemical varieties make different types of DNA, however, there are different types of cell. A human body contains about a thousand different types, and about 10^{15} different cells. There is a borderline between life and non-life: where do we place the virus (which reproduces but lacks some of the characteristics of a cell), or the nerve cell in an animal (which does not divide)? But generally speaking, the power of a cell to reproduce itself is essential to life.

When an amoeba or a bacterium reproduces, the cell simply splits into two parts. But the higher forms of life, including birds and mammals, have for the last nine hundred million years enjoyed sexual reproduction, which is vastly more complicated. Here the combined cells take male or female forms, and two special different cells from the male and the female (the gametes) must fuse in such a way that the number of chromosomes in each of the cells is halved (meiosis). The new cell is viable because it has the correct number of chromosomes, but these result in a mixture of the parents' characteristics: in other words, in a new individual. If the new individual is male, this is caused by the presence of one special chromosome (Y) among the forty-six. But no great space need be taken up by this operation. The zygote resulting from the fusion of a human egg with a human sperm weighs about thirty-four thousandths of a gramme.

In that zygote from which each one of us comes is stored a fraction of the genetic history of the Earth, continuous from the first living cell. Each one of us is part of that stream of life; and if we have children, we pass on the gene-line. And the more we look round with the eyes of science, the more we see how persistent, varied and productive has been the life that has struggled and swarmed on this planet.

In the Fig Tree chert of Swaziland have been found fossils of organisms which were alive about 3,400 million years ago. On the shores of Lake Superior are fossils of blue-green algae about two thousand million years old. In our world we can observe the tiny plants which survive in the snow and the sand. We learn that a single oyster may lay several hundred million eggs in a four-month season and that the relatively infertile codfish produces an annual average of fifteen million eggs of which all except about a dozen get eaten as part of the plankton on the sea. We are told that at the present day some three million species, over a million of them being species of animals, are sufficiently different from each other to be classified as alive; yet fossils suggest that the number of extinct species is vastly greater. It has been suggested that life has so far produced some five hundred million species.

Within each species, life is so massively overproduced that the Earth could not possibly support every individual born. Fortunately most animals die before they have produced any offspring, while most of the rest die before they have borne as many offspring as was biologically possible. Among wild birds, over three-quarters of the young die before breeding. In fish and insects, normal losses among eggs and among the immature are said to exceed 999 in every thousand. Few animals are strong enough or lucky enough to die of old age. But what Charles Darwin wrote at the end of *The Origin of Species* (1859) is also true: 'From the war of nature, from famine and death, the most exalted object which we are capable of conceiving, namely the production of the higher animals, directly follows.'

Not even the genius of Darwin could recognize the method used by nature. It had been the theory of Jean-Baptiste Lamarck (1809) that improvements in organs reward greater skill in responding to the environment and can be transmitted to descendants physically as 'acquired characters'. This suggestion was welcome to the Victorian businessman who liked to bequeath his profits to his children. Later on, it appealed to the authorities in Soviet Russia who made Lysenko's pseudo-science compulsory on this basis; it suggested that specially heroic workers deserved their rewards. Even people without such motivation accepted Lamarck's theory because they refused to believe that the behaviour of a favourite bird (for example) was not the result of merit handed on as a legacy to offspring. But the very quiet observation of garden peas by the abbot of a monastery in Bohemia, Gregor Mendel, began to be known in 1900, sixteen years after his death; and as twentieth-century genetics advanced from Mendel's discoveries, it became increasingly clear that 'acquired characters' cannot be transmitted to descendants physically, any more than the results of accidents can generally be transmitted. No experiment has ever shown that changes induced in an individual's body – for example, by cutting off a mouse's tail – produce corresponding changes in the DNA for genetic transmission.

So far from passing on the results of gains or losses in the organs, the genetic transmission of heredity preserves the stability and continuity of a species. Many forms of life are reproduced by the genes with an almost complete similarity. Even the greater variation made possible by sex does very little to counteract this basic conservatism on the genes. This is greatly to the advantage of the species, as is demonstrated by the fact that hybrids produced by inter-breeding between the species usually die quickly or are infertile. But a very tiny proportion of genes in a very rare individual may be damaged by X-rays, radioactivity, a chemical substance or some other harmful physical force so that the damage causes a significant fault in the copying of that gene when the individual breeds.

Almost always the 'mutation' is harmful and the individual who suffers from it dies prematurely and without breeding. Sometimes the gene affected may be one with little importance in the formation of the body, so that the total result is slight. But very occasionally the change turns out to be one that equips the offspring to respond more effectively to the environment. It is chance; there is no scientific evidence that the change has taken place in order to help the offspring. In the science of genetics, mutations are aptly described as 'random'. Yet mutations are supremely important in evolution when an individual, thus changed by chance, has more offspring than his less lucky contemporaries. In the scientific account of evolution as a whole, it is legitimate to speak of 'progress' because the random mutations are selected if they improve an organism's capacity to survive.

Darwin or the Darwinians popularized the resounding phrases 'Struggle for Life' and 'Survival of the Fittest' as explanations of the process by which the improved forms of life are selected by nature. But if narrowly interpreted, such phrases can mislead. Neither direct competition for food nor a gladiatorial duel to the death is the main factor in a far more complex process. Although individuals do compete (and the members of a few species such as haddock eat each other), often the advantage conferred by a random mutation concerns ability in food-gathering (a giraffe's neck), or speed in escape (a horse's legs), or camouflage (an ermine's fur, brown in summer and white in winter), or warning off rivals from a particular territory (a bird's song), or sexual attractiveness (a peacock's display), or nurturing the young (many birds), or sheltering the young in the placenta before birth (the blue whale's young are born twenty-three feet long).

What matters always is the improved capacity to survive. It is estimated that in most circumstances a species or variety with equipment improved by the random mutation of genes will replace the unimproved species or variety if it leaves only one per cent more offspring. Of course each species needs energy in order to survive and must get some of this energy from consuming less developed species, in the process intensively studied in recent years as the 'eco-system' or 'food-chain'. But it is importing human prejudice into this baffling scene if we call it a murder story. With greater justice we could call it a birth story.

One reason why it is impossible to reduce evolution to an immediately intelligible story in accordance with our moral and aesthetic convention is the sheer time the action takes. The story of the Earth covers only a part, perhaps the last third, of the story of the universe. But its length still sets an impossible task to any story-teller. In his *Science and the Christian Experiment* (1971), Dr Arthur Peacocke quoted a helpful analogy which compared the history of the Earth with forty-eight hours, each hour standing for a hundred million years. 'During the second half of the first twenty-four "hours" and the following morning and afternoon, primitive living matter evolved chemically, assembling and coagulating, and only at 6.00 p.m. in the evening of this second "day" do the first fossils appear. From 6.00 to 7.00 p.m. on this second day the seas fill with shelled creatures, but only at 8.00 p.m. can fishes be recognized. At 9.00 p.m. amphibians appear on land and at 10.30 p.m. the reptiles dominate the Earth. By 11.30 p.m. . . . mammals, including the first primates, spread across the globe. At 11.50 the monkeys and apes among the trees come to the ground. At 11.59 a primate stands on two legs and in the last thirty seconds of this day we see man appear, but only at the last stroke of the midnight bell can we recognize the earliest tools made by modern man, whom we can at last call *Homo sapiens*.'

The story there dramatized (by Professor David Nichols) has been told by F. H. T. Rhodes in *The Evolution of Life* (1976). Some six hundred million years ago the seas were full of sponges, jellyfish, starfish, shellfish and worms. They fed on the seaweed and other algae. Later on came the corals, oysters, mussels, squids, octopuses and the earliest fish in the seas. Slugs, snails, scorpions, spiders and cockroaches enjoyed life in the shallow pools. Then newts, toads and frogs explored the land while still having their real home in the water; there they returned to reproduce. Higher forms of life (including snakes and lizards but also much larger creatures now extinct) could settle on the land to eat the first plants, some four hundred million years ago. We still have contact with this early life – not only in the fossils, or in the species which have survived, but also in the coal and oil which the plant and animal life formed in death.

The early plants began to die out some three hundred million years ago. About the same time the reptiles began to rule the Earth – and some, having developed feathers and wings with other uses, discovered that they could fly to join the insects in the air. The most spectacular reptiles were the dinosaurs, dominant throughout the seemingly interminable Mesozoic times (from 225 to 75 million years ago). Physically they were the most impressive creatures ever to walk this planet. The modern recovery of fragments of their story through the discovery of fossils and footprints has fascinated many; the advance of our knowledge was presented together with some speculations by A. J. Desmond in *The Hot-Blooded Dinosaurs* (1975). But only the comparatively small crocodiles or the tiny lizards survive to give us an idea of what these 'dragons' or 'prehistoric monsters' looked like. For their dominance of the Earth ended completely and mysteriously.

Probably the main cause of their downfall was that the Earth itself changed. Huge areas of land were inundated by the seas, leaving many shells above the older fossils. Great new mountain ranges were thrown up. It became much colder. And the dinosaurs were defeated. Even if (as is far from certain) some of them were warm-blooded, generating the heat they needed from their own muscles and tissues instead of relying on the Sun's warmth as lizards do, they had other fatal handicaps. The enormous bulk of many of these reptiles cursed them with gigantic appetites for flesh or fodder. A skeleton suggesting a weight of a hundred tons has been found and it has been calculated a thirty-ton dinosaur consumed half a ton of vegetation each day. And although they were intelligent food-gatherers and also social with each other (footprints have been discovered which suggest that at least some of them moved in herds), their brains were not their strongest point. *Diplodocus*, for example, left behind bones and skulls suggesting a length of some eighty-five feet with a brain the size of a hen's egg.

What was created now – now, when so much of this planet's history was already past – was the Earth as man came to know it. Although some rocks accessible to man were in their present condition some 3,700 million years ago, it took long ages for continents of varying shapes and heights to grow and to split. At first there was one land mass, known to modern scientists as Pangaea. Then about 180 million years ago Pangaea split into two masses: Laurasia and Gondwanaland. Gondwanaland in the south itself divided some 175 million years ago. South America moved to the west; Madagascar, Arabia, India, Australasia and Antarctica wandered off to the east. Then India moved north to collide with Asia some forty million years ago – and the Himalayas mark where the collision took place. Laurasia divided when North America split from Europe about eighty million years ago, and the Rockies show where the journey had to stop. The Alps, formed twenty million years ago, are reminders of a time when Europe was itself on the move north until checked. This 'continental drift' – first detected by Alfred Wegener who died in 1930, and confirmed in detail in the 1950s – still continues; North America and Europe are drawing apart, Africa and Europe together. And earthquakes continue. But the land was stabilized sufficiently to be the scene of life more advanced than the dinosaurs.

The future in all these continents lay with warm-blooded creatures who had escaped the jaws of the dinosaurs by being small and agile – the birds and the mammals. Some birds migrated several thousands of miles every year. Others, such as the ostrich, could not fly at all. Most turned out to be great survivors such as the pelicans, at home on the ice of the Arctic or Antarctica. Comparatively few species made fatal mistakes. One was the elephant bird of Madagascar, who grew ten feet tall and found it too much. Among the mammals, the bat was at ease equally in land and air; the seal, the sea-lion or the walrus swam vigorously and could return to the land; the whale and the dolphin took to the water with brilliant success. But most mammals, exercising the cerebral cortexes in their brains and suckling their young, found enough scope on the land, now fertile with ferns, conifers and the first flowering plants.

Some of the earliest mammals to appear – the duck-billed platypus, the wallaby, the wombat, the koala bear, the kangaroo – have survived into our times in Australia. About fifty million years ago some of the mammals began to eat flesh as some of the dinosaurs had done; from these are descended the modern lions, tigers, leopards, foxes, wolves, cats and dogs. At about the same time the monkey began to develop from an earlier form which survives more primitively in the lemur. This monkey had a future. About ten million years ago one species of the ape evolved into the hominid known as *Ramapithecus*. He was the ancestor of man.

Although a great deal has been written in recent years about the beast that lurks beneath the skin of *Homo sapiens*, much of this material has been speculative. Whole varieties of man and immense ages of time in the human story are now known to us by only a few fossilized skulls and bones discovered by chance. Exactly where, when and how men and women appeared whom we should acknowledge as like us, how they behaved and what they were thinking – these are problems which are by their very nature insoluble. All that can be known is an outline of possibilities. On the basis of recent finds – one presentation was *Origins* by Richard Leakey and Roger Lewin (1977) – it seems that *Homo habilis* emerged in Central Africa from the more ape-like hominids more than two and perhaps almost three million years ago. *Homo erectus* ('Heidelberg' or 'Peking' or 'Java' man, who used fire and made tools of stones or bones) appeared more than seven hundred thousand years ago; a skull of about that date has been found at Petralena in Greece. Neanderthal man may have emerged in Africa more than a hundred thousand years ago, and Cro-Magnon man (from whom we are descended) in South-East Asia at about the same time.

The evolution of life takes place before our eyes today; in the industrial cities of Britain, for example, black moths are replacing the grey-and-white 'peppered' variety. But the evolution of man has so far been unique in its success. It was not mere human arrogance for Sir Julian Huxley to write at the end of his *Evolution: The Modern Synthesis* (revised in 1963) that 'progress hangs on a single thread: that thread is the human germ-plasm'.

Many pieces of equipment have given man his unique advantages. His binocular vision seems to have been developed when his ancestors among the apes had to leap accurately from bough to bough, but he stands upright on the ground and he can wield his short arms and cunning hands for many purposes. His striding walk was to his advantage as a hunter. He has rare equipment for touch and for speech. Many other marvels are produced by the million million (or more) cells making man's body. But above all man possesses two fistfuls of pink-grey tissue: his brain. It is by the brain's power over the motor nerves that he has gained so much control over his muscles; it is by the brain's strength to direct his fingers and thumb that all his manual skill is possible; it is by the brain moving his tongue and his vocal chords that he has developed speech, half-present in the apes; it is the brain that has laid the foundations of language, so surprisingly similar in all the human languages. Most amazingly of all, it is through the brain's potential that man can in some measure escape both from the random chance and from the physical necessity to be seen everywhere else in evolution.

The average weight of the brain is about fifty ounces in men and rather less in women; this is about one fortieth of the weight of the body. The brain, almost fully formed at the age of seven, covers about four hundred square inches when unfolded. The largest part of it, the cerebral cortex, already contains at birth about ten thousand million nerve cells (neurons). Each of these develops some twenty-five thousand interconnections. Its many other marvels are described in, for example, Steven Rose's *The Conscious Brain* (1976) against an evolutionary background. An essential stage in the evolution of *Homo sapiens* was the provision of space for a brain at least twice as large as that of his predecessor, the hominid or 'ape-man' *Australopithecus*, who by two and a half million years ago had at least doubled the size of the brain of the largest ape known to us. The room was available because the relation of spine and skull changed now that the ape-man no longer had to swing from the branches; and some bulky muscles were no longer needed to move the jaw.

It is possible that progress will come through some further physical improvement of the brain, which obviously is not perfect – and mankind's progress certainly does depend on more members of the species getting adequate protein so that the brain is fully formed in infancy. But meanwhile plenty of progress is possible for man using the brain he has. Already he can fly because of this brain; he can build computers which for limited purposes are quicker and more efficient than the brain itself; and many other technical feats seem to lie within, or only just beyond, his present brain's capacity. The most difficult problems he faces are emotional or social problems, but to solve these he does not seem to need more cells in his brain. He needs to learn and to remember more in the frontal lobe behind the forehead, in the temporal lobe above the ear, and above all in the hypothalmus which regulates the emotions of lust and rage.

Science leaves it an open question, whether man can learn well and quickly enough to survive. Certainly, however, science supplies warnings. The dinosaurs were the lords of the Earth for about one hundred and fifty million years – and became extinct. A race of *Homo sapiens*, Neanderthal man, ruled Europe for about fifty thousand years – and died out some thirty thousand years ago.

For all species now extinct, the fatal challenge came from the environment. The climate seems to have defeated the dinosaurs, and probably also Neanderthal man. In the Ice Age, which began some six hundred thousand years ago, the whole of North America and Europe was covered with ice some ten thousand feet thick. The last of the Ice Ages covered sixty thousand years, and ended only some ten thousand years ago. Since then many species are known to have become extinct as a result of relatively minor variations in the climate or other environmental changes; for example a change in the winds over the Atlantic dried up the Sahara. And presumably in the ages to come man and the other animals will have to cope with many such changes, including new Ice Ages. But the paradox in the twentieth century AD is that man's future is threatened not so much by his environment as by his emotions.

These emotions have served man well for most of his very long history. His sexual activity or desire is all-the-year-round and almost lifelong; this 'naked ape' is the sexiest of the animals. He has a fierce loyalty to a fairly small group defending a territory; he is the most territorial of the animals. And he has a taste for the hunt with its inevitable violence; he is the most brutal of the animals. Even in the most sophisticated civilization the entertainments we choose show that the emotions which we feel need to be released: the romantic novel or the sex magazine, the patriotic celebration or the football match, the war film or the murder story. In our rational moments we can see that these emotions can be fatally dangerous if uncontrolled. The sexuality – so useful in evolution as a bond between parents encouraging the care and education of the young, and as an incentive to the multiplication of the species – can lead to the overpopulation of the Earth and to the miserable degradation of human life. The skill and delight in co-operation and the territorial imperative – so useful as bonds between hunters – can become an obsession with alleged threats from enemies. The joy in the hunt and the kill – so useful in obtaining protein from meat – can lead to orgies of destructiveness. So emotional drives can become psychological diseases, as set out in (for example) Erich Fromm's *Anatomy of Human Destructiveness* (1974).

However, the portrait of man painted by science has a reassuring aspect. It seems that these emotions are not transmitted and implanted by the genes. If they were, they could never be changed – but it seems that they are not, so that they should be attributed to 'human culture' rather than to 'animal ancestry', to 'nurture' rather than to 'nature'. Konrad Lorenz's alarming *On Aggression* had a wide influence when translated into English in 1966, only to be denounced as too 'squeamish' by Richard Dawkins in *The Selfish Gene* ten years later; but the comparisons between men and other animals were oversimplified in such books. A more cautious treatment is outlined in Ashley Montagu's *Man and Aggression* (1968). We all know that mobs of people can behave worse than packs of wolves. But it is unfair to blame such behaviour on the beast in man. Animals do not, it seems, enjoy inflicting pain or killing except for necessary food or in self-defence. It is people who have learned to behave like that.

As Robin Ardrey has shown so dramatically, even luridly, in his books leading up to *The Hunting Hypothesis* (1976), these grossly human emotions did benefit man's survival in the past. But today they do not have biological value unless they are disciplined for the sake of social co-operation. The bad old habits could presumably be replaced by new learning. Fortunately for men, the learning needed would not be completely new. Peaceful and co-operative emotions have already proved their value in man's own history; for example, in guiding him to rear his young. Similar behaviour is very plentiful among animals, as among ants, fish and birds; in the wild apes are normally rather gentle and highly social creatures. It seems reasonable to suppose that by using the magnificent brain he has, *Homo sapiens* can survive and progress. His murderous, and therefore ultimately suicidal, reflexes can be controlled. His social wisdom can catch up with his technical skill. If evolution means survival, this is what evolution now means for man.

So science leaves us with the obvious truth that man needs to learn love at a new depth – love for his whole species, and not just for the fellow-member of it who for the time being arouses his sexuality; and love for his whole environment, and not just for his own territory. The student slogan 'make love not war' is perhaps one way of putting this. Another way of putting it is to say that man needs that conquest of the ego which is religion.

4 Science and Religion

Our trouble is that religion is thought to be unscientific. Fundamentally this is the reason why a highly civilized Englishman such as Lord Clark ends his exposition of what he holds dear with these words: 'The trouble is that there is still no centre. The moral and intellectual failure of Marxism has left us with no alternative to heroic materialism, and that isn't enough.' But what is meant by calling religion 'unscientific'?

It is certainly pre-scientific. Some fifty thousand years ago Neanderthal people buried at least some of their dead in a crouched position, first sprinkling them with red ochre; and many modern scholars believe that such customs represented the hope of a continuing life. Before the end of the last Ice Age the Cro-Magnon peoples who replaced the Neanderthals in Europe painted very beautiful pictures of hunting on the walls of caves, presumably to assist magic or prayer. A large part of the early history of religion seems to be occupied by primitive man's attempts to explain natural phenomena by saying that they were the work of gods or spirits; for the time being this impressed as an explanation. As more and more natural phenomena were understood well enough to deprive the gods and spirits of such jobs, the gods and spirits were in effect deprived of existence. God himself was driven (it seemed) into the gaps of scientific knowledge.

It was for a time believed that there was scope for one God who was needed to intervene from time to time in order to put the natural processes right by a miracle. The scientific genius of Isaac Newton in the seventeenth century was fully compatible with that belief in one miracle-working God; that was why Newton was as interested in biblical prophecies (which he thought foretold future miracles) as in scientific experiments. As the age of science has progressed, however, most thoughtful believers in religion have abandoned the crude concept of miracles being wrought by God in order to rectify mistakes or fill in gaps. 'Miraculous' events are increasingly understood as being natural events which arouse wonder because of what they signify to man's spiritual life. However, this translation of traditional religion is not an easy process. Still less easy is it for religion to develop new images to express its sense of wonder. Most of the images still loved in religious circles derive from periods before our science-based civilization; thus God is a king or a craftsman, Christ is a shepherd or the 'lamb of God' offered in sacrifice.

And religion is certainly non-scientific. The history of the universe as known to modern science is so staggering that any selection of items in it as keys to an understanding of the rest must be a risky business and a matter of opinion; it must be subjective, not scientific. Religion is of course not the only attempt which people have made to make sense of the world around them, even after the rise of science. Morality is another such attempt, and it too depends on choosing certain items in the history of the universe as being more valuable than the rest. In his *Ethical Values in the Age of Science* (1969) Paul Roubiczek showed that the basic distinction made by Kant in the eighteenth century between knowledge and belief still stands and is vital to all ethics, which must always involve belief. In his *Evolutionary Ethics* (1968) Antony Flew has displayed the variety of moral beliefs that can be held even after a modern knowledge of natural phenomena. In the nineteenth century the 'Social Darwinians' of America argued that evolution applauded the survival of the fittest in the capitalist system of *laissez faire*; yet Karl Marx asked permission to dedicate the English translation of his *Capital* to Darwin because he was convinced – and his English collaborator Engels was even more convinced – that evolution supported Communism. J. H. Huxley, who popularized Darwin, argued with passion that human morality must fight against nature – Tennyson's 'nature red in tooth and claw'. His grandson Sir Julian Huxley, on the other hand, believed that his new, highly civilized, religion of Humanism and his distinguished work for the United Nations were inspired by his scientific work on evolution.

When we enquire how twentieth-century Christian theologians have related their religion to science, we find a tendency to draw a sharp distinction, so that religion and science may have ceased to be in conflict at the cost of ceasing to be in contact. In his Preface to Volume III of his massive *Church Dogmatics*, dealing with 'The Doctrine of Creation', Karl Barth declared: 'There can be no scientific problems, objections or aids in relation to what Holy Scripture and the Christian Church understand by the divine work of creation'. In his

Jesus Christ and Mythology (1958), Barth's great rival Rudolf Bultmann explained why he had not discussed nature. 'The affirmation that God is Creator cannot be a theoretical statement about God as *creator mundi* in a general sense', he claimed. 'The affirmation can only be a personal confession that I understand myself to be a creature which owes its existence to God.' Probably most theologians now consider that both Barth and Bultmann drew too much of a distinction: after all, both religion and science have to describe the same world, for it is not actually possible for man to experience two worlds. But that there is a sharp distinction between the scientific and religious ways of knowing this world is emphasized generally. A book such as Don Cupitt's *The Worlds of Science and Religion* (1976) is representative.

The distinction made by theologians generally is, it seems, accepted by most scientists who are Christians. In the seventeenth century Francis Bacon advocated the experimental method of science as the best way of handling the 'book of God's works' and he urged those who, like himself, still accepted the Bible as God's word to make sure that 'they do not unwisely mingle or confound the two learnings together'. Blaise Pascal, a genius both in science and in religion, luminously explored the nature of faith as something very different from science's certainty. The distinction was worked out with reference to more recent science and theology in, for example, Ian Barbour's *Issues in Science and Religion* (1966) or in the more personal *Man, Science and God* by John Morton, Professor of Zoology at Auckland, New Zealand (1972). Morton argues that faith in a good and sovereign Creator can be held nowadays by an intelligent, honest and well-informed scientist; he holds it himself. But this belief is not to be deduced from nature. 'Let theologians beware,' he says, 'of too readily acclaiming the evolutionary process as a guide to God's nature ... Evolution is thus given a moral content that is highly dubious ... If I am asked what the study of evolution can of itself tell me about God, the answer – if I am honest – must be bleakly "Nothing".'

Is religion, then, anti-scientific – as Marxists (for example) assert unless they happen to be courting religious believers?

Professor Morton tells us that he is a Christian, but he recognizes that this puts him against the intellectual stream. He refers to the opinion which many of our contemporaries prefer: that the world is 'not explicable at all' – since 'whatever internal coherence science may find in the natural order, man is ultimately alone in a meaningless world'. Is all religious belief the wrong choice to make, now that we have science to tell us the facts about our world? Are 'God' and 'soul' words which should be banished as those mythical entities, 'phlogiston' and 'ether', have been?

They certainly are not words which ought to be found in a scientific sentence, except in the course of descriptions of religious believers' opinions and behaviour. They point to realities which, if they exist at all, lie beyond the scope of science. 'God' is clearly not a grandfather in the sky who occasionally interferes with the Earth, and 'soul' is clearly not a ghost within the chemical mechanism of the body. But is there any reality behind such words? That is a question which the scientist cannot answer as a scientist. As Lord Ritchie-Calder wrote in *Man and the Cosmos* (1968): 'The scientist who says "I am an atheist" is being dogmatic and unscientific. *As a scientist* he would have to show that God does not exist. He can, and must, say *as a scientist*, "I am an agnostic", meaning "I do not *know*. I cannot prove that God exists." ' But it does not follow that as a human being a scientist or anyone else must keep silence completely. There has therefore been an immeasurable quantity of religious language in the history of mankind – and there has been a considerable effort in recent years to clarify its status, the best introduction to this discussion being Thomas Fawcett's *The Symbolic Language of Religion* (1970).

Nowadays 'God' and 'spirit' are often said to be words used in myths – but by 'myth' can be meant, in this context, not a completely false and valueless statement but a story which, while not literally or exactly true, is a suggestion or reminder of a truth too deep for words. Religious words are models – meaning by a 'model' a man-made object which, while not a completely accurate representation, may serve man's purposes as an image of a reality too big to be reproduced. And these words are used in paradigms – meaning by 'paradigm' a small example which can be pointed to in order to indicate a far wider pattern.

Professor Ian Barbour, who is a physicist as well as a theologian, has compared the uses of *Myths, Models and Paradigms* in science and religion (1974). It might seem that no comparison is possible. In fact, however, there are myths which science itself creates as tools to make sense of the otherwise baffling complexity of nature; one example is the idea of evolutionary 'progress', which implies that evolution has a purpose to get us where we are. There are models which science uses in order to explain otherwise unintelligible phenomena, such as the model of light as particles or the rival model of light as waves. And there are paradigms or patterns which are really fashions in science, tendencies to concentrate on particular facts and to group all others around them. In *The Structure of Scientific Revolutions* (1962) Thomas Kuhn impressively argued that the ablest scientist needs to rely on textbooks for most of his knowledge and on the climate of opinion in the scientific community for guidance in his research. There is a vast background of 'received' knowledge behind practical science. Kuhn suggested that a scientific revolution occurs when a Newton, an Einstein or some other genius opens up a whole new way of seeing things and this new way is gradually accepted in the scientific community. Thoughtful students of religion need no persuading that myths, models and paradigms all occur frequently in that field. So there seems to be profit in comparing the scientific and religious ways of knowing as human activities which both deserve a critical respect.

Religious knowledge, although it has to be expressed by using myths, models and paradigms, arises out of experience which is real enough. It is experience that anthropologists, historians, biographers, psychologists and sociologists can study (and their work was usefully assessed in, for example, John Bowker's *The Sense of God*, 1973); but as is the case with a good many other human activities, really to understand it one has to experience it. At the heart of religion the experience of being confronted by an ultimate reality that seems to lie beyond as

NOT A FLUKE BUT A PURPOSE

well as within everyday things; beyond as well as within other people; beyond as well as within one's own self. Many have compared it with a child's experience in being confronted by the personality of a parent. Across the centuries and around the globe, religion is present in every society of which we have evidence. It may even be that it is present in every individual, although there is often a great reluctance to talk or even to think about it.

Religion in all its varied manifestations is all, in the last analysis, man's concern with this ultimate reality; and the experience that gives rise to this concern seems to be as real and as frequent in the age of science as it was in the last Ice Age. For example, it inspired Teilhard de Chardin to see the whole panorama of man's evolution – and he had expert knowledge of the fossils as a palaeontologist – in the light of his religious vision as a devout French boy and Jesuit priest (*The Phenomenon of Man*, translated into English in 1965). For a century others combining some religious experience with some scientific knowledge had been seeing much the same thing, as Ernst Benz recalled in his *Evolution and Christian Hope* (translated into English in 1967). One of them was A. N. Whitehead, Bertrand Russell's collaborator in advanced mathematics, who eloquently rejected Russell's atheism because, unlike Russell, he had reached the conclusion that religious experience – and that alone – could illuminate the dark mystery surrounding human life and the whole process of evolution.

If the philosophical systems of Teilhard and Whitehead are thought to be too visionary and jargon-ridden, the work of Theodosius Dobzhansky, the distinguished geneticist and author of *Mankind Evolving* (1963), may be preferred – particularly his short book on *The Biology of Ultimate Concern* (1963). Sir Alister Hardy, formerly Professor of Zoology at Oxford, has asked in a number of books which of his activities man has reckoned most valuable after his evolution from less complex forms of life. In *The Biology of God* (1975) Sir Alister summed up his argument that *Homo sapiens* is supremely the 'religious animal'. Such books remind us that religion is not merely a world-escaping mysticism, or simply an emotion fed by myths with no basis in reality. Religion is indeed partly mystical because it transcends the everyday categories of perception, reasoning and duty: it is about glory, not about the commonplace. And it is indeed partly moral because it advocates certain patterns of behaviour, and claims to guide and strengthen those who pursue them. But religion habitually claims to describe what really is the case in the world, and it stands or falls by people's acceptance or rejection of that claim.

What, then, is the world as seen by religion?

One of the ancient Indian *Vedas* has this to say about the creation:

> Both being and not being were not yet,
> No air was then, nor any sky.
> Who kept the world or bounded it?
> Where was the abyss and where the sea?
>
> No day was there, nor was there night,
> No death was then, nor immortality.
> Then breathed in windless, pristine might
> One without duality.
>
> The whole world was like a lightless field,
> An ocean in a dark domain.
> Then what had so far been concealed,
> The One, arose through power born of pain . . .
>
> Who, then, could be the arbitrator
> To tell about creation's source?
> The gods came into being later.
> Who knows from whence it took its course?
>
> He by whom all was first begot,
> Who looks from heaven's apogee,
> Who made it, or perhaps did not,
> He knows it – or not even he?

One of the Taoist scriptures declared in ancient China:

> There is a being, wonderful, perfect;
> It existed before heaven and earth.
> How quiet it is!
> How spiritual it is!
> It stands alone and does not change.
> It moves around and around, but does not suffer.
> All life comes from it.
> It wraps everything with its love as in a garment.
> Yet it claims no honour,
> It does not demand to be Lord.
> I do not know its name, so call it *Tao*, the Way.
> And I rejoice in its power.

It is now possible for our science-based civilization to gain access to the treasures of Hinduism. Many not born in India can share the glimpse of the one uncreated Lord (*Ishvara*); the pictures of the many lifetimes, many worlds and many universes being born and dying in cycles of painful existence. Similarly it is possible to study the ancient Chinese 'Way'. Even non-Muslims can now appreciate the sublime visions of the creative power of God in the Koran and subsequent Muslim literature – for example, *Surah* 55 with its celebration of the beauties of nature and its refrain repeated thirty-one times: 'Which of your Lord's blessings would you deny?'

Some Indian, Chinese and Muslim scholars have compared those sacred treasures with the modern accounts of evolution which they also accept. But here I want to concentrate on the Jewish-Christian tradition, originating in the religious experience which is reflected in the Bible. I want to ask whether that tradition has been totally discredited by the rise of science.

All the standard histories show that (although Chinese and other early technology should not be forgotten) modern science grew out of European soil, which had been soaked for centuries in Christianity and in the Jewish faith which Christians inherited. Most of the early modern scientists left behind apparently sincere expressions of a basically Jewish-Christian attitude. They regularly worshipped God within the tradition and they understood their scientific activity as 'thinking God's thoughts after him'. They were actually encouraged to pursue science (whatever discouragement some authorities of the Church might offer) because the God of the Jews and Christians was a rational being and the Creator of an orderly universe. Thus they expected their own reason – part of the 'image' of God in them – to be able to probe nature successfully, and they hoped to find an intelligible and reliable order everywhere. Today we know that they underestimated the amount of randomness or chance in the universe. But at the time it was probably a useful mistake. Had they not made it, they might have not had sufficient trust in the intelligibility of the universe to become scientists.

It is impossible for honest and informed people today to treat the Christian Bible with the innocent credulity that marked the theological work even of the great Isaac Newton in the seventeenth century. It is certain that the Bible does not possess the kind of authority that a good modern scientific textbook possesses. Indeed, it is also certain that even the best of scientific textbooks does not possess an authority so complete that it ought not to be questioned. Thanks to the questions which scientifically minded people rightly insisted on asking, we know that the Bible contains much mythological material. The Bible begins with a creation in six days. The total time that its story covers, from the creation to Paul's arrival in Rome, is a little more than four thousand years. But here I want to ask whether the essential teaching of the Bible, which comes out of profound spiritual experience rather than mythology, is as out-of-date as it is often assumed to be.

I do not think that there could be a more important question. For I agree with what J. A. V. Butler (who is far from being an orthodox Christian) writes at the conclusion of his *Modern Biology and its Human Implications* (1976).

'What is needed,' he declares, 'is a new covenant on the basis of human life, which is compatible with all the scientific knowledge of the era but does not accept its supremacy or its sufficiency. While it should not reject any source of human inspiration, it has in its hand as its most likely basis for Western people the teachings of Jesus, the man, which are already inextricably embedded in all Western thought, culture and institutions and which provide a reservoir of feeling which has accumulated around them for two thousand years. If it is rejected probably nothing is left to hold together Western civilization and its final decay will be inevitable.'

5 A View of the Creation

The literature of the Bible is so shot through with the sense of the presence of God, and is on the whole so innocent of philosophical refinement, that it can easily convey a false impression. We may suppose that a naïve belief is essential to it – the belief that every event is immediately controlled by God, or it may be a devil. And this belief seems to have been discredited by science. Thus J. A. V. Butler observes in passing: 'it is no longer possible to credit that events in the natural world are under the control of supernatural intelligences'.

But it is necessary for a modern reader to ask rather carefully what this literature, taken as a whole, means by the ideas to which Dr Butler refers when he uses the three words 'control', 'supernatural' and 'intelligences'. Does the Bible as a whole say that every event is completely under God's control or the devil's? Does it say that God or the devil is supernatural in the sense of being entirely above nature, or of being knowable apart from man's physical senses? Does it say that there is a perfect symmetry between God's life (or the devil's) and the life of an intelligent man? The answer to all these questions is, surely, *no*.

The Hebrew scriptures as we have them were collected by men who had seen the two little Israelite states blotted out, Jerusalem and its temple destroyed, and many an individual's life reduced to the misery of Job. The Christian Bible was put together by a community under persecution and is dominated by a teacher well aware of the moral indifference of nature: 'Your Father makes his sun to shine on bad and good people alike ...' (Matthew 5:45). The Christian knows that the necessary preface to Bible study is provided by the terrible words of the deserted and doomed Jesus: 'My God, my God, why did you abandon me?' (Mark 15:34 quoting Psalm 21:1). In Rudolf Otto's justly famous phrase, the God of the Bible is the 'tremendous and fascinating' mystery. The conventional image of God dies in a tragic world, yet he is still there – 'my God, my God' – beyond all complacent and trivial ideas about him. He is revealed most movingly not in a thunderstorm or even in a wild flower but in the patient suffering of Jesus.

Going to the heart of this storm of suffering the Bible affirms that everything is from God. 'In the beginning, when God created the universe...' (Genesis 1:1). Paul sums up the faith of Ancient Israel and of the Christian Church in words which the New English Bible translates: 'Source, Guide and Goal of all is' (Romans 11:36); 'from whom all being comes, towards whom we move' (1 Corinthians 8:6); 'over all and through all and in all' (Ephesians 4:6). A hymn which may have been familiar to the early Church is used in the Revelation of John (4:11):

> Our Lord and God! You are worthy
> to receive glory, honour and power.
> For you created all things,
> and by your will they were given existence and life.

The word *bara*, translated as 'created', is used in the Hebrew scriptures only when God is the subject. That special word for a unique activity is a reminder that the Bible knows that the comparison between the Creator and a craftsman, although inevitable, does not completely explain the mystery which inspires worship. In particular, the comparison with a human worker who then rests does not sufficiently stress the fact (as the Bible sees it) that God is always active. Jesus takes it for granted that 'it is God who clothes the wild grass' (Matthew 6:30); and the whole of the fourth gospel affirms that the Father is 'always working' (John 5:17).

The celebration of God the Creator in the Bible can be valued without making the claim that the Bible supplies an accurate account of the Creator's methods. Indeed, few Jews or Christians are 'Fundamentalists' or 'literalists' in that sense today. The first chapter of the Bible belongs to the 'priestly' tradition, one of the latest elements in the Old Testament, and it is accompanied by a number of earlier mythological pictures of the creation; one of these is found in the Bible's second chapter. In his study of *Creation* (translated into English in 1974) the Old Testament scholar, Claus Westermann, concludes that 'reflection on creation meant to rehearse, in the present world and in man's dangerous situation, the beginning, when what is now came to be.' What appears to be an historical narrative is but 'a reiteration of the reality by virtue of which the world continues to exist'. This interpretation of the Bible corresponds closely with the conclusions of modern scholars about the surviving traditions of primitive tribes. The significance of the first chapter of Genesis is best brought out by comparing it with the Babylonian creation myths – against which it was, most scholars think, an exiled Jew's manifesto. Scientifically the Jews were inferior to the Babylonians (whose divisions of space and time we still use in the degrees, minutes and seconds of longitudinal measurement and in the hours, minutes and seconds of the clocks). But that is not to say that the ancient Jews have nothing to teach modern men religiously. An introduction to the modern discussion of the significance of their myths has been supplied by Norman Young in *Creator, Creation and Faith* (1976).

To the Bible this universe is an astounding unity. When the Hebrew poet looked at the heavens he understood far less than a scientist does in one sense, but he was moved to ask God: 'What is man that you think of him, mere man that you care for him?' (Psalm 8:4). He worshipped the God who alone had stretched out the heavens and made the Earth (Isaiah 44:24); before whom the inhabitants of the Earth were like grasshoppers, its peoples like a drop from a bucket (Isaiah 40:15, 22); by whom the host of the stars had been counted, named and kept in existence (Isaiah 40:26). When doubts invaded him, Hebrew man clung to the thought that God alone laid the foundation of the Earth; he alone confined the sea; he alone commanded the Sun, the snow, the rain, the thunder, the stars (Job 38).

To the Bible, the universe is one because it has this single Source, Guide and Goal; because it all comes from the divine 'word' or 'wisdom'. This conviction can be put very simply: 'God looked at everything he had made, and he was very pleased' (Genesis 1:31). But the conviction can be also held when the thought of the distances of heaven and earth has almost overwhelmed the worshipper (as in Psalms 19 and 139), or when there has been some contact with Egyptian and other wisdom about nature (as in the books called Proverbs, Ecclesiastes and the Wisdom of Solomon). In the New Testament the thought of the unity of the universe in its divine origin is expressed in two dramatic ways. One is the teaching that the 'word' or 'wisdom' of God glimpsed in all the creation – 'not one thing was made without him' says John (1:3) – is to be seen among men as Jesus. The other is the prayer of Jesus himself. For the Source, Guide and Goal of the universe can be addressed as *Abba*, 'Father' (Galatians 4:6; Romans 8:15).

To the Bible the universe is marvellous but not divine. Man must respect it but is at liberty to explore and use it. Features of the creation myth that begins the Bible are its denial of pantheism (the belief that everything deserves worship as divine) and polytheism (the belief in many gods, usually including many natural phenomena regarded as divine). From first to last in this story, one God alone is active; what exists is what he makes; and the climax of his creation is the making of man with a mandate to 'fill the Earth and subdue it'. In the Babylonian creation myth, on the other hand, many gods are active along with Babylon's own Marduk; the Sun, the Moon, the stars and the Earth are made out of the body of the defeated goddess, Tiamat; and the climax is the building of Babylon's temple. To the Jew or the Christian, the Earth itself is the great temple honouring the invisible God – as Paul is said to have told the Athenians (Acts 17: 22-29). It has been argued that the Bible has encouraged a scornful attitude to nature, leading to the ruthless exploitation of the Earth; it is sometimes alleged that the Jewish-Christian tradition was in this way among the historical roots of our ecological crisis. But that is not a fair assessment. To the Bible, the universe is sacred because it is the work of the Creator. Many passages in the Old Testament and the gospels praise the farmer's skills as he co-operates with the natural processes, and they draw spiritual lessons from a countryman's close knowledge of nature. The main consequence of the biblical understanding of nature – set out in, for example, *Man and Nature*, edited by Hugh Montefiore (1975) – has been to encourage not a ruthless exploitation but a reverent enjoyment and exploration. The monks who at the beginning of the Middle Ages practised and spread efficient agriculture were faithful to this tradition; as was Abbot Mendel, who by watching the peas founded our modern knowledge of genes.

The famous *Canticle of the Sun* by St Francis of Assisi is a particularly lovely example of the Jewish-Christian tradition that the Sun, like the rest of nature, is to be celebrated but not worshipped. Sun-worship has been a favourite activity in the long history of religion. In the Old Testament it is an accepted fact about many peoples – but not about the people called to worship Yahweh, the God of Israel (Deuteronomy 4:19). The power of the Sun was so deeply imprinted on the religious imagination of the biblical world that an early Christian could find no stronger climax to his description of the victorious Jesus than to say that 'his face was as bright as the midday sun' (Revelation 1:16). But in the psalms the Sun is put in its place. The strength of the Sun is like a bridegroom's ardour, and nothing is hid from its heat, but only the law of God is perfect (19:4-6). A king can claim that he was promised a throne as enduring as the Sun, but he knows that once God's wrath is aroused he is rejected (89:36, 38). The Sun itself will be included when the heavens wear out like a man's clothing and are thrown away (102:26). The Sun rules the day (136:8), but its task is to praise its Maker (148:3). And there are some religiously revealing touches in the Priestly creation myth. On the third day, when there is as yet no Sun, God decrees: 'Let the Earth produce all kinds of plants, those that bear grain and those that bear fruit . . .' On the fourth day, when God gets round to making the Sun, the Moon and the stars, it is only because they will be convenient 'to separate day from night and to show the time when days, years and religious festivals begin; they will shine in the sky to give light to the Earth' (Genesis 1: 11-15). This is not science but it is a magnificent downgrading of the divine Sun into a calendar and a lamp.

Even before the rise of modern science there were devout believers who saw that the essential teaching of the Bible did not depend on its mythology about the Sun. In the Old Testament a picture of the universe has been adopted from surrounding peoples. It is a picture of the Earth as a flat surface covered by a hemispherical dome. Both the Earth and this dome ('heaven') are surrounded by water and the Sun moves across the dome. But the medieval Christian picture, found for example in Dante's *Divine Comedy*, was very different from that Old Testament mythology. It was the picture resulting from the work of the Greek astronomer Ptolemy in Alexandria about AD 150. Ptolemy taught that the Earth was a sphere around which the Sun and the stars moved in perfect circles. When in 1543 Copernicus taught that the Earth moved around the Sun in a circle (not an ellipse: that was Kepler's discovery), he was opposing Ptolemy's theory by his own. In 1633 the Roman Inquisition condemned Galileo for teaching that Copernicus was basically right, and Ptolemy basically wrong, according to his own observations through his telescope. They claimed that they were defending the sacred scriptures; but in 1582 on a Pope's authority the work of Copernicus had already been used as the basis of the Gregorian reform of the calendar. What the Inquisition was really defending – with such disastrous consequences for science in Roman Catholic countries – was the prestige of Ptolemy. Already in the Middle Ages it had been recognized that the Old Testament had not said the last word about the cosmos.

The Bible celebrates the joy of life. Psalm 104 gives thanks that, surrounded by the rain, the clouds, the winds, the thunder and the lightning, the Earth is set on such sure foundations that it cannot be shaken. The seas are curbed although they once stood above the mountains, and the springs gush forth to water the beasts. The birds sing in the trees, the cattle chew the grass, the goats take refuge in the hills and the badgers in the rocks. The lions roar for their prey in the night and sleep peaceably in their dens by day. The sea teems with fish and is crossed by ships. Perpetually all living beings are fed and, even when death comes, after it the Earth is renewed. Amid such life, man finds plants to cultivate, wine to gladden his heart, oil to make his face shine, innumerable causes to sing to the Lord while he has being. The observant delight which Jesus took in the nature around him at Nazareth comes out in many of his parables.

In particular the Bible celebrates the joy of human life, with its marvellous mixture of body, mind and spirit. This is the wonder in the ancient picture of God breathing life into *Adam* (man), made of earth (Genesis 2:7; I Corinthians 15:45-49). It is hard to tell how far this creation myth was taken literally. If the primitive people studied by modern anthropologists are anything to go by, it was at one level or in some moods; but at another level and in other moods it was regarded as an old tribal story not to be treated like everyday, matter-of-fact observations.

Certainly the Bible (which includes the erotic Song of Songs) is full of the facts of sex – and full of man's links with the rest of life. In Genesis 1 the creatures of the sea, the birds of the air and 'all kinds of animal life' must appear on the Earth before human life is possible. Man is told to get to know the animals, to name them and to take care to control them (Genesis 2:19; Psalm 89:5-8). The animals must be rescued when the Flood rains down; otherwise man on the Earth will not have a tolerable future (Genesis 7). God's covenant with Noah is also with the animals (Genesis 9:10). The Bible contains a number of pictures of animals drawn with loving care and detail. Job finds the power of God in the creation of the lion, the ox, the ostrich, the horse, the hawk, the hippopotamus, the crocodile (Job 38:39-41:34). Some of the laws of Ancient Israel protected birds and animals; for example, taking the mother bird along with the young or the eggs in the nest was prohibited (Deuteronomy 22:6-7). Paul quotes: 'Do not muzzle an ox when you are using it to thresh corn' (Deuteronomy 25:4). When he adds: 'Is God concerned about oxen?' (1 Corinthians 9:9), he falls below the Bible's own standards of sensitivity to the animal kingdom. He was a townsman – not a village boy like Jesus.

The abundance of life, revealing the patient power of the Creator of life, is praised rather than explained in the Bible. It strikes one ancient writer that the rain pours down to carpet the desert with grass and flowers (Job 38:25-27). It strikes Jesus that scattered seeds produces corn with up to a hundred grains – 'first the tender stalk, then the ear, and finally the ear full of corn' (Mark 4:1-9, 28). And Jesus notices that the mustard seed, by tradition the smallest of all seeds, produces a plant so big that birds make their nests in its shade (Mark 4:31, 32). The mercy of God is as abundant as this life which needs mercy. Over a stormy world is set the vision of God's patience 'as long as the world exists' (Genesis 8:20-9: 17). Over the memory of the impatience of Moses and the people is set God's self-revelation as 'a God who is full of compassion and pity, who is not easily angered' (Exodus 34:6).

The Old Testament's insight that the mercies of God are 'new every morning' (Lamentations 3:23) is a prominent theme of the teaching of Jesus. He compares God with the farmer who lets all the weeds remain among the wheat until the harvest (Matthew 13:24-30); with the housewife who waits until the bread is all levened (Matthew 13:33); with the fisherman who knows that his net will catch useless fish (Matthew 13:47, 48); even with the absentee landlord who puts up with many insults from the tenants of his vineyard (Mark 12:1-9). As Paul contemplates the patience of God, he is driven to exclaim: 'How great are God's riches! How deep are his wisdom and knowledge! Who can explain his decisions? Who can understand his ways?' (Romans 11:33).

According to the Bible, God maintains, expresses and accomplishes his purpose by selecting small groups and individuals. The central theme of the Old Testament is the covenant between God and his chosen people, Israel, but even an Israelite could see the numerical insignificance of his people in the ancient world (Deuteronomy 7:6-8). Within this agreement between God and Israel, individuals are called out of the crowd, as when David is chosen as a king or Jeremiah is chosen as a prophet; and it becomes the duty of the crowd to follow those individuals. Characteristic of the whole Old Testament is the story told of how the army of 32,000 had to be reduced to three hundred before God would give the victory (Judges 7). The same theme runs through the New Testament. At times Jesus is presented as being utterly alone, the sole remnant of the servants of God. In a city only a few – and those society's rejects – may be Christians (1 Corinthians 1:27-29). Yet all the time God does not forget the many. As Psalm 145:8 sings:

> He is good to everyone
> and has compassion on all he has made.

Jesus proclaims a God who sets no limits to his compassion. Paul preaches that 'God has made all people prisoners of disobedience, so that he might show mercy to them all' (Romans 11:32).

If we ask what is the purpose behind God's strange behaviour, the Bible does not answer that this purpose is clearly seen throughout the existing world. That was the mistake made by later Christians who felt obliged to argue for the existence of the Creator from the evidence of the watch-like 'design' which they claimed was so clear in nature. The Bible, on the contrary, has to come to terms with apparently triumphant evil. Repeatedly the Bible insists that in this often tragic world 'our life is a matter of faith, not of sight' (2 Corinthians 5:7). Even the seer who glimpses the Beginning and the End knows that he and his Christian brothers are called to patient endurance (Revelation 1:9). And the Bible does expect the endurance to be possible without the faith that the End, like the Beginning, lies in God. (I tried to present the 'eschatology' of the Bible in *The Last Things Now*, 1969.)

The End, according to the Bible, is to include the glory of man. The Bible does not say that man is the only intelligent creature in the universe; it is full of pictures of angels and demons. Least of all does the Bible say that man is perfect, or always rational, or thoroughly good; it is full of murders, beginning with Abel's in its fourth chapter. But an ancient tradition claims that men and women – equally – are made in God's likeness (Genesis 1:27). Another tradition puts man in a garden of beautiful trees. Only two of these trees are out of bounds – meaning that man is not immortal and cannot make the ultimate decision about what is good or bad in life before death. Subject to these restrictions Adam is the lord of the Earth (Genesis 2:8, 9). By his own fault Adam loses that paradise, but Paul calls Jesus the new Adam (Romans 5:15-21), in keeping with the Christian conviction that the Old Testament's highest claims for man have been fulfilled in the victory of Jesus (Hebrews 1:1-2:9).

One of the visions that unites the two Testaments occurs first in the book of Daniel (7:13, 14) when a mysterious figure looking like a man is given rule over the whole Earth. That lies behind the New Testament's description of Jesus as the 'Son of Man' through whom 'many sons' share the glory (Hebrews 2:10). Through him 'people from every tribe, language, nation and race' become 'a kingdom of priests' (Revelation 4:9, 10). And Paul envisages even more. 'All of creation waits with eager longing for God to reveal his sons'. Creation will 'one day be set free from its slavery to decay and share the glorious freedom of the children of God'; and meanwhile 'all of creation groans with pain, like the pain of childbirth' (Romans 8:18-22).

Obviously the image of a cosmic childbirth is not easy to interpret in precise terms, but Paul does offer some help. As God's purpose reaches its triumph – as 'the complete number of the Gentiles comes to God' and 'all Israel will be saved' (Romans 11:25, 26) – bodies made of the Earth will be exchanged for imperishable spiritual bodies (1 Corinthians 15:35-37). Paul agrees that the idea of a 'spiritual body' is 'a mystery'. Nowadays we should call it a myth. But the myth expresses the conviction that the completion of the divine purpose running through all creation depends on man entering eternal glory, having prepared for it in physical existence.

Beyond this glory for man is briefly glimpsed in the Bible the fulfilment of God's purposes in the whole universe: 'God will rule completely over all' (1 Corinthians 15:28). Obviously here, too, the pictures given are mythological, as when we are told that 'lions will eat straw as cattle do' (Isaiah 11:7) or that 'new heavens' will be created after 'the Day when the heavens will burn up and be destroyed' (2 Peter 3:12, 13). But this End-myth arises out of the Christian experiences. God's power experienced at the birth of 'Christ in you' is felt to be a foretaste of God's complete victory everywhere (Colossians 1:20-27), because God is now known to be 'able to do so much more than we can ever ask' (Ephesians 3:9-21). God is capable of making this whole universe what he wants it to be – and of preserving for ever, in his own life, everything he values in the universe after its necessary death. Already a psalm of Ancient Israel (102:24-27) conveyed a vision of the ground of this hope:

> O Lord, you live for ever,
>   long ago you created the earth,
> and with your hands you made the heavens.
> They will disappear, but you will remain;
>   they will wear out like clothes.
> You will discard them like clothes,
>   and they will vanish.
> But you are always the same,
>   and your life never ends.

6 A Choice for This Generation

I have now completed the experiment of placing the main teachings of modern science about man and his circumstances alongside the main teachings of the Bible as summaries of the religious experience of Jews and Christians; or at least, I have completed as much of this experiment as is needed here. I have made the experiment not for academic purposes but in order to answer the question whether the essential claims of the Jewish-Christian tradition can still make sense in the age of science. For I am convinced that with that question is bound up another: is the sense of the 'incomprehensibility of the new cosmos', the 'lack of confidence,' the 'terrible loss of nerve' to which Kenneth Clark and Jacob Bronowski referred really necessary for a civilization based on science?

To these crucial questions the truthful answer is, I think, that we are *not* compelled to abandon the religious experience and attitude. So we are *not* forced to surrender to the 'terrible loss of nerve'. Let me try to put very succinctly the choice that is still, I believe, open.

To the person who chooses not to believe in the Creator, the modern discoveries about the origins of the universe are all that can be known; all talk about the God beyond, as well as within, those origins is simply nonsense. To the believer, on the other hand, modern science is a breath-taking revelation of the Creator's methods – beginning so far as we are concerned with the primeval egg of elementary particles and beginning again with the first living cell.

To the unbeliever, the regularities in the universe are so amazing that they cannot be compared with any human activity. The modern believer still finds it helpful to speak of the 'laws' of God. To the unbeliever, the attempt of some churchmen to suppress Galileo's research into the relationship of the Earth and the Sun, and the later attempt to discredit Darwin's work on evolution, are typical of a long history in which religion and science are irreconcilable enemies. To the modern believer, despite the mistakes of the past religion and science need not be enemies but can be two eyes looking at the universe which has its 'Source, Guide and Goal' in God.

To the unbeliever, the evolution of higher forms of life from the interplay between the environment and the random mutations of genes needs not God but only immense amounts of luck and time. To the modern believer, evolutionary progress is the work of God – although the control which God exercises over the complex process is far more subtle than previous generations of believers thought. Out of a total picture which is certainly astounding, the unbeliever chooses to stress the apparent chance in the mutations and the apparent cruelty of the fates of less improved forms of life; while the believer chooses to stress that the end product is progress and that along the way much is found that seems full of joy and beautiful.

To the unbeliever, *Homo sapiens* is the highest form of life in the universe – but perhaps not high enough to survive for much longer on the Earth. It is also reckoned (except by those who have rejected religion but accepted the essential claims of spiritualism) that there is no possibility of the individual personality surviving the brain's death. To the believer, on the other hand, the mental or spiritual life which man's brain has made possible is supported and guided by the Creator's love which is father-like. That divine love need not be frustrated by man's folly or terminated by man's death. On the contrary, God's love is what holds a personality in God's own life, eternity.

Salvador Lauria in his *Life the Unfinished Experiment* (1973) apologized for the almost inevitable human tendency to find a purpose in nature – a tendency shown in the title of his book. 'I have sometimes referred to evolution – that is natural selection – almost as if it worked with a goal in mind . . . In describing these events there is a tendency to use words such as goal or purpose or plan because one comes to think of genes or cells or organisms in human terms. But genes are merely molecular structures, cells chemical factories, and organisms pawns of the blind monster, evolution. Man is alone in knowing the joys and torments of conscious will.' Professor Lauria's assessment of the human condition is this: 'Man is but one product, albeit a very special one, of a series of blind chances and harsh necessities. As with all evolution's creations, his biological fate is to make do, to survive as a species by the skin of his teeth.' But that leaves out religious experience and the vision to which religious experience gives rise. As a result of experience the believer is of the opinion that, while genes, cells, organisms, planets and stars should certainly be depersonalized there is present in the universe a will higher than man's will but certainly not inferior to it. Man is not alone.

Evidently the argument between religious belief and unbelief can never be settled on scientific grounds. That this really is 'the creation', under its Creator, must always be a matter of opinion. But what modern science can do for religion is to show that *if* the Creator is real, if God exists, then the actual creation is revealed in the discoveries of science. The actual creation is of a universe imperfect (how else could it differ from the perfect God?) but alive everywhere with some part of the activity of God. The size of the universe – great beyond anything we can observe, calculate or imagine – shows the Creator's boundless delight in creativity; and the unity and intelligibility of the creation are reflections of the unity of its only ultimate Source. Man is invited to explore and to use this universe as a child is invited to explore and to use a home. All the marvels of the Sun and the Earth have at least one clear function: they make life here possible if not probable. This life is made so rich in its variety by methods which astonish us – but which were, it appears, best, given the nature of the universe.

Such methods of the Creator call for what we can only call 'suffering' in him as in his creatures, but any other methods would have been less efficient for the Creator's purposes and therefore, in the long run, less beneficial to his creatures. The will of God is done sometimes by small groups or individuals, but always God works out his purposes for all. There is real freedom or chance in this process, but it is freedom or chance allowed within God's purposes – because not to allow it would be less beneficial to the progress of the whole. God's purposes lie beyond the full comprehension of his creatures, but some of these purposes are fulfilled when his physical existence makes man capable of entry into a deathless life with God. Difficult as this is for us to believe, the prize of the fulfilled creation must be so precious that it justifies what is done or endured in the process. When man looks at the universe around him, he sees the way in which the Creator has expressed his own character in striving for this prize; and when man looks at himself, he sees the way in which the Creator has expressed himself more fully than in all the lifeless stars; and when man looks at the future, he sees the Creator's reward.

An estimate of man's place in the universe suggested by this combination of modern science with the religion of the Jewish-Christian tradition seems powerful enough to lay a foundation for what Jacob Bronowski most wanted ('an understanding of man himself') and to remove the heart of darkness that Kenneth Clark most feared ('the incomprehensibility of our new cosmos'). It demands a leap of faith as does any religion or morality, but it is not a leap which must be made in defiance of scientific knowledge. It suggests ethical values urgently important for the age of science and its spiritual crisis – reverence for the Creator, reverence for the whole creation, and reverence for the human animal who is, more than any other creature, like the Creator.

For this generation the choice is, I believe, still possible. And I think that means: hope for humanity can still be judged to be reasonable.

At the end of his brilliant reconstruction of *The First Three Minutes* in the creation, the physicist Steven Weinberg wrote: 'The effort to understand the universe is one of the very few things that lift human life a little above the level of farce and gives it some of the grace of tragedy'. But at end of his *The Universe: Its Beginning and its End* (1975) Dr Lloyd Motz, Professor of Astronomy in Chicago, drew the conclusion that man's 'development towards perfection' is 'inevitable' – because the 'dominant role' in evolution must be assigned not to random mutations or to natural selection but to 'the potential for change in a certain direction'; and the direction seems to be 'the appearance of intelligent life' after the whole process reaching back to the fireball at the beginning of the universe we know. And at the end of *Animal Nature and Human Nature* (1974), W. H. Thorpe, Emeritus Professor of Animal Ethology at Cambridge, wrote: 'The task of mankind is perhaps greater and his activities for good or ill more momentous now than ever before in the history of the world. It is tragic that such multitudes are today oppressed and rendered impotent and ineffective by a failure to find meaning in their lives when in fact the potential fullness of human life has never been greater or more obvious for those who have eyes to see. It is indeed both a joy and a terror to be living in times such as these – joy at the fullness of life and the opportunities for greater enlightenment; terror at the danger and disasters threatened by evil forces – for never has the human race had greater opportunity than now to rise above itself and to bring the human spirit to new levels of transcendence. To do this we must be inspired by a glimpse of the timeless vision of Dante who saw in the ineffable climax of his pilgrimage, in perhaps the greatest poem in the history of man, that all creation and all time are bound up, like the pages in some vast volume, in God – "the love that moves the Sun and the other stars." '

Part Three

NOT DOOM
BUT LIBERATION

1 Are We Doomed?

While I was at King's College, Cambridge, an eminent anthropologist who was Provost of the college, Dr (later Professor Sir Edmund Leach, broadcast some Reith Lectures about the future. They were later published under the title *A Runaway World?* (1968).

Their point was that a glorious future lay ahead, if only the present generation would get a grip on the world. 'Men have become like gods,' the Provost began. 'Isn't it about time that we understood our divinity? Science offers us total mastery over our environment and over our destiny, yet instead of rejoicing we feel deeply afraid . . . Can we accept responsibility for changing the life span of individuals, for altering the genetic endowment of human beings, for restricting the balance of competition between all living things? . . . All of us need to understand that God, or Nature, or Chance, or Evolution, or the Course of History, or whatever you like to call it, cannot be trusted any more. We simply must take charge of our own fate.'

In contrast, a fairly typical book of the 1970s was Gordon Rattray Taylor's *How to Avoid the Future* (1975). Mr Taylor saw doom everywhere. The climate was entering a new Ice Age. An alternative disaster was that the output of carbon dioxide would overheat the atmosphere and cause the Arctic and Antarctic ice to melt. But anyway the cities were doomed by the violence of their own inhabitants – not to mention the greed that had caused suicidal inflation. 'Where social structure will crack first is a rash thing to prophesy. Possibly in Italy? My guess is that it will be in Great Britain . . .' And Mr Taylor was the man chosen to write the book connected with the 1977 exhibition of technology in London, *A Salute to British Genius*!

Dame Barbara Ward's two books *Only One Earth* (with René Dubos) and *The Home of Man* (1972-76) were prepared in consultation with many experts for the great international conferences on 'the Human Environment' and 'Human Settlements' in Stockholm and Vancouver. But these carefully researched, well pondered and superbly well expressed books could not be described as optimistic. The key quotation in *Only One Earth* was from Adlai Stevenson about the Earth as a little spaceship on which we all travel together, 'dependent on its vulnerable supplies of air and soil'. The second book, on urban problems, had a key section entitled: 'Is the Future Possible?'

Perhaps the authors of such books were worried and weary British intellectuals, only listened to by UN conferences, if by them? But it was an Australian lecturer in politics, Joseph Camilleri, who wrote the best book yet published on *Civilization in Crisis* (1976), with careful notes about most of the other books. It was an Australian professor of biology, Charles Birch, who told the Assembly of the World Council of Churches at Nairobi in 1975 that 'the world is a *Titanic* on a collision course' and that the 'de-development' of the rich nations was unavoidably necessary 'if we are to continue to inhabit the Earth'. And it was an Australian zoologist, Angus Martin, who wrote *The Last Generation* (1976). He quoted a fellow-scientist in Melbourne: 'We're the last generation who can eat a steak any time we like, chop down a tree if we feel destructive, and have as many kids as we want. So what the hell? Let's make the most of it!' White Australia's time was almost up because it could not remain isolated from a starving Asia; and the opening sentence was a grimly approving quotation from *The Population Bomb* by Paul Ehrlich (1968): 'The battle to feed all of humanity is over'. Dr Martin interpreted the scientific evidence to mean two things: probably man is doomed to destroy himself, and at the same time to refuse to believe that he is doing so.

In the extensive literature, journalism and TV coverage of doom which inaugurated the last quarter of the twentieth century, the statistics naturally differed from author to author and year to year. But the message was always the same. Nature is beginning to hit back.

The end of our oil and natural gas supplies is in sight. Other resources are also finite. Metals and minerals are listed with predictions of the years when there will be no more unless consumption is drastically curtailed. Gold and silver, the idols of many generations, are near the head of these depressing lists. Food supplies are assessed and famine is seen as the inescapable doom of the multiplying millions. If fishermen reap the harvest of the seas more thoroughly, other species may follow the whales now near extinction. If peasants can be encouraged to grow more by massive political and economic reforms, oil-based fertilizers will be too expensive; or the improved seeds will produce crops which will be destroyed by new diseases; or the sprays used to kill pests and weeds will also kill the soil and breed pests resistant to the sprays; or irrigation will bring not only water but also disastrous amounts of salt. If industry can be made more productive – assuming, that is, that the raw materials will be there, with the energy to turn them into what man desires – it is feared that the waste will be such that the rivers will become sewers and the air itself will be poisonous. Already the great pest-killer, DDT, is swept from the crops on the land to the plankton on the ocean's surface, and so into fish, and so into men's stomachs. Some of the lead in America's petrol ends up in the ice of Greenland. Lakes are dying through lack of oxygen and the Mediterranean may soon join them. While these doomsters argue with each other about which disaster will come first, all agree that man is not going to get away with his treatment of nature – even if the cities do not explode with their own citizens' violence and even if the stockpiles of armaments are never used.

To the doomsters, man is by nature incapable of responding to this multiple challenge. In the words of Angus Martin, man is 'the pig who is being asked to fly, the chimpanzee being asked to paint the Mona Lisa'. To be sure, man has a long record of self-condemnation. Within the twentieth century the First World War shattered self-confidence and produced many despairing statements of the human condition. Two little books of 1930 and 1931, Sigmund Freud's *Civilization and its Discontents* and Aldous Huxley's *Brave New World*, have in fact never been bettered as cynicism. But since 1945 the years of peace – or of the absence of world war – have brought a new dimension to man's intellectual and moral attack on himself: man is exhausting and polluting his planet like a bird fouling its nest. Indeed, the prophecy of man's well deserved doom has become so frequent that it may have become self-fulfilling. The key sentence in Robert Heilbroner's influential *Inquiry into the Human Prospect* (1975) was: 'The question, then, is how we are to summon up the will to survive . . .'

The evidence suggests that during almost all his history man has known famine as his neighbour, has seen death strike repeatedly in his family, has not expected to escape his own death much longer, and has felt that his descendants' survival on the Earth was very perilous. In 1798 an English clergyman, Thomas Malthus, published his *Essay on Population*. In the same year the economist David Ricardo published his *Principles of Political Economy and Taxation*. Malthus and Ricardo had noticed (in the classic words of Mark Twain's father) that 'they are not making land any more'. So they revived the fear that population growth would soon outgrow the productivity of the land and of any industry. Today the world's population is four times what it was at the end of the eighteenth century. Improvements in agriculture and industry have so far been enough to keep the people alive. Indeed, the population of England doubled in the half-century after 1798. Resources were dangerously stretched in the Hungry Forties, but after 1850 growth both in production and in population began climbing again. But there have been some horrible warnings about the risks being run. One of them occurred in a country then united politically with England. After the potato famine caused by a plant disease in Ireland in the 1840s, about two million died and about two million emigrated: together, about half the population. Many now ask whether this sort of disaster could happen again globally.

Since the population explosion in the 1950s and 1960s these and other ancient fears have been voiced; and a new voice has been added to the disheartening chorus. The end must be near for the computer says so, and the computer is a more reliable instrument than the unaided mind of doomed man. That was the argument of *The Limits to Growth* (1972), the sensational report sponsored by the industrialists and scientists of the Club of Rome and based on computer work organized by a prestigious team at the Massachusetts Institute of Technology. Their conclusion was that 'if the present growth trends in world population, industrialization, pollution, food production and resource depletion continue unchanged, the limits to growth on this planet will be reached some time within the next one hundred years. The most probable result will be a rather sudden and uncontrollable decline in both population and industrial capacity.' Their proposal was that 'a condition of ecological and economic stability' (zero growth) should be established as quickly as possible.

During the ensuing discussion, it emerged that the computer programming in this 'world systems analysis' had not been rigorous enough. More variations ought to have been allowed between those areas most likely to be hit first by famine and those which would use their greater agricultural skills to grow more food and their greater purchasing power to buy it; between those areas likely to be hit hardest by pollution and those which would remain too poor to be polluted; and so forth. More delays ought to have been allowed for in the collapse of the world's economy because some people would be able to think of devices to postpone the evil day. In the computer industry's own jargon, there would be feedback from the world on the way to doom. These criticisms were put forward with special force by the experts in the University of Sussex who compiled *Thinking about the Future* (1973), and those who had sponsored *The Limits to Growth* acknowledged their substantial justice. Still, the main argument of *The Limits to Growth* could not be faulted. It was that the world could not endlessly continue to double its population every thirty years, and consumption of energy every fifteen; yet precisely that was the pattern at the beginning of the 1970s. Even to feed the mouths already in the world, and the mouths of the children now bound to arrive, would be a physical task greater than any faced by man before. Industry could not help if it endlessly multiplied its consumption of non-renewable materials and its discharge of poisonous waste. The conclusions were reiterated: there are severe limits to the Earth's man-carrying capacity, as there are severe limits to man's recognition of this fact. *Mankind at the Turning Point*, the Club of Rome's 1975 sequel which was intended to be less pessimistic than *The Limits to Growth*, quoted a Dr Gregg as saying: 'The world has cancer and the cancer is man'.

The debate about the future of nuclear power has provided a focus for most of these fears. Here the physical limits of nature's gifts to man are dramatically evident – as are the psychological limitations of man's response to the dangers.

When the atomic bombs were dropped in 1945, horror spread everywhere. Robert Oppenheimer said that the physicists had known sin; and the world gradually added that so had the politicians. But then came a curious lull in the alarm. The conventional wisdom grew to be that there were great consolations in the new era. Nuclear weapons, retained by the United States, the Soviet Union and Britain as the world's super-powers, could keep the peace by deterring aggression with the fear of massive retaliation. The secrets of the atomic and hydrogen bombs could be used to produce abundant and cheap electricity. 'Atoms for peace' would thus make real the new world of science fiction – where, whatever else might be in short supply, there was never any lack of energy. People would surely be sensible enough to refrain from unleashing nuclear war: thus a 'balance of terror' would be struck and held, and under the protection of this admittedly bizarre arrangement a peaceful and prosperous future could be secured. Bikini, the atoll in the Pacific which the US Navy cleared of its inhabitants in order to test nuclear weapons in 1946, was remembered only as a name for girls' swimsuits on happier beaches. But then the horror came back. Slowly the perils of reliance on the threatened use of nuclear weapons – on that flash 'brighter than a thousand suns' – began to dawn on imaginations and consciences. The arms race between America and Russia became a nightmare, with each side boasting that it had more than enough to exterminate the other but claiming that it 'needed' yet more to feel secure: it 'needed' a stockpile able to destroy a million Hiroshimas. Eventually it was calculated that the nuclear arsenals of the Americans and Russians, when combined, would provide sixteen tons of explosive power for every human being on the Earth. The perils were accentuated as other nations including China and France developed nuclear weapons and refused to allow the original owners to reassert their club's exclusiveness. The prospect seemed to be that every nation would soon consider its own nuclear missiles as essential as its own airline to its self-respect: in both cases, whatever the cost. And in the 1960s the alarm grew about the peaceful uses of nuclear energy. This story is told in, for example, Walter Patterson's *Nuclear Power* (1976).

The development of nuclear power stations proved to be far more difficult and expensive than had been foreseen. Then it was realized that the uranium on which the whole process of nuclear fission depended was a finite resource, like oil itself – but much, much scarcer. Then people learned with dismay how poisonous was the radiation from the plutonium to be produced as a waste by the 'fastbreeder' reactors which were to be fifty per cent more efficient in their use of uranium. Just as it is taken for granted that nations cannot be trusted completely and for ever to keep nuclear weapons under lock and key, so it is assumed that nations, however peaceful, cannot entirely discount the possiblity of something going terribly wrong in a society based on plutonium. Terrorists can make use of plutonium, which has to be moved to the stores where it is to be held, actively dangerous, for hundreds of thousands of years. A more innocent example of human carelessness can frustrate the elaborate safety devices in any nuclear power station, and of course the accidents have been headlined. The safe storage of plutonium will mean considering the possible effects of coming Ice Ages, thus neatly combining two nightmares.

It was inevitable that there should be massive public protests about these dangers. In the late 1950s famous wise men – Albert Einstein, Albert Schweitzer, Bertrand Russell – aroused opinion. International movements such as the Pugwash Conference began probing the possibilities seriously. In Britain the Campaign for Nuclear Disarmament was started in 1958 and its echoes have been heard around the world. Later resistance grew in America and elsewhere to 'atoms for peace'. The World and British Councils of Churches were among the bodies sponsoring inquiries which combined the technical and moral approaches and produced impressive reports (*Facing up to Nuclear Power*, 1976, and *Nuclear Crisis: A Question of Breeding*, 1977). But to protest is evidently not enough. The Campaign for Nuclear Disarmament failed to persuade any British government to renounce its own 'deterrent'. Similar protests have failed in other countries. Despite hesitations it is most unlikely that the reliance of Britain or of other nations (rich or poor) on the prospect of nuclear energy in peace will be reversed.

Many people now sense helplessly that the world is running away to doom. They feel that they have become not like gods but like demons. They are terrified lest the amazing but still very limited mastery over their environment given to them by science will merely succeed in enabling them to achieve a complete disaster. In the titles of two widely discussed books by Alvin Toffler, the early 'future shock' can easily grow into a near certainty about the coming final terror of the 'eco-spasm'. And people are not reassured by even the ablest of reporters of science (I have in mind a book such as John Maddox's *The Doomsday Syndrome*, 1972) when these reporters try to poke fun at the prophets of doom without fully confronting the possibility that the prophets may be right. Men do not trust themselves to master the crisis now upon them; instead they know themselves only too well – and they know their moral powerlessness. To be human is, they fear, to run towards a tragic fate.

I shall now attempt to assess this defeatist mood – which I have often shared – in the light of the facts, so far as these can be known. I am not an expert in any of the academic disciplines involved. But in this society which is so often said to be running away to doom, I believe that it is the duty of everyone to find out the facts.

2 A Hope

Doom has been pronounced on modern man from so many angles that it seems likely that at least some of the warnings are valid – and any one of them, if valid, is enough to make a profound alarm realistic. It seems reasonable to suppose that an effort is demanded to escape from the trap sprung by the twentieth century: an effort as great as *Homo sapiens* has ever achieved. It seems no overstatement to say that if civilization does survive, it will be a society transformed by this effort. In other words, modern man will not survive. It is post-modern man who has a chance.

It also seems reasonable to suppose that if post-modern civilizations are built in the millions of years to come, they will never enjoy a limitless abundance. If they are free to eat what they want it will be because they are not free to have as many children as they want. Whatever energy they use, it will not be derived from the fossil fuels: oil, natural gas and coal. Whatever metals they use, they will have to re-use scraps if they share the modern taste for a number of metals; whatever else the future may be, it will not be golden. Most of their wealth will come from their own technology, not from the soil – and their confidence that their own human nature can sustain the technology and its application is unlikely to be limitless. In other words, any future now conceivable for man is likely to be as much a battle as any period in the past. The one real hope is that the battle may not be lost.

Even this austerely limited optimism certainly requires justification. That in turn must involve cautious predictions about food, industrial raw materials and energy as the material basis of the first post-modern civilization. Obviously I cannot attempt detailed predictions. But I can write down simply what I have gathered from the experts in a good deal of anxious reading and listening.

I hope that I do not take lightly the fact that in the world where I live there is much hunger and some famine. If the experts say that the main problem in the world's food supplies is at present distribution, not production, that calm reflection does not fill the bellies of men, women or children. Nor do I want to treat lightly the warning that the world received in 1972-74 of an actual food shortage after an appalling combination of floods and droughts (leading to huge Russian purchases of American grain, to soaring prices world-wide, and eventually to the modest success of the Rome conference). However, it does seem reasonable to believe that our planet could support a population larger than its present four thousand million. The Russians assured the 1974 conference that, if run scientifically, the world could support a population ten times larger; the Chinese, that the whole of the Third World would develop satisfactorily if only the First World would stop exploiting it. The views which I accept are more complicated, but are not very much more doom-laden.

I hope that this is not only because as an Englishman I am aware that the UK increased its food production by about forty per cent in the twenty years 1950-70 (as did Russia). Experiments in the USA have shown that vegetables can be grown without soil, but it is more to the point that both in Latin America and in Africa a vast amount of arable land has never been cultivated or could be reclaimed for agriculture. The FAO calculate that the present farming area could be increased by some fifty per cent without unreasonable exertion, investment or ecological danger.

Specially in India and South-East Asia agriculture has not got anywhere near the attainable standard of efficiency; on average, the Indian farmer produces four times less than the Japanese. Improved seeds, fertilizers, irrigation, weed-killers and pest-killers have already produced much better crops that it seems reasonable to hope for further improvements, including technical answers to problems thrown up with the new methods. The Green Revolution, pouring science into the soil, need not come to a halt in the 1970s when it has just begun. On the contrary, the next stage of this revolution is obvious. It is to extend the advance of agricultural science in such a way that its blessings reach small farmers and retain rural employment all over the world – instead of concentrating, as at present, on the estates of large landowners in non-Communist Asia who then reduce the labour they employ. One clear essential is to use human and animal dung to make fertilizers for the ground and methane gas for cooking, instead of burning it as fuel. Another is to secure more variety and rotation in crops, which would be good both for the land and for the people's diet. Still another is to do much more to protect the crops from damage and waste when they have been harvested. Still another is to distribute the crops by co-operation between farmers' communes and governments. Already the prosperity that has come after only modest use of machines or scientific advances sets an appetizing example.

The main emphasis must obviously lie on the Third World feeding itself. 'Food aid' – meaning the disposal of some of the surplus of North American farms without charge in India and elsewhere – may have been a genuinely humanitarian response to famine in the 1960s, but is now generally reckoned to have done more harm than good because it discouraged the battle to increase Indian farmers' productivity. But it also seems realistic to hope that in the years to come grain will be purchased from North America for the Third World's cities. Then North America would be freed from the restrictions placed (formerly by governments, latterly by its farmers) on its capacity as the world's granary. For most of this century surpluses have been the problem in American agriculture. That was why all the science of the Green Revolution in the land of its birth resulted only in economizing on farm labour and swelling the national unemployment problem; in the period 1950-70 US agricultural employment was almost halved and US agricultural production rose by one per cent. As late as Spring 1973 the US government was paying farmers not to produce. (Much the same pattern is true of Canada, Australia and Argentina.) As the Chicago agronomist D. Gale Johnson argued in *World Agriculture in Disarray* (1973), the American farms have been all too typical of world-wide policies which have not maximized production.

The elimination of the tsetse fly in Africa is, we are told, now possible and would release an area comparable with the USA for crops or pasture. Cattle farming is obviously capable of immense improvement. One necessity is to replace or supplement grain or grass or fishmeal as feed; the answer may be the use of those parts of many crops now thrown away (stalks, etc.) or of fast-breeding, single-cell proteins. Another essential is to breed cattle not for adornment but for consumption and the market. At present all over Africa tribal custom favours large numbers of scraggy cattle as a substitute for currency. Fewer cattle could be fatter cattle. In India cows are too sacred to be slaughtered. If an increased population is to have enough protein, however, it seems essential to supplement minced meat with soya beans, which have a similar protein content.

Fish farming is another line full of rewards once it is followed up in the determination to get more protein. Lakes and ponds, natural or artificial, could teem with fish. The oceans could yield much more if fished more scientifically. This means more careful conservation of stocks which are threatened by overfishing. It also means more adventurous fishing in new areas – and more imaginative treatment of the 'trash fish' now thrown away. *The Limits to Growth* said that fish yields could be doubled. Most experts seem to think that this estimate was far too cautious – if only men on the seas and on the lakes, as on the land, can progress from hunting to careful agriculture.

The truth has now dawned that the raw materials of industry are not in limitless supply, and that the known reserves of some metals and minerals are dangerously low. But it is equally plain that what matters decisively is not what is there physically but what is there at a price which consumers are willing to pay. As proven reserves are depleted the price usually rises, providing more resources to discover fresh supplies, to improve the efficiency of mining and to use scrap in recycling; and these three responses are likely to prolong the availability of most raw materials. If it becomes economic to recover the minerals from the continental shelves in the oceans, a huge new supply will be available. The greater scarcity and cost of traditional natural materials also stimulate the search for substitutes, either natural or man-made. Famous examples are aluminium and silicon replacing copper and iron, man-made fibres replacing cotton, and artificial rubber replacing the natural product. At present the tendency of the rich nations to develop substitutes for their imports from the Third World is probably a bigger problem for the world than any threatened exhaustion of natural resources.

The production of substitutes such as silicon or man-made fibres uses a great deal of energy. A good many new materials (plastics, for example) are oil-based. The whole tendency of modern industry is to depend on more and more electricity and the popular demand in an industrial society is for centrally heated homes stuffed with electric gadgets. These familiar facts have naturally given rise to many fears about future energy supplies. But it does seem possible that advanced industrial nations will be able to prosper without copying or exceeding the recent American rate of energy-consumption. President Carter, for one, has argued that the United States could in every sense afford to economize on energy. His argument is supported by the fact that in the 1970s Sweden enjoys a standard of living comparable with America's, and France a standard of living superior to Britain's – but based on half the energy-use per head. In the United States or in Britain, about half the heat produced by fuel is, it is reckoned, simply wasted; endless gallons of petrol are burned up in engines which are far too pretentious, in cars which are far too large, for the uses to which they are put; and industry is (to its own commercial loss) profligate in using up fuels which come from fossils laid down over millions of years. It seems perfectly possible to insist on more effective insulation in homes and offices, and to trust that economic pressures will result in smaller cars and less 'energetic' factories. And one additional reason for expecting the rate of growth in energy-use to diminish is that the rich countries will never again need the work of the 1950s and 1960s in the introduction of central heating and air conditioning.

Clearly oil will never be cheap again. As reserves run low – probably within the lives of those born in the 1970s – this 'black gold' is going to be so priced, and if need be so rationed, that it is kept primarily to supply fuel for aviation and oil bases to fertilizers, plastics and other manufactures. But the higher price of oil will mean that oil beneath the oceans can now be exploited – not only in the Caribbean and North Seas but elsewhere. A higher price still, with improved technology, would lead to the commercial use of sources on land such as oil shale in the USA and tar sands in Canada.

Even pessimists agree that there is enough coal in the world to last for at least three centuries to come and that some oil can be extracted from coal. The problems are economic – how to finance mechanized means of extraction; how to pay the remaining miners enough; and how to transport the coal. There are also large, although more limited, reserves of natural gas.

There has been much talk, and some research, about substitutes to replace oil, coal and gas. The fact is that technology needed to make alternatives safe, cheap and abundant has not yet been developed, and it is here above all that prediction becomes a matter of guesswork. But hopeful guesses can at least claim to be supported by science's utterly amazing and wildly encouraging record of solid success. It does not seem foolish to hope that nuclear power based on the plutonium-producing 'breeder' reactors (or their alternatives) will be no more dangerous than the factories of the chemical industries are at present; and a great deal less dangerous than the petrol-driven motor car, which every year inflicts over one hundred and fifty thousand deaths on the world's roads. It also does not seem foolish to hope that the 'fusion' process for the production of nuclear power – imitating the Sun itself (roughly), based on deuterium from sea water and not producing waste – will be developed within the twenty-first century if not within the twentieth. That will be the decisive breakthrough into industrial prosperity – if, as is hoped, it produces power safely, cheaply, and with no limits other than the limits of finance and technical manpower.

Nuclear power seems the necessary centrepiece for industrialization; the alternative, as Sir Fred Hoyle argued in his *Energy or Extinction* (1977), is a cold and hungry, and therefore a very violent, world. Nuclear power also seems likely to make practical some fascinating developments – electric vehicles (mostly public transport) for cities and the desalination of sea water (by heating) to help agriculture. But in recent years research has rightly been encouraged into other possibilities likely to take their place as extremely useful supplements. Energy cascades down from the Sun; heating systems using this solar energy, at present very clumsy, could become cheap through the development of fuel cells. Other energy beyond reckoning could be wrested from the winds and the waves, and in some areas from hot rocks beneath the Earth's surface. Most expert discussion – and there has been plenty of it – suggests in the end that the energy crisis, although grave, is not insoluble.

The population explosion rightly causes great alarm, for here the evolutionary drive to reproduce has been in a head-on collision with the evolutionary drive to survive. But as the UN discussions (especially the Bucharest conference in 1974) have gradually made plain, the world's population problem is not one problem to which there is one answer. Some governments still go to international conferences in order to say that their countries are under-populated; or they worry about a stable or declining birthrate because it may leave too few workers supporting too many pensioners. Even countries usually reckoned overcrowded, such as Britain, do not always rejoice when the population declines (as it is expected to do in Britain in the 1980s); on the contrary, their taxation policies usually encourage parents to have children. Certainly some population growth is compatible with great economic growth, as the USA and Japan show (and even in the relatively backward Britain, 1952-68, the population increased by $12\frac{1}{2}$ per cent and the gross national product by 140 per cent). Experts usually agree that both Latin America and Africa could feed many more people – if most of those people were efficient agricultural workers.

The nightmare of overpopulation can at present be reduced to a few very alarming facts. The world's population could not safely grow for ever at its recent rate, for the food would run out as it does for birds and animals who overbreed. There must be a cut-off point somewhere in the future, near or far. Already in the 1970s the moderate expectation in expert circles is that there will be 6,500 million mouths to feed in the year 2000.

And already famine has struck the drought-prone area running across Africa from the Sahel to Ethiopia.

But the dangers implied in these facts can be conquered. It is, indeed, as certain as anything can be in the business of population – prediction that the rate of growth will slow down even if no more birth-control measures are introduced. The phenomenal recent growth is a result of the death-control introduced with the elements of modern hygiene, medicine and technology. For example, the conquest of malaria by DDT has saved many millions of lives. Above all the rates of infant mortality have sharply decreased. No comparable combination of changes prolonging human life seem likely in the future, so that left to present-day birth-control methods the world's population is reckoned to be likely to double only every forty or fifty years. But even this reduced rate of growth, leading to perhaps 30,000 millions by 2100, is not thought by most experts to be really likely unless the world's resources do grow proportionately.

In an encouraging number of Asian countries birth rates have recently been stabilized at levels which can be supported by the agriculture and industry now available. Such evidence as is available about China suggests that this has been achieved there by the pressure of public opinion enforcing later marriages, encouraging the use of contraceptives and punishing any mother whose pregnancy has not been agreed on in advance by neighbours and fellow-workers. That is a solution acceptable in a society prepared to accept a high degree of regimentation. Other Asian countries (including Taiwan) have, however, achieved the same ends by stressing the economic advantages to individuals of small families, and in 1977 Mrs Gandhi's downfall after her sterilization campaign suggested that only after subtle pressure will the Indian people agree to have fewer children. *The Limits to Growth* itself made the point: 'In general, as gross national product rises, the birthrate falls. This appears to be true, despite differences in religious, cultural and political factors'.

Whether through the pressure of a Maoist commune or through the promise of affluence to a more liberal society, the essential point is to persuade parents in the poorer nations that it is not to their advantage to have a large family. At present parents in such countries see that almost all work in the fields or at home demands hands which need not be skilled; and the cheapest hands available are their own children's. Parents expect some or most of their children to die young; so that in order to be sure of a son surviving to support his parents in their old age, it seems to make sense to have six or seven children. The expectations of parents and children alike for food, shelter, clothing, education and recreation are very modest, so that even while they are dependent on their parents children seem to be good investments; indeed, they may be the only investments possible. A man expects to be admired for his manliness, and a woman for her womanliness, when many children can be produced as certificates of sexual skill. Should a woman rebel against this fate, she will find that a male-dominated society uses many methods of crushing rebellion. A whole web of expectations has to be broken if a small family is to seem desirable.

In one country after another, however, the pressure of public opinion is beginning to be felt. Whether driven by the fear of famine or lured by the prospect of affluence, people are beginning to *want* birth control, which itself is the decisive step. The next step is to make simple and effective contraception available everywhere. That is a Herculean task, but it ought not to prove an impossible one – specially if, as seems probable, a 'morning after' or 'once a month' pill without side effects can be invented for mass production and can be accepted for mass distribution. If they think that it is in their interests, women will take that pill. Even men might help.

If agriculture can be made more efficient on land which the peasants control, and if the population of the world's villages can be stabilized, it is unlikely that the drift from hunger in the countryside to unemployment in the town (where it is more expensive to feed people) will continue at its present catastrophic rate. Given a genuine choice, most people would probably prefer to stay where their roots are, surrounded by the familiar countryside and the extended family. But certainly the urbanization of man is a new, striking and very dangerous development. Present trends suggest that by the end of the century more people will live in towns than in villages, for the first time in history. If the towns have too little industry, the unemployment will breed the politics of despair. But if the industry is as harmful to man and his environment as was the first industrial revolution in a country such as Britain, the pollution will lead to disaster; the rapid industrialization of the 1960s and early 1970s was polluting the globe at a rate expected to double every fourteen years.

But here, too, remedies are within man's reach. The essence of the first industrial revolution was using hands to help the machines in the factories – but that may not be the pattern of the period into which we are moving. The world looks like being divided sharply into the countries which fear overpopulation and those which fear a declining birthrate. In the former, industry ought to provide as many jobs as possible; in the towns as in the countryside, 'intermediate' or 'appropriate' technology is all that is needed, removing some of the drudgery without removing the employment. In these vast areas, it ought to be possible to limit pollution by limiting mechanization. In the industrial nations a technology is needed which will be designed for cleanliness and which will be so productive that economy will be able to finance stringent action against pollution. Already, with present day technology, it has been proved possible to curb pollution by insisting on safeguards. This has been conspicuous in the United States since President Johnson made conservation official policy in the mid-1960s. The concern has spread around the world, monitored by the UN Environment Programme ('Earthwatch') based in Nairobi. In Britain some of the results have been dramatic. Because of cleaner air the number of hours of winter sunshine in London doubled in the period 1960-75. The River Thames is cleaner than it has been for a century and a half. No doubt the battles against pollution will never end, but the evidence – set out in, for example, *Environment and the Industrial Society*, scientific essays edited by Nicholas Holmes (1976) – suggests that the battles can be won. The poorer countries need not be dirty; and the rich nations can afford to be clean.

Peace is the necessary background to all these battles for the survival of our civilization. But peace, too, is not impossible.

Despite all the conflicts and tensions since 1945, peace has been kept between the great powers. It has been kept by the universal terror of nuclear war. For more than thirty years after the use of the atomic bombs on Hiroshima and Nagasaki, nuclear weapons were not used again. In the perspective of human history, that is a great achievement. At once one adds the qualifications. Despite the agreements eventually reached between the USA and the USSR to restrict testing, nuclear weapons have remained in existence and have spread to new countries – causing a waste of money and scarce skills tragic beyond computation, creating a danger to mankind horrific beyond the imagination. And despite the agreements to renounce biological and chemical warfare, it has proved impossible to 'ban the Bomb' as the demonstrators of the 1960s demanded. Yet the non-use of this Doomsday machine has been a fact – a fact which can justify a cautious hope.

Peace between the great powers has been kept amid cold wars which in the pre-nuclear period would almost certainly have been allowed to escalate into hot conflicts. Peace was kept when Russians and Americans viewed each other with much the same hatred as Germans and Frenchmen in the first half of the century. Peace was still kept while the Russian and Chinese propaganda machines hurled insults at each other; while the Russians suppressed the rebellions of the Eastern Europeans; while the Chinese affected to believe that the American giant was a paper tiger. The nuclear deterrent deterred – and all the time ever more elaborate precautions were being taken against its accidental or impetuous unleashing.

No less significant as an austere sign of hope for peace has been the unwillingness of any public to pay the consequences of a major war. Over many years Russians were encouraged to believe that their fatherland was encircled by ruthless enemies; the Chinese marched and chanted in their millions, first against the Americans and then against the Russians; the French had to accept the humiliations of defeats first in Indo-China and then in Algeria; the Americans, brought up to believe that the purity of the American dream was whiter than white and destined to prevail, had to swallow the first large-scale defeat in their history in the Vietnam war. But none of these peoples, when it came to the crunch, could face the prospect of retaliation by their enemies in the nuclear age. The Americans could not even face their own television screens which showed them what their soldiers were doing to their enemies, and the revulsion of the American conscience against the horrors of Vietnam raised the question whether any people would ever tolerate a prolonged land war in the age of television. Would the trenches have been tolerated had they been filmed and shown night after night in living rooms in 1914-18?

Of course nationalism and militarism have remained strong emotions; the armed forces have enjoyed immense and obviously excessive prestige and power in many countries; about £350 thousand million a year, some seven per cent of the world's gross product, is going into armaments – but the world has entered the last quarter of the twentieth century knowing in its heart that no major war can bring glory or profit to anyone. However corrupted it may be by its use in propaganda, 'peace' is a word which corresponds with the deep longing of mankind. Those who misuse it pay tribute to this fact, for hypocrisy is always the tribute which vice pays to virtue.

Moreover, peace today is generally seen to mean more than the absence of violent conflict. In the famous phrase of Pope Paul VI (*Populorum Progressio*, 1967), development is another name for peace; and it is increasingly recognized that no one nation can develop in disregard of all other. The man who photographed this planet from the moon – thus perhaps justifying all the expenditure on the Moon Race – imprinted an image on the conscience of our time: the fragile coloured ball in the big black sky. For just as the food-chain ties plants, fishes, birds and animals together because they need each other, so on this small planet the intricate web of modern economic life does actually unite the nations. Of all the nations, Britain has perhaps the best reasons to know this. Britain has profited greatly from the general agreement embodied in the International Monetary

Fund that no nation can be allowed to go bankrupt, because all the others would also suffer. The prices in Britain's foodshops vary week by week according to the world price levels, and British unemployment statistics climb up or down according to the state of world trade. Dependence on modern sea and air traffic means that 'this England' is no longer Shakespeare's 'fortress built by Nature for herself against infection'. Britain also knows that it is capable of polluting other countries; the sulphur in the smoke of British factory chimneys comes down in acid rain on Norway.

The United Nations Organization, so far from acting like a world government, is perpetually deep in debt, strangled by an expensive bureaucracy even in its specialist agencies, and torn by political conflicts even in its special conferences to ponder world problems. But at least it has been a forum where the nations were willing to meet and argue face to face; and at least the nations using this forum to make propaganda have felt obliged to speak in terms of justice and peace. At least we can see soldiers wearing UN insignia on guard in some of the world's trouble spots, and we can hear spokesmen of the UN monitoring the world's economic follies. And at least the UN has been more effective than that European debating society, the League of Nations. It says much that the USA eventually consented to the admission of Red China, in 1971; it says even more that China wanted to be admitted. Over the crises and disappointments since its first Assembly in the Methodist Central Hall, Westminster, the UN has built up a tradition. It is a new tradition for a human race which has for so long wallowed in the rivalries of villages, tribes and nations. It guards man's best political hope.

3 Zero Growth?

The call for a simplification of life in the nations now rich has been a response to the world's crisis. But it has not been helpful that this response has been pushed to silly extremes. For example, Professor Charles Birch, addressing the Assembly of the World Council of Churches at Nairobi in 1975, called on the rich nations to 'de-develop'. He claimed that it was morally wrong for any nation to live at a standard which the Earth could not afford for all. Such an extreme is not, I believe, the factually or morally right conclusion of the recent debate.

Certainly some simplification is both possible and desirable. The American way of life guzzles energy, demolishes mountains of protein, habitually throws away rich food on almost every plate, and creates about a ton of material waste for each person each year. Yet the average expectation of life is no higher in the United States than it is in Russia (about seventy-one years). Superior medical care is, it seems, offset by less exercise and a less healthy diet. As an example of what is desirable, since Vance Packard's *The Waste Makers* (1960) it has been clear that one of the most urgent needs in advanced industrial societies is to make the recycling of garbage and sewage an economic proposition. At present fantastic amounts of valuable material, from paper to bread, from bottles to dung, are wasted by being burned, buried or washed away instead of being sorted and processed for further use.

But it does not follow that Professor Birch's call to 'de-develop' the already rich countries was either practical or moral. In the 1970s Britain had a curious experience. At the beginning of the decade there was some feeling of surprise, and even guilt, about the new affluence. Were not people – or at least, other people – becoming greedy and soft? Yet Britain during the 1970s actually managed to achieve 'zero growth' and the curious result was this: it did not turn out to be the road back to Paradise.

I have asked myself what would happen were any British government to adopt the *Blueprint for Survival* produced in 1972 by the *Ecologist* monthly magazine. That plan called for the halving of Britain's population over the next hundred years to the level where the island could grow its own food (using organic fertilizers only). It also demanded the break-up of the cities so far as possible into self-supporting neighbourhoods. Its anger at the ugliness and inhumanity of Britain's cities and suburbs corresponded with a good deal of anti-urban, anti-industrial and anti-scientific talk in the United States and elsewhere (for example, in the books of Theodore Roszak). It sounded youthfully rebellious with its alternative vision of a natural simplicity, and in this was as attractive as the talk about a 'new consciousness' to be found in the new American jeaneration (for example, in Charles Reich's 1970 vision of *The Greening of America*). But my sober answer is that the greening of Britain, or of the other industrial nations, would lead to much misery.

It would have to be enforced. Although the advocates of this vision are democrats with a tendency to anarchism, the changes involved would have to be so great and so rapid that it would be naïve to expect them to come about by private initiative or with universal consent. Government propaganda and intervention, massive and ruthless, would be needed to prevent the births of children, to enforce the decentralization and general de-development of economic life, and to compel the population and the economy to maintain the desired low levels. It is hard to see how such a government required to take such action could in practice be less than totalitarian.

It is also hard to see how the century of transition to the new low level of economic life could avoid misery. The problem of caring for the old in a shrinking population would be immense, unless the old folk were liquidated. The dispersal of the cities and the dismantling of their industries, the supply of homes (however basic) and public services (if permitted) in approved locations, the general switch from urban to rural occupations – all these moves would all create a staggering range of human problems at a time when human and material sources to cope with them were being deliberately diminished. And it does not seem likely that all this dislocation would lead into a period of contentment. Unless all other industrial nations agreed to transform themselves similarly, or unless all communications with the outside world were cut, the impoverished population would know that many comforts and conveniences were available in other countries but not to them. To rub salt into the wound, memories would be handed on of their own past affluence.

The more one contemplates the prospect of the 'de-development' of a rich industrial society, the more one realizes how different the process must be from anything that has happened in the past. The results of a fall in population can be acceptable in the long run when a society is prepared to take the plague or famine as an 'act of God' and when the fewer labourers left can earn higher wages on the farms. It appears, for example, that in England after the plague of the Black Death in the fourteenth century the population was more or less stable until the industrial revolution in the eighteenth – and during most of this period the ordinary man was better off than he had been before the Black Death. But the problems of de-development *after* industrialism are, it is clear, on an altogether different scale. In fact, human suffering of vast dimensions would have to be imposed by what was manifestly an act of government.

It can be argued that industrialism is already such an unhappy business that its end would be welcome. There is a widespread feeling that many features of industrialism have been dehumanizing. The industrial cities are not enjoyable communities to live in. The factory, office or shop work needed seems meaningless to the workers. Consumer goods are poured out and the pressure is on to find some meaning in life by the competition to consume most of them – with disillusionment inevitable. Meanwhile public services and amenities are allowed to degenerate into squalor because they do not fit into the picture of life as making and spending money. Such a criticism of industrial society was popularized in the last century by English prophets such as William Morris and John Ruskin. It has been taken up in our own country by economists analysing the highly sophisticated but also highly unsatisfactory economy of the United States. A whole row of American laments from J. K. Galbraith's *The Affluent Society* (1958) to Tibor Scitovsky's *The Joyless Economy* (1976) has made an impact not only on thoughtful Americans but also on those who in other countries see that American trends are likely to be copied. As an economist, Professor Scitovsky asked: 'If so much that contributes to man's satisfaction is left out of the National Product, why do we attach so much importance to its size?' A professor at the London School of Economics, E. J. Mishan, has actually argued that economic growth in an industrial society has been, is and must be the enemy of human happiness (*The Economic Growth Debate*, 1977).

In the past much of the rejection of industrialism has been made by people whose own preference was for the pleasures of the aristocracy or at least of the countryside. The university professor was pleased by the beauty of ancient lawns outside his study; the businessman liked to retreat at the weekend to rural sports or at least in the evening to a suburban garden. But recently it has been recognized that however a democracy might huff and puff such pleasures, separating the privileged from the common herd, simply could not be extended to all. In his *Social Limits to Growth* (1977) Fred Hirsch argued that the pursuit of affluence has bred dissatisfaction because affluence has been understood in terms of 'positional goods' (called by others status symbols). The world can never produce limitless supplies of exotic food, fashionable neighbourhoods, eye-catching clothes, rare antiques, exclusive schools, private surgeries, exceptionally fast cars on deserted roads, restful tourist spots or country cottages in quiet areas of outstanding beauty.

Obviously, then, dissatisfaction with industrialism and its rewards exists and has many symptoms. But it serves no good purpose to exaggerate the present gravity of this disease. Most Americans show a proper gratitude for being the most privileged people ever. Even in Britain public opinion polls consistently show that while most people feel that they need a bit more money the overwhelming majority is 'satisfied' at work and 'happy' at leisure. Certainly there is no sound case for killing the patient in order to cure the disease. It is far more constructive to think out the human uses to which the growing profits of industrialization can be put.

Fred Hirsch was surely right up to a point: if the members of a rich society are to be happy, they will have to accept a more standardized equipment for happiness. Industrialism will have to be valued not because it can indefinitely extend the privileges of the few as the few have known them, but because it can raise living standards for the many by making possible a universal improvement in diet, housing, clothing, furniture, education, medical care, transport and recreation. Satisfaction will have to be derived from the contentment, not the envy, of others. And in another psychological revolution it will have to be accepted that one of the main rewards of the new style of work is more time off work, rather than the competitive accumulation of material goods. There is already promise in the fact that new industrial processes have made possible shorter working weeks and longer holidays (in Britain the working week of male manual workers fell on average from $47\frac{1}{2}$ to $39\frac{1}{2}$ hours in 1960-76, while the percentage of all full-time workers entitled to more than two weeks' paid holiday rose from three to 99). Paradoxically, further industrial development seems to be the necessary prologue to the age of leisure.

Even in the United States the limits to morally desirable economic growth still seem far off – whatever may be physically possible, which is certainly more than the doomsters believe. The millions of unemployed, the squalid inner cities, the rural poverty . . . America still needs to buy its way out of many problems. In Britain in the 1970s the limits have been even further off with three million Britons on 'supplementary benefit' from the State as some recognition of their poverty. The sheer fact that people live longer challenges those at work (fewer than half the population) to provide more; in Britain by 1975 there were $2\frac{1}{4}$ million men alive over sixty-five, and $4\frac{1}{2}$ million women alive over sixty, whereas the figures for 1901 were half a million and $1\frac{1}{4}$ million. And in Britain there is not yet an excess of 'consumer durables', whatever the new Puritans may think; in 1975 approximately half the households in

Britain had no car, no telephone or no colour television. (I can recommend to my fellow-moralists in Britain the benefit of brooding over the publication of the Government Statistical Service, *Social Trends*, in conjunction with Wilfred Beckerman's *In Defence of Economic Growth*, 1975.)

Moreover, it should not be assumed that the development of industrialism must have as its sole or main purpose the production of consumer goods as contrasted with social benefits. On the contrary, once the cake begins to grow it is possible, and can be fairly painless, to decide to allocate some, most or all of the new growth to purposes which are believed to benefit society as a whole. A ruthless allocation of scarce resources is seen every day in the centrally planned economics of Communism; thus housewives were simply informed – or were left to learn – that because Russia must have sputniks in order to compete with the American space programme there would not be many domestic refrigerators available. But it is equally obvious that in a society where consumers are also electors, and where the cake is stable or shrinking, it is difficult to persuade them to renounce either consumer goods or social benefits; that has been the experience of Britain in the 1970s. Human nature being what it is, it is economic growth that makes social progress compatible with democratic freedom.

It is not difficult to make a list of social benefits which an industrial society can earn. The most obvious example is generosity in payments in pensions, unemployment pay, family allowances and other social security benefits. In Britain 1950-75, public expenditure on such purposes increased sevenfold after adjustment for inflation. Whatever improvements are needed in the system, that is not a record which people who want a more prosperous society will be quick to condemn. In Britain as in other countries the 1970s have also brought other benefits to workers in the shape of job security or redundancy payments. This, too, has amounted to an immense tax on industry.

More prosperous people can afford better homes. In Britain the record here is less impressive, and similar problems still exist in other nations now considered rich. Surveys of British housing at the beginning of the 1970s reported that many people found their accommodation unsatisfactory. About a million homes, one tenth of the total, had no fixed bath. Partly this situation results from the strange priorities which people have in their own spending (despite the famous love of the British for home life, they spend more on alcohol plus tobacco than on housing) – but such a bizarre pattern of expenditure seems to reflect the despairing feeling that decent housing for all has not been within the British people's reach. Wherever one looks, money is what housing needs. In Britain large numbers of new houses need to be built (despite a stable population) at prices to attract builders; rents need to be raised to encourage investment by landlords; houses built for a local authority need to be transferred to private ownership through mortgages (to encourage pride in their maintenance and to reduce the present irrational system under which tenants who may be quite prosperous have their rents heavily subsidized).

Overcrowding in the inner city has been reduced by the new patterns of industry and business and could be reduced further. Thus the population of inner London was almost halved in the period 1900-75; the population of inner Liverpool was halved in the period 1950-75. New factories and offices can be made far more attractive than the old, and those employed in them can be housed pleasantly near them; in the 1970s a prodigious waste of resources was suggested by the fact that the British people spent more on transport than on housing. The new towns created in Britain since the 1950s show what can be done, for all their growing pains. There can also be a far greater emphasis on the provision of public services and amenities if only there is the money to pay for them out of public revenues. In Britain, for example, much discussion has already led to some action in reversing the run-down of public transport. During 1960-75 employment in the medical services increased from just over $\frac{3}{4}$ million to just under $2\frac{1}{4}$ million, and employment in education grew from some 960,000 to $1\frac{1}{4}$ million. In the late 1970s public expenditure on such purposes has had to be cut; yet no one could say that the British people is too healthy or too educated (the proportion of young people from working class homes in the universities, about twenty-five per cent, scarcely changed over forty years after 1935). Many of the much needed amenities – entertainment, sport, libraries, parks, the restoration of historic buildings, the conservation of nature – can benefit from taxes on the profits or wages resulting from a prosperous industrialism.

But there are snags . . .

4 The Self-Preservation of the Rich

In the nations now rich, the philosophy of the schools is to encourage self-expression. Youth has few doubts about what it wants and is entitled to, here and now. Even parents sometimes demand the right to be themselves. For adult workers the twentieth century has been the liberating age when rights have been recognized as never before and year by year the extent of the rights claimed and granted has grown. The idealism motivating such a society has received expression in the major work by the American philosopher, John Rawls: *A Theory of Justice* (1971). To Professor Rawls, the ideal is that each person is to have 'an equal right to the most extensive total system of equal basic liberties compatible with a similar system of liberty for all'. Rawls reckons that justice is based on a sense of fairness reached in agreements between co-operating individuals. In such a society some inequalities can be tolerated, but only if they are reasonably expected to be to everyone's advantage in the long run and if they are attached to positions open to all. Probably even in the rich nations officially Marxist most people would recognize this as the ideal.

So self-expression in freedom is acclaimed by all. Yet quite another theme emerges from almost all the discussion about a sustainable future for the rich nations. The theme is that the rich will have to discipline their behaviour and their wants in a radically new way; that for them self-restraint is the key to self-preservation.

In the United States, where futurology has become yet

another profitable industry, the end-product is almost always the advice to use a giant's strength with restraint. The future is not what it used to be in the days when the whole continent seemed to be a virgin awaiting the white man's self-expression. Restraint, too, is the outcome of the less optimistic analysis elsewhere. In Britain, for example, the media and pressure groups have endlessly probed the British disease and have predicted the outcome which is inevitable unless the patient stops day-dreaming and takes his medicine. Many groups sponsored by the Churches have joined in by offering a diagnosis in similar terms – as may be seen in Margaret Kane's *Theology in an Industrial Society* (1975) or Trevor Beeson's *Britain Today and Tomorrow* (1978). Running through all this consideration of the future is the theme that there must be strong self-restraint and therefore a clear vision of society's corporate purpose. The individual has to accept a great deal of restraint – not merely because the demands of others for equal liberty are the irritating catch about this business of freedom, but because the individual's demands simply have to be limited, and limited severely, if his society, and he as a part of it, are to survive. For the rich as for the poorer nations, the name of the game is now survival.

The reason is plain. Although the limits may not be as near as some doomsters believe, there certainly are physical limits to the material consumption that is possible even for the richest – as there are 'social limits' to growth because the supplies of the status symbols which not-so-rich people covet cannot be endless. This is the challenge to 'liberty for all' which the economic crisis of the 1970s has begun to drive home, but it would seem that not everyone has yet counted the magnitude of the psychological cost of recognizing it. Competitive materialism with no limits in sight has for many years had the same effect on the rich nations that the Frontier had on nineteenth-century Americans. To produce material goods in ever greater abundance has seemed the essence of serious work and has been the constant theme of the moralizing exhortations of national leaders. To possess and consume these goods more and more luxuriously has been the criterion of success – not only in public attitudes but also in private self-esteem. Inside the fat society there have been a thousand million people all earnestly struggling to be fat, and in particular to be fatter than the next man. If the indoctrination in this creed is ever questioned, the heresy is beaten down by that giant industry, advertising; and if the advertisements do not stretch daydreams far enough, a new literature of fantasy, science fiction, offers the picture of a universe where material restraints are unknown. The whole character of the rich society in its present shape means that the acceptance of limits to economic growth must involve a psychological reorientation and, with it, all the pains of a society's rebirth.

But as the physical and social limits to growth come in sight and the lure of competitive consumption diminishes, there will certainly be consolations. For the new psychology may ease some all too familiar social problems.

If we use an evolutionary perspective, six thousand years of city life (and how small most of the old 'cities' were!) are only yesterday. This recent innovation has been compared with putting other animals into a zoo, and it is not surprising that the modern city has produced so many symptoms of stress. Children have to control their noise, motorists their impatience . . . the hourly challenges to self-restraint are too familiar to be worth listing. The American literature on urban sociology already almost scrapes the sky and an 'introductory reader' for the problems mounting on the other side of the Atlantic has been provided in *Cities in Modern Britain*, edited by Camilla Lambert and David Weir (1975). Faced with so many signs that human nature rejects city life, many have seen no hope until the cities are ploughed to grow more carrots – but it would have been equally sensible to abandon the medieval towns, where there were plenty of miseries and riots. Others have more usefully studied the detailed problems and have taken action. Here I simply mention the book *Built as a City* by David Sheppard, Bishop of Liverpool (1976), and I give a single quotation from *The Human Zoo* by Desmond Morris (1969). 'The stakes are rising higher all the time, the game becoming more risky, the casualties more startling, the pace more breathless. But despite the hazards it is the most exciting game the world has ever seen. It is foolish to suggest that anyone should blow a whistle and try to stop it.'

The rich society is, unless self-restrained, a society that breeds vandals and muggers. The American plague of violence, endlessly glamourized by television, films and novels, is now notorious throughout the world. But the same disease has spread to 'peaceful' Britain, to the rest of Europe and to Japan. In England and Wales during the quarter-century 1949-74, known crimes of violence against the person rose from some 4,800 to 62,800 a year and violent crimes against property from 92,000 to 493,000. It was a war against society. Before 1914 the total number of reported crimes in England and Wales was around one hundred thousand a year. Sixty years later the figure had risen to two million. When supplying these facts in his *Policing a Perplexed Society* (1977), Sir Robert Mark added the unanswerable comment that no police force could conceivably be strong enough to prevent crime on such a scale or to ensure its conviction. Those who know the prisons are agreed that, whether run on hard or soft lines, they probably breed as much crime as they punish. There is only one real answer ever offered in all the debates about crime: a rich society must be its own police, and the contentment of its members must be the effective deterrent. But no one has ever yet suggested a way of making enough people content if the sole standards of achievement are those endlessly advertised in an acquisitive society.

The advertisements in the typical modern city also flaunt unrestrained sex. Clearly the old standards of reticence and Puritanism are most unlikely to be revived – and in any case they were accompanied by much hypocrisy and much unhappiness, as the numbers of prostitutes in Victorian London showed. But even in an age which is deliberately (and probably permanently) permissive, most people would agree that some restraint in sexuality is right; that it is just as important as the restraint of violence to the welfare of mankind. When the taboos which are enforced in so-called 'primitive' societies are lifted, a rich society's emotional life can become primitive unless there is self-restraint. If explicit sexuality in advertisements, magazines, films, live performances and behaviour on the streets is not banned by the censor, it can be restrained only by a free people's sense of what builds up human dignity. If sex outside marriage is not liable to lead to unwanted babies (although in Britain in the 1970s nine per cent of all live births are illegitimate), or if venereal disease is regarded as acceptable (although in Britain in the 1970s it amounts to an epidemic), then the new freedom to enjoy sexual intercourse can be restrained only by a mature people's sense of the relationship of sex to love. If women who want their babies to be aborted are not to be denied this freedom over their bodies, abortion can be restricted only by the conviction that the foetus shares at least potentially in the dignity of man. Because *Homo sapiens* has been left by his history to date with such strong urges to sex and violence (often mixed), his self-restraint here may be the most important indication he can give that he is determined to continue his evolution in a direction he can want and respect.

Other ravages produced by their unrestrained acquisitiveness have formed the central themes of the rich nations' economic news.

It is always tempting, because in the short run easy, for a sophisticated society to believe that it can decide all the rules in the economic game. The supply of new money by government-controlled banks can be increased not because the increase corresponds with real wealth or realistic credit but in a gamble that printing more money will swell economic growth. In the early 1970s a British government (Conservative) yielded to that temptation and met catastrophe. Or a government can increase public expenditure not by raising taxes but by raising vast loans at artificially high interest rates which draw money away from investment in industry. Successive US governments yielded to this temptation in order to finance the Vietnam war. So did a British government (Labour) in order to meet the popular demand for the expansion of the social services in the 1970s. Such cheating incurs a fate all too familiar to rich societies – a retribution analysed in (for example) Irving Friedman's *Inflation: A World-wide Disaster* (1973).

It is not only a lack of self-restraint at the heights of government and finance that can cause a ruinous inflation. The pay packet is also prominent; even in Russia workers need a bonus if they are to produce above-average efforts. It has become a very familiar fact that wage demands enforced by the most powerful trade unions, particularly those who control energy and transport, can also produce inflation. In Britain, inflation was being contained before 1970; in the period 1965-70 wages rose by eleven per cent and prices by eight per cent. But once trade unions insisted on pay rises well above $2\frac{1}{2}$ per cent average annual growth in the economy, disaster followed. By 1975 inflation was running at over twenty-five per cent a year and one worker in every twenty-five was unemployed. Britain then looked into the abyss and was duly alarmed. Yet – as Aubrey Jones, the former Chairman of the Prices and Incomes Board, had already recorded as he looked back in his *The New Inflation* (1973) – no democratic government can resist demands for increases in wages and salaries in the absence of overwhelming public support for restraint. Accordingly, the social contract between the Labour government and the Trade Union Congress, replacing previous attempts to enforce a statutory incomes policy, did not last beyond the summer of 1977. This British experience points dramatically to one burden which every rich society must now carry: the burden of deciding – whether by a nationally agreed policy or by local or individual bargains – the realistic limits to pay.

So the rich nations have many teachers of the lesson of self-restraint – a sober sequel to the philosophy that the essence of justice is 'liberty for all'. Yet the rich nations have no hope of learning this lesson if 'self-restraint' sounds a dreary negative or an order from on high. Except perhaps during a war, the puritanism of telling people to go without simply invites them to make rude signs to the puritans. Not even the tyranny of Stalin, or Maoism in China, can permanently impose a completely rigid social discipline. What, then, is to be done?

A rich society seeking to restrain its suicidal impulses needs – literally *needs* – to stress in every possible way the alternative satisfactions offered by non-material goals. Fortunately these are already relished within most people's daily experience, supremely in family life. Countless people without any claim to moral heroism give themselves every day to please husband, wife or children more than themselves. They do not count the cost and the reward which they expect is not chiefly to do with material comfort or physical sex. In the rich societies there are many well-known strains imposed by modern conditions on family life; in Britain, where the divorce figures are lower than in the USA, the statistics of the 1970s are of over 300,000 first marriages a year but also over 130,000 petitions for divorce. If the human misery behind such a divorce rate could be lessened, that would be one of the most obvious ways in which to make a rich society happier. But it needs to be remembered that young people are in the uneasy position of semi-independence at home for longer than in previous generations; and that older married people live longer, prolonging the problems as well as the pleasures of marriage (in Britain, 1911-51, the number of married people almost doubled). All the evidence points to the family as an unexhausted and inexhaustible source of satisfactions which are not material.

There are, of course, many other satisfactions open to those who will accept a certain discipline of concentration. Innumerable fans are extremely well-informed and enthusiastic about pop music or particular teams. More and more adults learn from happy experience that the pleasures of good food depend chiefly on cooking. Above all there is television. In Britain this consumes an average of almost twenty hours a week for every person over five (except in high summer) – half the average working week. TV, the 'idiot-box', is often said to breed square-eyed zombies. In fact it has enriched life beyond measure as entertainment, as education and as a source of information; and as the novelty wears off and people watch it more selectively, the obvious hope is that more and more people will actively pursue interests glimpsed on television. Surveys suggest that in Britain only about half the population has a hobby which they enjoy regularly; only a fifth takes an active part in sports or games; only a fifth belongs to a social or political club; and less than a fifth reads books regularly. The hope that a rich society will increase its non-material satisfaction means in practice the hope that more and more people will lose themselves and find delight and contentment in active recreation. In his book *Towards a Society of Leisure* (1967), Joffre du Mazedier was surely right to say that 'the tendency to find fulfilment in leisure rather than work could be the beginning of a humanistic mutation more fundamental than the Renaissance'.

Human psychology being what it is, the hope that new goals will be accepted also means the hope that more and more people will take a positive part in the work of defining those goals. It was sensible of the World Council of Churches to announce in its title for its big 1979 conference that the 'just' society nowadays must be both 'sustainable' and 'participatory'. No society can be stable if its members do not think it just.

At present in all the rich societies it is a fact, and a very dangerous fact, that most of the citizens do not feel that they have shaped their own lives. Consequently they do not feel deeply committed to preserving the societies in which they live. Even in a society such as Britain – more egalitarian in its income distribution than either the Soviet Union or the United States – dangerous numbers do not feel that they have a real stake in society.

For one thing, too few people own property. In the mid-1970s in Britain, half the population do not own, and are not buying, their own homes. Eighty per cent own only sixteen per cent of the personally held wealth, while the top five per cent own over half. But mainly the sense of powerlessness and therefore rootlessness has been caused by the more subtle ways of excluding the majority from the decisions. Even in a country such as Britain where 'ordinary' people have the right to vote secretly in free political elections and enjoy much protection from the law and grants from the State when they withdraw their labour, they still do not feel fully involved in the affairs of their neighbourhood or firm. They habitually refer to the decision-makers as 'them'.

The war-dance of the strike – harming families, damaging profits (sometimes fatally) and inconveniencing customers (sometimes severely) – is a symptom of what is wrong. Many studies conclude that strikes are often motivated not merely by the wish to add extra money to the pay packet but also by a longing to add an occasional excitement to life. But the truth must be that the excitement which a rich society wants most is the excitement of constructing a way of life which will in every sense be rewarding and satisfying.

Increasingly in rich societies the most effective wealth-creators are machines controlled by computers. But such machines still need some looking after, and industry as a whole still needs its human element. An urgent necessity is therefore to secure the agreement of workers to the installation of the new machines and their co-operation in making these machines do most of the work. In a free society agreement and co-operation do not come except after consultation; and a country such as Britain has known for many years to its cost that the lack of consultation between the 'two sides' of industry can hold up modernization. If a rich society is to be continuously innovating in order to stay rich and grow richer, it must be continuously at work on the problems of human participation.

These problems include the adjustment of the machines to suit the people remaining in the factories and offices. In the past industry has often seemed to treat workers as inefficient machines which unfortunately it could not yet replace. Now it has been learned by much bitter experience that in an industrial society human nature remains essentially what it was when man was a hunter, a farmer or a craftsman – and human nature clamours for fulfilment. The processes of production or administration must be shaped in order to reduce boredom to the necessary minimum and in order to fulfil the human instincts to work in a group, to do useful and respected work by methods accepted by that group, and to take a pride in a creation achieved or a service rendered. Some experiments (for example, the replacement of the assembly line by team work making Volvo cars in Sweden) have promised excitingly that the old methods of individuals doing repetitive, low-skilled and deadening jobs without seeing the end-product will soon belong to the barbaric past. The future of industrialism must belong to the team which finds satisfaction in making something together;

otherwise the explosion of frustrated human nature will wreck the new machines as the Luddites wrecked some of the early machines of the first Industrial Revolution.

Karl Marx analysed the problem of industrial man's 'alienation' brilliantly, but never came up with a workable answer. Romanticizing the past before 'alienation', he insisted on Utopia after it. Pending Utopia, the increase in the power of the Marxist state appears to have done little if anything to reduce the Russian worker's 'alienation' in practice. Disillusionment with the psychological effects of nationalizing industries has increased the conviction that state ownership is not a sufficient answer. The only answer, it seems, is that in every factory, office or neighbourhood people must be set free to shape their own lives for themselves. And this is a burden. At first 'self-management' (the Yugoslav phrase) sounds an entirely attractive idea. But in our century enough experience has been accumulated for the snags to appear. The first difficulty is to know how best to organize the social services or local government or 'industrial democracy' so that more people are both able and willing to participate. In Britain the debates on both topics have been fierce and long, and despite the reorganizations of the 1970s it seems most unlikely that the right solutions will be found without many more burdensome studies, discussions and experiments. Some of the problems were analysed by John Lucas in his *Democracy and Participation* (1976).

What, for example, is to be the place of trade unions?

They were founded to fight the exploitation of the underdog by working for Socialism, and that seems to be generally the image they retain of themselves; but to think about their real place, it is necessary to forget the rhetoric. In Communist countries, where Socialism can be thought of as already having come to its full flower, trade unions are virtually powerless. Their sole function is to assist the State; since the State is 'the workers' state', no problem can arise – in theory. In the poorer nations, where pressure from the underdogs is most needed, trade unions usually have an equally limited life because there is not the freedom, and perhaps not yet the capacity, to organize. In fact a vigorous trade union movement goes with a vigorous private sector in a fairly advanced economy. The freedom of workers to combine in order to sell their labour dear can be regarded as one of those 'market forces', like the freedom of capitalists to charge for their products as much as the public can be persuaded to pay. Yet in practice every rich nation has found that it has had to limit the free play of the market forces, whether by law or by public opinion – and this means curbing the unions as well as the businessmen.

The problem of the unions has proved greater than any wisdom or courage which Britain could muster in the 1960s and 1970s. The problem has arisen for Britain not because this nation has a worse record of industrial strife than other nations (its record has usually been better) but because the power of the unions has seemed such a flagrant breach of the general principle that all the British live under laws made by Parliament. Beginning with Labour's proposals *In Place of Strife* (1968) successive governments have been attracted to the idea of bringing the unions 'under the rule of law' – curbing strikes by insisting on a postal ballot before official 'industrial action', and penalizing unofficial disputes. But both Labour and Conservative governments have found that their proposed or actual legislation was stillborn because union members refused to accept it, while the general public did not wish for a confrontation worse than the strikes which the new law was supposed to 'cool off'.

In 1977 the Bullock Commission, going to the opposite extreme, proposed that representatives of the unions should have an equal number of seats with representatives of the shareholders on all boards of companies employing more than two thousand people. This proposal deliberately aimed to place the seven million workers in the private sector of the British economy under this radically new control because it was believed that no less radical step would end the alienation of the shop floor from management. Neither works councils (with limited powers) nor supervisory boards (without day-to-day managerial responsibilities) nor the direct election of workers' representatives (without involving the unions) would be enough.

The West German pattern, which left the last say with the shareholders, was not enough. Brushing aside such compromises, the Bullock Commission said simply: the unions' power must be increased. This proposal, like the Labour and Conservative plans for Industrial Relations, ran into so much trouble that it was unworkable. Owners, managers and unions all rejected it. French industry, also deeply divided into 'two sides', has also failed to agree on worker-participation in running firms. But the problem will never leave any industrial society which allows workers freedom to combine as it leaves shareholders freedom to invest – yet also depends on their self-restrained willingness to co-operate.

Probably the least difficult proposal is that a 'code of good industrial practice' should be the basis on which all have to co-operate. Many attempts have been made to draw up a national code; or more effectively, to work one out in local practice. It is at least plain that much candid discussion is needed about problems which crucially challenge morality, and in the last resort also law, in an industrial society.

Another snag about participatory democracy is that when it prevails leaders cannot lead, and followers cannot follow, in the style of an old-fashioned army. The Director of the Manchester Business School sums up in a sentence the new concept of the manager. 'His specialism is that of the taking and implementing of decisions about what shall be done, but in doing this he is interpreting "the law of the situation" to those not placed or equipped to see it clearly and to see it whole' (W. Grigor McClelland, *And A New Earth*, 1976). Great personal understanding and much self-restraint are implied in this new style of management – for so much of any situation is human. To consult when one used to issue orders; to argue patiently when one is the best informed; to study human nature as carefully as the technical problems; to see the second-best technical solution adopted because it is democratically acceptable – all this is to be the boss's burden. But contrary to what they expect when they first hear about this possibility, the people who have been bossed in the past have to carry the biggest burden if they are now to participate in decision-making. For participation if it is to work needs time – time to attend meetings; time to investigate the problems; time to study the regulations; time to listen to colleagues, experts and bosses; time, in short, to share the manager's own responsibility for a total situation so that its 'law' may be grasped. Much of this time has to be taken from private pleasures including family life – and it has to be given without the manager's hope of a superior financial reward. One of the present facts of life in Britain (for example) is that only a handful of people are willing to spare this time and to be candidates for office in trade unions, works councils or local government. Often it is only a minority that is willing to accept the bother of voting in elections. Notoriously, the enthusiasts who obtain office in this travesty of democracy are likely not to be true representatives.

The members of a rich society must also accept the burden of finding new jobs, many of which will mean that they become each other's servants.

As technology changes continuously in an advanced industrial society the willingness to move to new work becomes essential, as does a willingness to re-train; and the far greater willingness of the Americans in comparison with the British goes far to explain why they have been twice as prosperous. Fortunately in the 1970s the British government's Manpower Services Commission has begun publishing studies and making experiments which show both the size of the tragedy of unemployment in this nation and the only way out of it. For more than twenty years after 1940 'full employment' seemed possible in Britain; but with twenty-six million wanting work, the total number of unemployed exceeded a million in 1972 and five years later seemed horribly steady at one and a half million, 450,000 of whom were under twenty-five. 750,000, mostly women, are expected to swell the total of those looking for work in Britain, 1978-81. If the present overmanning of old jobs were to be ended at least another half million might be put out of work. The only realistic way to find those extra jobs is to train and re-train for the work which a developing industrialism really does require. Artificially protecting jobs in inefficient or out of date industries, or creating jobs out of taxes, is no long-term answer. But this burden of accepting continuous change in employment leads a rich society straight to yet another burden.

Already in the United States more workers are 'white-collar' (salaried) than 'blue-collar' (paid by the hour or the piece). Their jobs are not hard in the sense of being dirty, but they are expected to serve efficiently and pleasantly – which many people find harder. All over the advanced industrial world, this is the trend. It would have been the trend more rapidly in Britain had not the unions resisted all attempts to reduce the notorious overmanning of large sections of manufacturing industry, with a consequent disaster for Britain's competitive position. But it is estimated that already in Britain in the 1970s unskilled or semi-skilled operatives directly engaged in manufacturing constitute under fifteen per cent of the total work force.

The trend means that increasingly employment is going to be available only to those prepared to be patient and expert with the often irritating problems of machines and of other people. Men and women whose fathers earned their living by brute strength are going to have to earn theirs by nimbleness and tact. Increasingly, too, the employment available is going to be in administration, contacts with the public, transport, catering or the new 'leisure industries'; and it is burdensome to have to put oneself at the disposal of others in these 'service' jobs. As many raw materials become scarcer and therefore more expensive, many goods are going to be made to last longer and if something goes wrong with them they are going to be repaired, not replaced – another test of people's patience and adaptability. And behind the new industrialism is going to stand the greatest industry of all: knowledge. People will face the choice between 'going back to college' and going forward to the scrap-heap; and by the same token, the rich society is going to need many patient and relevant teachers. Daniel Bell has analysed this shift from goods to services in America in his *The Coming of Post-Industrial Society* (1973).

'Service' is not a word that attracts rich societies in the 1970s. In Britain it suggests the exploitation of domestic servants in Victorian households. But perhaps it can be rehabilitated by being linked with another stratum in Victorian society. In 1873 the Cambridge economist, Arthur Marshall, looked forward to the day when manual work would have been made so much less demanding that 'by occupation at least, every man is a gentleman'. A century later, Anthony Giddens analysed *The Class Structure of the Advanced Societies* (1973) so as to suggest that this day was dawning. But in such a day it would be right to remember that part of the old idea of a gentleman was that he was willing to serve with a professional dedication and a constant consideration of other people's feelings – with, in one word, self-restraint.

And there remains the burden of service to the world, in action to help the poorer nations help themselves. World development is the price of the rich nations' ticket to world peace; and peace is a price tag attached to the rich nations' prosperity. By the year 2000 the population in the rich countries may be related to the population in the poorer countries in the ratio of one to six (in thousand millions); another guess is that it may be in the ratio of two to seven. In the 1970s half the world's population is under fifteen. This preponderance of the poor and the young is being accompanied by a steady build-up of anger against the rich and the ageing, reflected in international meetings from the United Nations to the World Council of Churches. Television and transistor radios mean that the privileges of the rich cannot be kept hidden from the poor. The need of politicians (and even of military strong men) to appeal to the masses means that the grievances of poorer countries' governments in international relations will not go unmentioned among the people. If the poorer countries' desperation increases, it is bound to explode in action against the rich.

Such action may imitate the oil producers, who quadrupled their prices in 1973-4. Already the 1970s have seen dramatic rises in the prices obtained for tropical countries' products. But it is far more difficult to organize a cartel to enforce high prices for bananas, or even phosphate, than it was for the oil producers to win their way. The slow rate of progress on the producers' proposals for long-term 'commodity agreements' bears witness to the fact that market forces when left to themselves do not always push consumers to agree on prices which suit producers. Not even pressure from the oil producers can easily persuade the rich North to pay the prices suggested for the non-oil products of the South, since it is unlikely that the oil producers will cripple themselves in order to help Asia, Africa and Latin America as wholes. And all the resolutions of the United Nations cannot alter this pattern of self-interest reigning in economic bargains between nations. Nevertheless, it stands to reason that if the producers of raw materials and food which the rich nations want can increase *both* their own populations *and* their own purchasing power, they will wish, and be able, to keep more of their own products for themselves unless the rich nations offer tempting prices. That will be the time when there is more equality in bargaining strengths.

Is it in the interests of the rich nations that they should help the poorer to reach this position? At first sight the answer seems 'no'; and that is the answer which is accepted without much thought by the majority of consumers who are also electors in rich nations. So the challenge to the rich to send at least one per cent of their gross national products to developing countries in aid or investment, at least 0.7 per cent being in official aid, has been endorsed in theory by the United Nations – but not acted on. (The challenge was first heard in 1964, but ten years later only 0.3 per cent went in official aid.) Trading agreements favourable to the poor have proved very hard to negotiate, and in 1977 the much-vaunted 'North-South dialogue' to inaugurate a 'new international economic order' collapsed in frustration.

But 'no' to the poor would be a short-sighted answer. In the long run, the self-preservation of the rich is bound up with the survival of the poor on terms which the poor think tolerably fair. And it has become crucial that the rich nations should respond to this challenge of the Third World, as after World War II the United States responded to the challenge of a ruined Europe with the Marshall Plan for reconstruction.

One reason why this is so is that knives do not remain on

empty plates indefinitely. The poor whose lives are reckoned cheap can always spend those lives in violence against those whom they hate as the exploiters or envy as the privileged. Whether or not the poorer nations ever use or threaten to use nuclear weapons against the rich, they can send their desperately heroic young men and women to destroy some of the installations on which international trade depends or to engage in terrorism in the privileged cities. The rich North could be held to ransom as some of its jet airliners have already been hijacked by Palestinians; and if the feeling grew that the great majority of the world's population applauded such terrorism, it might take only a few incidents or threats to get public opinion in the rich countries thoroughly alarmed. Even if such direct action is not taken, the poor nations can certainly bring pressure to bear by accepting the leadership of China against America or Russia or both in international politics. Already in the 1970s the growing Communist influence in Southern Africa has alarmed the Americans – who were taught by the Vietnamese that a modern army, however well equipped and however ruthless, cannot be sure of defeating a determined peasant movement. But even apart from military action or political alignment, the poor nations certainly have one weapon they can use against the rich. As they die of famine they can rely on plagues spreading. They can also rely on those plagues reaching the rich.

It is clear that a world divided into those who worry about slimming and those who worry about starving 'cannot endure permanently', as Abraham Lincoln said about a Union divided into slave and free. But it is more constructive to consider the long-term economic advantages of building up the nations now poor. Stable arrangements in prices lead to stable supplies of products. If – and only if – the poor nations are given higher prices for these products, they can afford to purchase fertilizers, machinery, manufactures and insurance and distribution services; they can become partners in a mutually profitable trade. The much-discussed point at which the internal markets of the rich nations become saturated with consumer goods may actually be reached within a century or so, leaving markets in the nations now poor as the main hopes of expanding or maintaining production and therefore employment in the North. The North also stands to gain in the long run if the more labour-intensive industries (textiles, leather and timber in particular) are concentrated in the South and are allowed to trade freely with the North, for industries which give employment to the poor also give cheap prices to the rich peoples.

I have, however, not yet mentioned the most powerful reason why it is in the interests of the rich that they should help the poor to help themselves. This reason is psychological or moral. Were the rich to refuse to pay any attention to the growing misery of the mass of humanity – were they to sit back and watch millions die on television – the quality of their own lives could not be unaffected. To condemn most human beings in one's own generation to hunger, rioting and disease before premature death would be to dehumanize oneself. To become complacent would be to become brutal. So the famines of the South could also kill off the spiritual heritage of the North – a heritage which everywhere praises sensitivity, compassion and the search for justice. Alternatively the famines in the poorer nations could create an intolerable burden of guilt among the privileged, or so arouse the indignation of the sensitive that every rich country would be torn apart from within.

For this variety of reasons, it is right for the rich nations to help the poorer. That obviously involves a great deal of self-restraint. But does it mean ceasing to be rich?

The proposals for a 'new international economic order' worked out by the poor nations in the 1970s – or on their behalf, as by Professor Tinbergen and his colleagues in *Reshaping the International Order* (1977) – put the challenge precisely. The rich nations have to be rich enough to reach the UN targets in aid and investment for world development, and to cancel or ease the poor nations' crushing debts to them. They have to be rich enough to allow the poor countries much more access to the International Monetary Fund (which has been too much absorbed in supporting inefficient rich economies such as Britain's). They have to be rich enough to offer open and stable markets to the poor countries' products – and to pay well. They have to be rich enough to pay their own farmers not to take profits away from the Third World's (for example, a rich Europe ought not to grow sugar beet if it means excluding tropical cane sugar). They have to be rich enough to release science and technology to help the poor nations' industrialization, and to redeploy their own industries where these compete with the Third World's (in the manufacture of clothing, for example, or in labour-intensive electronic goods). And they have to be rich enough to be prepared to leave the poorer nations with more of the food which they grow. At present many crops and animals are raised in the Third World for export; the cash is badly needed for imports of fertilizers, machinery and other goods all requiring foreign exchange. In the years to come the poorer nations ought to be able to make more of these things they now have to import and they will increasingly face resistance from their own hungry peoples to the export of cash crops. In that situation, the rich countries could use their political and financial muscle in order to insist on receiving this food which the poor will need for themselves and their children. Or they could use their riches to explore new sources of food, such as the oceans.

It is natural and right that the present appalling contrast between the rich and the poor, world-wide, should have produced feelings of guilt in the more sensitive citizens of the rich nations. The facts are certainly unforgettable: one tenth of the world's population consumes three-quarters of its resources while millions of children go to bed hungry; the USA, which has six per cent of that population, consumes about forty per cent of those resources; more than a quarter of the world's grain production becomes animal fodder so that the rich can eat meat . . . The simple slogan has been heard widely: 'Live more simply so that others may simply live'. But it has not persuaded, for this slogan is too simple. A policy is needed with more to recommend it to the hard-headed. For example, if American cattle were given less grain (as enthusiasts for aid frequently recommend) very little of the grain saved would find its way to the children of Bangladesh. All the experience of American agriculture in this century suggests that American farmers would merely grow less. In the outcome the world's poor would not be helped – any more than the cocoa farmers of Ghana would be helped if the British were to eat fewer chocolates. It would be better for Americans happily fed on steaks (but not on too many of them) to give generously to the poorer nations, to leave more manufacturing to them, and to pay handsome prices for what the poor want to sell. It is not desirable for the women of a rich nation to walk the streets barefoot. It is desirable for them all to own large collections of shoes made in India.

One of the few solid achievements in the trading negotiations between North and South has been the Lomé Convention between the European Economic Community and ex-colonial nations in Africa, the Caribbean and the Pacific. That treaty gave those forty-six nations (there were subsequent additions) duty-free access to a huge market for their industrial goods and eighty-five per cent of their agricultural products, in the initial period 1975-80. It did nothing to help the desperately poor peoples of South Asia and Latin America; indeed, it made life harder for them. But by liberalizing the terms of trade it was an encouraging example of what rich societies can afford to do with some self-restraint.

It seems that a good slogan would be: 'Live more richly so that others, too, may prosper.' That, surely, is not too frightening a way of stating what is vital to the self-preservation of the rich nations as well as to the survival of most of humanity.

5 The Self-Liberation of the Poor

When discussing the prospects of the poorer nations, I try simply to echo those Third World voices which seem to be realistic. I am white and a citizen of a comparatively rich country, but I am persuaded that too much of the discussion about 'world development' has been carried on by rich whites who, however generous or expert they may be, lack the one necessary qualification of belonging. The future which the poorer nations build must be their choice, built by their wisdom and work, within the limits set by the real world which they know by living in it. Otherwise the future will not appear except as a paper scheme – or if it does appear, it will not endure.

The very word 'development' may conceal this reality, suggesting that someone else is going to 'develop' the poor acceding to someone else's ideas (whether these ideas are commercial or idealistic). It is, I have learned, much more useful to think about the self-liberation of the poor. Every new mouth arriving has a brain attached to it. Every brain can have a dream. Within the limits of the real world every dream can come true. Obviously the dismantling of colonialism, from the expulsion of the British Raj from India to the expulsion of the Portuguese Empire from Africa as late as 1975, was absolutely essential to self-liberation. At the same time, however, the *self* in self-liberation needs to be stressed against the Marxists. Whatever the material benefits may be, it is not true liberation if the wretched of the Earth exchange their present fate for life under a totalitarian regime. Their scientists and technologists need freedom to question, to experiment and to innovate; it seems that even in China the lack of such freedom has been felt as a great disadvantage about the Maoist 'liberation'. The poorer countries' managers, craftsmen and shopkeepers need freedom to invest, to risk and to create wealth for themselves and for others by their own hard work; their citizens have often won success in that way in the past and it would be a great loss if all such enterprise were placed under the deadening control of bureaucrats. Above all the poorer countries' farmers need freedom to run their own lives in their own villages. The shrewdness of the peasant is no myth. What peasants have lacked has been information about modern methods relevant to local needs, and the incentive to use these methods intensively. The peasant needs this help far more than he or she needs to be liberated by any Communist or managed by any bureaucrat.

It is also sad that this idea of 'liberation' has been degraded by propaganda (not only Marxist propaganda) into a call to war to the death against every ex-colonial power. If such propaganda is valid, it means that the wretched of the Earth will never know freedom until Latin America, for example, has thrown out every investment and every expert sent from North America; until no white man is left at work in Africa; and until there is not an office of a multinational company in the whole of Asia. In effect a world-wide race war would be needed to accomplish such a liberation, and it would seem madness to imagine that peaceful and mutually profitable trade between the rich and poorer countries would continue during it, or resume rapidly after it. It would also be highly optimistic to think that the rich nations which had seen their investments go up in smoke and their expertise rejected contemptuously would be quick to send fresh investments and new experts overseas. If the Yanks were sent home as the slogans on the walls so often demand, they would be likely to stay at home. It is more than doubtful whether the poor would gain. India, Bangladesh and Pakistan have not gained on the whole by being unattractive to international investment and trade.

Certainly it is necessary for ex-colonies to complete their achievement of political independence by achieving the end of 'neo-colonialism' – if by that term is meant a system where the key economic decisions affecting a poorer nation are taken without the prior consent of the government of that nation. The necessity of that step is not always acknowledged by those who appear as friends of the Third World. Rich countries may seek credit for supplying as 'aid' arms or machinery or experts or capital or loans which are in fact designed to tie the poorer country more closely to the donor. Such 'aid' has its uses, but it should not be called aid. It is an expense incurred while pursuing a foreign policy, or an investment to promote trade. Real aid is given in such a way that the decision-making power of the recipient is not diminished but increased. A study by Teresa Hayter of the US-dominated World Bank's relationship with Latin America, *Aid as Imperialism* (1971), explored these issues. On the other hand, it is still possible to have a mutually profitable relationship when it has been recognized what 'aid' truly is. Aid can be, and is, given both by voluntary agencies and by governments – aid without strings. Investment can be, and is, both given and welcomed alongside this aid.

NOT DOOM BUT LIBERATION

What, then, are the poorer nations to do for their own liberation?

Realism is essential. Talk about the poorer nations taking off into 'modern development' within a few years was heard in the 1960s but was always unrealistic apart from a few exceptional cases such as Singapore, Hong Kong, Taiwan and South Korea. The economic progress which most of the poorer nations have achieved since 1945 has been faster than most of the progress to be seen during the nineteenth century in the nations now rich, but the talk about the 'take-off' did not do justice to the immensity of the psychological, political and physical problems. What is necessary is an escape from privations often like those under which Europe, for example, suffered through the long centuries of the Dark and Middle Ages. And the talk about the poorer nations 'catching up' with the rich was always totally unrealistic. By the 1970s one American was consuming resources which would have kept fifty Indians alive, and he faced a future radically different from India's; the increase in the gross national product related to the population that the USA can achieve in one year would take India a century. The Earth's resources simply would not sustain the consumption needed for the fifty Indians to 'catch up' with the American consuming at this rate. It is inconceivable – and also undesirable. Such an economic revolution would totally wreck the social traditions which have been built up over thousands of years all over the Third World and which are still a great source of happiness to the peoples of that world. Almost all Third World thinkers therefore now prefer to think in terms of the Third World's own self-chosen path, combining more but still modest consumption with a stable society.

Adequate nourishment is essential – particularly in infancy, when the brain is being formed. At present coloured people are often slower-thinking and slower-working than white people. They are more prone to disease and to early death. Yet they are also more apathetic to their discomforts. History teaches as its first lesson that these characteristics are not due to the lack of whiteness in skins. Egypt, Persia, India and China were highly civilized when Europe and North America were wildernesses. The twentieth-century achievements of countless coloured people who have been given a fair chance teach the same lesson that genetically equality exists between the races. Any slowness in the coloured poor generally results from their food, not their genes. Vitamin A deficiency causes blindness; Vitamin D deficiency causes rickets; iron deficiency causes anaemia; iodine deficiency causes cretinism; protein deficiency causes swollen bellies, scrawny limbs, scaly skins. The remedy is partly to grow more food; partly to resist imported nonsense foods like Coca-Cola or artificial milk for babies; and partly to check, and if necessary change, traditional diets in the light of modern knowledge of nutrition.

Hygiene is essential – particularly hygiene in the home. At present disease is bred by the habits of life in countless villages and shanty towns. This is not because the people are naturally dirty. Many tribes far more primitive than these people are known to be skilled in avoiding disease. The reason is often that enough of the twentieth century has reached these places to double the traditional numbers in the village, or to crowd people into a shanty town which falls far below the village in its level of hygiene. What is needed most urgently is advice by fellow-villagers or fellow-townsmen who have received a basic training in modern hygiene adapted to local conditions. To give such advice with life-changing effects is the work of China's 'barefoot doctors', and almost everywhere such hygiene-workers are needed more urgently than are highly skilled, professional doctors (who may stay to work in the rich countries where they have received their expensive training). Often clean water is the most important need of the people, and its provision does far more credit to any local authority than does a gleaming modern hospital. But of course doctors, too, are needed. An appalling amount of human suffering is suggested by the estimate that about forty per cent of the world's people have no access to a doctor.

Education is essential – particularly education in the techniques of efficiency in the home and at work. At present ignorance is a fact of life, as life-destroying as any famine or drought – not because the people are stupid but because no sustained effort has been made to reach them with the training they need. Literacy is obviously important; it is reckoned that over thirty per cent of mankind including some seventy per cent of Indians are still illiterate. But all too often such education as has been provided has been far too bookish, designed by schoolteachers (it has often seemed) in order to produce more schoolteachers. The education of an elite as members of the international community is important, but all over the Third World education has been too absorbed in the languages, customs, histories and psychological diseases of the ex-colonial powers. The training of an elite to be scientists, technicians, administrators and managers is important, but too much of the emphasis has been elitist, and education instead of awakening the consciousness and ambition of the masses has actually helped oppression because it has adjusted the educated to the values and purposes of the exploiters. Modernization through education is important, but all too often the schools have encouraged what Ivan Illich (*Tools for Conviviality*, 1973) has called 'the accountant's view of the value of time, the bureaucrat's view of the value of promotion, the salesman's view of the value of increased consumption, and the union leader's view of the purpose of work' – views which the modern industrial societies are themselves questioning.

The end of discrimination is essential. Although Gandhi's defence of India's untouchables made such a deep impression at the time, in many Third World countries there is in practice (whatever the constitution may say) discrimination against people of a particular race, tribe, religion, caste or class. In fact, it is difficult to think of one country in which such discrimination is not rampant. The loss of the loyalties and talents of the despised and excluded groups must be prodigiously damaging to the nation. Of course the rich countries do not set edifying examples of social equality; of course white racism is the worst, most notoriously in South Africa; but the challenge to the poor nations is to enlist the help of all in nation-building at a time when no one's contribution can be rejected safely.

The equality of women is even more important in the poorer nations than in the rich. All over the Third World women are kept in virtual bondage by the force of tradition, often sanctified by religion. They are probably not given the elementary education which men may receive. They are not allowed to seek jobs, to choose their husbands, or to decide the number of their children. When they have cooked the food they may not be allowed to eat it until the men have taken the best bits. Yet both at home and in the fields they usually work harder than the men. Worn out by child-bearing and by these labours, the women die prematurely and before the men. The whole system is hostile to one half of the human race.

The curbing of elites is essential. Tragically often political independence has led to the rule of a small elite in the new nation's life. Elites are necessary in human societies. They become unjust when they extract from the economy more than a fair reward for their enterprise, leadership and skills. There can be little doubt, except among members of the elite concerned, that in many Third World countries the rewards taken by the privileged few have far exceeded their contributions to the national life. It is estimated that in Latin America, for example, the average incomes of the top five per cent are twenty times greater than those of the bottom fifty per cent – more than double the contrast in North America. All too many of the profits of agriculture or industry, which ought to be ploughed back in wages or investment, are dissipated in luxuries or invested in other countries which (understandably) are regarded as more 'stable'. These bloodsucking elites are often unhealthily dependent on the rich countries both financially and culturally; and too much foreign 'aid' increases this dependence. Their pride is to keep up with foreign fashions and to enjoy holidays abroad. They cannot lead the people because they do not respect them; indeed, they meet them (apart from their servants) as little as possible. Communists are surely right to argue that such elites deserve to be overthrown. And not only Communists! Summing up many studies in his 1970 book on *The Challenge of World Poverty*, the eminent Swedish economist Gunnar Myrdal stressed the degree to which its own elitism was repeatedly the major obstacle to the Third World's development; and because the reality has remained tragic Susan

George in her explosive *How the Other Half Dies* (1976) went so far as to suggest that the World Bank ought to insist on action before making grants or loans. That suggestion is politically impossible – but it is possible for the peoples of the Third World to take their own action against their own fellow-citizens who exploit them.

A proper mix in the economy is essential. Almost every economy in the Third World has been shaped in the interests of foreigners and an urban elite. Any roads or railways tend to help movement towards cities on the coast, founded as ports to ship crops and raw materials to the colonial countries, and in the smarter districts of those cities the elite can be found enjoying life (when at home). If the economy is to be freed from that past, determined action has now to be taken to stop the drift of the landless rural poor to the cities, to encourage many of these people to return to a revitalized countryside, and to employ those remaining in labour-intensive industries. A better mix of agriculture and industry is needed; China seems to have some lessons to teach, but everywhere the task is colossal. In many of the poorer nations, one or two crops are dangerously predominant because that was what the capitalists of the imperial nation wanted in the days of colonialism. If that harvest is poor one year, or if the world production is too large so that prices fall too low, the whole nation can suffer terribly through the loss of foreign exchange and other effects. A better mix of crops is essential – which does not make it any easier. More trade with the rest of the Third World is essential – and is unlikely to happen unless there are much stronger Common Market arrangements within Asia, Africa or Latin America.

Consistent government is essential. It is extremely unlikely that one form of government will be preferred by all the peoples of the world. It is also very unlikely that one form of government will be found to be indispensable in economic development. But it is clear that progress is greatly handicapped if changes in government policy are so frequent that long-term planning becomes impossible. Thus if a people decides that it wishes to develop its economy in partnership with foreign investors, it is essential to give those investors and their governments confidence that the investments will not be confiscated. If a people decides that it wishes to follow an economic policy which concentrates power in the hands of the State, that Socialism will not work if it always seems about to be overthrown by a coup of army officers in league with businessmen. The twentieth-century history of Latin America is littered with proof.

Efficient government is so essential that in most countries it is evidently reckoned by the people to be more important than the Westminster style of Parliamentary democracy. It is notorious that the politically 'liberated' Third World has suffered under many corrupt and inefficient politicians. One country after another has therefore consented to the overthrow of the politicians by the Army, and many of the military regimes have provided, at least for a time, clean and strong government. But over and over again the military regimes have in their turn become ineffective and unpopular. Army officers have seldom had any training either in the management of an economy or in handling the public with tact. Their constant temptation is to beat the drums of nationalism and militarism more loudly as the people drift away. So they are usually overthrown in a fresh coup – perhaps by fellow-officers, perhaps by politicians staging a return. There is no simple lesson to be learned about which form of government is best; that must be left to the nation concerned. But twentieth-century experience definitely teaches the ancient lesson that efficient government is one of the great blessings.

A Third World government, if it is to serve the people, has to fight (with more than presidential speeches) landlords, capitalists or foreign investors who are extracting more profits than they deserve out of the fields, the towns and the flow of trade. These are very difficult battles for a government to undertake if it is not backed up by an efficient civil service and if its own members are unduly influenced – perhaps paid – by the enemies they are supposed to be fighting. It is not surprising that so many Third World governments have so frequently been outmanoeuvred by their own landlords and businessmen, by foreign embassies and by multinational companies. Europeans or North Americans who are critical (often while taking cruel advantage of the situation) need to remember for how long in history their own governments were pitiably weak – but they are surely right to think that governments more worthy of the peoples of the Third World are essential to that world's self-liberation.

The liberation of workers so that they can work out their own salvation is essential. At the time of the World Employment Conference at Geneva in 1976 there was emphasis that several thousand million new jobs would be needed by the end of this century. Whatever the statistics may be, it is surely clear that one of the supreme duties of governments now is to put into hands of the people of the cities and villages the power to plan and work for themselves, harnessing the human energy which at present so largely goes to waste. In the cities of the Third World unemployment is a tragedy which is in its own way as lethal as the bomb on Hiroshima; and the answer is industrial co-operatives with appropriate technology. Expensive machines are seldom needed. What is most needed is some initiative by the State – to encourage the plentiful labour to organize itself productively, and to provide the necessary minimum of equipment.

In the countryside there is also some outright unemployment among the landless, but there is much more *under*employment among those who work or 'half-work' on other people's land mainly for other people's profit. It is estimated that in Latin America ninety per cent of the land is owned by about seventeen per cent of the landowners and over a third of the population owns altogether one per cent of the cropland. The redistribution of the land to the communes in China has aroused world-wide interest and general admiration, but land reform has been undertaken successfully elsewhere by military or democratic regimes, and where the tribal ownership of land is traditional that provides the starting point. Much experience and much analysis point clearly to certain steps as essential. The State must maintain and enforce a register of who owns what. Individually or in groups, those who work on the land must own it – or at the very least must have solid reasons to trust the landlords as 'good' and as efficient. In their own collectives or in services provided by landlords, those who work on the land must be able to rely on an adequate supply of water, seeds, fertilizers, storage, transport, wholesaling and credit – all things the individual peasant cannot provide for himself. Those essentials are as plain in Taiwan as in Red China, Denmark, Japan, Israel or Tanzania. In the world scene this is the example to follow – not the concentration on huge 'agribusiness' in the United States (where the number of farms halved, 1945-75). In India's half-million villages, this above all else is what it would mean for the peasants to be free.

6 Man's Decision

The prospects of the human race are therefore fearfully uncertain both in the countries now rich and in those now poor. It is plainly no time to revive the fantasies (abundant in the literature of European optimism before 1914) that men have become like gods, able to take charge of their own fate and to assume total control over their environment. On the contrary: the survival of man, or at any rate of civilization, depends on understanding, respecting and co-operating with the environment. It is the Superman who is under the illusion that he is at liberty to play God who becomes a destructive black hole in nature. But equally, this is no time for predictions of an inescapable doom – predictions which fulfil themselves if, and only if, they are believed. In the perspective provided by some knowledge of man's history and pre-history it seems unlikely that man has come such a long way merely in order to be defeated here; and altogether more likely that he has begun to acquire, or to recover, the wisdom that shows him the limits he must face and the burdens he must accept.

At least man now knows what decisions are necessary if he wishes to survive in conditions worthy of his past and his nature. The present pattern of international relations – an uneasy mixture of the armed pursuit of national interests with

NOT DOOM BUT LIBERATION 141

some acknowledgement of wider loyalties – will not survive; chaos will grow or co-operation will grow. Rich countries will not remain rich in their present style. They can preserve their wealth if they will accept the necessary self-restraint, or they can collapse. The poorer countries will disappear in famine and plague if they do not limit their populations, grow more food and employ their labour in their cities. And they will not do these things unless they free themselves from social and political systems which at present frustrate human energy. For rich or for poor, there seems to be no third option after the straight choice: doom, or radical change leading to self-liberation.

One who accepts modern science's story of the evolution of man is likely to find in this choice now confronting man a crisis such as a species often experiences. When the sea gets overcrowded, life is challenged to explore the land, and when the land is fully occupied, the air. The dinosaur and the man are both challenged by cold – and it is the man who responds by using and making fire. Man creates his own new mental world by language, and masters the world around him by the wheel. Man is challenged to feed his children and he begins agriculture; to feed his mind and he begins civilization. At the turn of the twentieth and twenty-first centuries AD the challenge is again of such dimensions.

Arnold Toynbee, the historian of civilizations, expounded this theme in many books – most finely in his posthumously published dialogue with Daisaku Ikeda of Japan, *Choose Life* (1976). He saw the human race brought to the brink of disaster by its greed, exhausting and polluting the Earth's resources. In particular he smelled doom in the barbarism of the nation state: 'today fanatical nationalism is perhaps ninety per cent of the religion of perhaps ninety per cent of mankind'. He found hope in the common emphasis of the great religions – he shared it with the Buddhist Daisaku Ikeda, for example – that man's supreme task is to master himself. Toynbee thought that man had been made self-centred and greedy by the harsh necessities of his evolution. The offer of salvation through any of the great religions is, he saw, to purify the desire – to direct it away from the self towards the whole human race, this whole planet, the universe and the ultimate spiritual reality.

And one who believes in a God who is ultimately in control will want to add a point about the alternative now facing man. It is a *crisis* in the original sense of the Greek word, for it is a judgement – the judgement of man by God. According to this understanding, God has put the alternative to man – and as man makes his choice, he will reveal his true character and turn to his preferred destiny. The will of God is, many believe, that rich and poor nations alike should liberate themselves, indeed that man should increasingly liberate himself from self; and many would add that God has given to man both the physical and the spiritual capacity to achieve this. But his Creator has, it seems, such respect for man's freedom that the possibility exists that man may choose self and greed. If the same God who has given to man the doom-defying capacity has also given to man the genuine choice of bringing doom on himself, it is in accordance with the insight in the Christian scriptures that 'this is how the judgement works: the light has come into the world, but people love the darkness rather than the light, because their deeds are evil' (John 3:19). That insight goes back to still older words: 'I am now giving you the choice between life and death, between God's blessing and God's curse, and I call Heaven and Earth to witness the choice you make. Choose life' (Deuteronomy 30:19).

But frankly, has the Bible any relevance at all to the facts and the fears just outlined?

Obviously the ancient scriptures did not prophesy the latest world-crisis in the sense of predicting its exact nature, and the efforts that have been made to extract such predictions from the book of Daniel, say, or the book of Revelation were merely wasted ingenuity. The Bible did not expect the Assyrians or the Romans whose brutality it recorded to launch intercontinental missiles. It did not worry about the planet's overpopulation; when the last word in it was written, the world-wide population was still, it seems, well under three hundred million. The Bible described a world which was indeed poor by the standards of today's rich nations. Adam is told: 'You will have to work hard and sweat to make the soil produce anything' (Genesis 3:19). Abraham, Isaac and Jacob had to be constantly on the move because in no other way could their herds find pasture. Jesus expected his hearers to miss a single lost sheep or lost coin desperately, and to be 'worried about the food and drink you need in order to stay alive' (Matthew 6:25). We also read that a prophet named Agabus 'predicted that a severe famine was about to come over all the Earth; it came when Claudius was emperor' (Acts 11:27). But the particular nightmares of our time are not found in the Bible. Despite its great funeral songs for the wicked cities of Tyre (Ezekiel 27) and Rome (Revelation 18), the Bible knew so little of modern urban problems that it called both Babylon and Bethlehem cities. In the parables of Jesus, when the foolish girls ran out of oil they could be told to 'go to the shop' since this oil grew on trees (Matthew 25:9); and when a foolish boy was caught up in a famine he knew that he was still within walking distance of food (Luke 15).

It is therefore an obvious waste of time to comb the Bible for exact prophecies of events in today's news – or of doom (or plenty) just around the corner. But I have been driven to see that it is worthwhile to put the broad pattern of the Bible's interpretation of history alongside the news, as I have already put the Bible's essential teaching about the creation alongside the revelations of modern science. The Bible does not give us a pattern of assured prosperity or automatic progress. Instead, it displays a pattern of man responding, or failing to respond, to one crisis after another. That is what makes it instructive to hold the Bible in the one hand and today's newspaper in the other.

The whole point of the great prophets of Ancient Israel was that they warned their hearers that disaster would come if they did not respond rightly to the challenge of the prosperity that had accompanied the reigns of David and Solomon, about a thousand years before Christ. The prophets saw in the society around them deep and growing divisions between rich and poor, and between rulers and people. They saw the cynical oppression of the poor; and they saw the rulers relying on military power or diplomatic manoeuvres instead of on justice. In actions or words of imperishable splendour Elijah, Elisha, Amos and Hosea denounced the northern kingdom of the Israelites; and Micah, Isaiah and Jeremiah spoke against Jerusalem itself. When Samaria fell to the Assyrians in 721, and Jerusalem to the Babylonians in 597, this stern prophetic tradition was vindicated. So in their defeat the Hebrews collected their scriptures, where the centre was occupied by these prophets and by the law of God to which they appealed over the heads of the rulers of the day. Near the beginning of these scriptures they placed the figures of Abraham, challenged to leave the familiar city, and Moses, commanded to leave Egypt and to enter a covenant with God in the wilderness. These were men reckoned righteous because of the faith they showed in their response to a crisis.

Jesus and the first Christians evidently did not expect history to last long – but the New Testament shows a consistent expectation that the months or years remaining would bring the challenges of history to a climax. Almost all of the parables of Jesus were warnings about the coming crisis or promises to those who responded wisely to the warnings. A typical New Testament passage (Mark 13) speaks of wars and famines as being 'like the first pains of childbirth' as the great crisis comes to life. Many such passages concentrate on the terrible sufferings accompanying the fall of Jerusalem to the Romans – a disaster which could be seen coming long before it came in AD 70. Scholars dispute about the extent to which these warnings have been edited before being written down in the gospels, but few can fail to hear the voice of Jesus pleading: 'You can predict the weather by looking at the sky, but you cannot interpret the signs concerning these times!' (Matthew 16:3).

According to the Bible, it is not so much in quiet times of peace as through the crisis that God acts, summoning man and if man responds saving him. Parts of the biblical literature – for example, the book of Daniel – are called 'apocalyptic' from the Greek word for 'revelation'. For, according to this teaching, it is precisely in the crisis – for example, in the persecution of the Jewish religion at the time when the book of Daniel was compiled – that the true and living God reveals his power.

Luke's gospel is typical of this strand in the Bible when it urges its readers to rejoice when 'whole countries will be in despair'. 'When these things begin to happen', it advises, 'stand up and raise your heads, because your salvation is near' (Luke 21:28). The last book of the Bible is also typical in expecting the final appearance of Christ in triumph to be preceded by the four horsemen – the two tyrants on their white and red horses, the announcer of famine on the black horse, and Death on the pale-coloured horse (Revelation 6:1-8). It is only after such forecasts that the seer glimpses the fulfilment of God's purposes in 'the Holy City, the new Jerusalem, coming down out of heaven from God' (21:2) – the city into which 'the peoples of the world' and 'the kings' come, through gates which are never closed (22:24-26).

The Bible does not offer a detailed prediction about the future of the world. It offers something better. It suggests a basic attitude to all the successive crises which offer new life – or which, when unheeded, bring doom on the selfishness and greed of man. And it says: 'choose!'

Part Four

NOT MARXISM
BUT EUROPE

1 Conserving Socialism

When a hope matters, we do not leave it in dreams, books or conferences. We put it into a society. I therefore turn to face the question: what kind of a society can embody the hope that is real in the last years of the twentieth century? An American must think about 1976-2076; an African about the realities of freedom achieved; an Asian about China long after Mao and India long after the Gandhis; an Australian about an age when Australia will be considerably closer to Asia. I can write only about the answer which seems to be emerging in Britain.

All over the world people are wondering what is the matter with Britain. Throughout the Commonwealth they suspect that in her old age mother may have gone a little mad. In the American half of the English-speaking world they often find it difficult to speak with conviction about Britain's future. But as I see it, Britain has a future – and it is now functioning as a laboratory to test possible futures.

Britain was the birthplace of parliamentary democracy and, wishing to preserve this freedom, has combined with other parliamentary democracies to begin the formation of the United States of Europe. The first direct elections to the European Parliament in 1979 are rightly understood as a landmark in this journey. And the journey may be of interest in other continents. In 1776 the new United States of America could be based on a large measure of unity in language and culture. If the far more diverse Europeans can work out a new federal system, that may one day assist the United States of Africa or of Latin America or of South-East Asia. Meanwhile the growth of the USE will offer Europeans, including the British, much of what has been made possible for Americans by their federal unity.

But Britain was also the birthplace of Marxism and as the twentieth century approaches its end it seems possible that the British will turn to Marxism, feeling that their social tradition of a thousand years is now exhausted. Certainly Britain's long-term choice seems to lie between Marxism and Europe, for either the one society or the other is needed to be a society of hope. And this choice is of interest outside Britain, for throughout today's world Marxism has set the terms of serious political debate. In any nation the first thing to do nowadays, once one is of age intellectually, is to make up one's mind about Marxism.

How has the situation arisen in Britain?

The failure of the Social Democratic Federation to win a substantial working-class following was the failure of Marxism on its home ground. After the birth of the Independent Labour Party in 1893 it seemed that the movement would always be largely non-Marxist. It became a cliché that 'Labour owes more to Methodism than to Marxism'. The Nonconformist conscience was certainly influential, and many a chapel trained many a young man such as Ernest Bevin. But the movement was also inspired by a more secular idealism (*England Arise!*); by the Fabians' impatience with the inefficiency and needless injustice of capitalism; and by the fight of the unions for wages. By Marxist standards, none of these elements in the Labour movement showed much 'scientific understanding of historical processes'.

Accordingly the General Strike of 1926, provoked by cuts in the miners' wages, led in the end not to the Revolution but to the unions' retreat and the MacDonald-Baldwin National Government. This thoroughly British and therefore untheoretical character of the alliance called the Labour Party was what made Churchill's first radio broadcast in the General Election campaign of 1945 ludicrous and disastrous. 'Socialism is in its essence an attack not only on British enterprise', Churchill declared, 'but upon the right of the ordinary man and woman to breathe freely without having a harsh, clammy, clumsy, tyrannical hand clapped across their mouth and nostrils.' Actually as the Leader of the Labour Party Clement Attlee was extremely moderate, a master of understatement associated more with the public schools than with the secret police. In the 1950s a large area of consensus ('Butsksellism') emerged in British politics, and as part of his sympathy with the Conservative policy-maker R. A. Butler the new Labour

NOT MARXISM BUT EUROPE

leader, Hugh Gaitskell, dismissed the famous Clause 4 in the constitution of the Labour Party as 'theology'.

However, Clause 4 stayed put – and it continued to proclaim the necessity of 'common ownership of the means of production and the best obtainable system of popular administration and control of each industry or service'. Indeed, Labour's defeat in the 1970 election was attributed by many of its activists to its failure to be sufficiently Socialist; and since then, both in the party and in the unions, there has been a steady move to the Left, only halted by the need for a tactical alliance with the Liberals. During the 1970s it has begun to seem possible that the British Labour Party will end up in a position not very far from the Communists of France and Italy, with whom the non-Marxist Social Democrats have formed tactical alliances. The Marxist attitude has, of course, always been that Socialism is a stage on the road to Communism.

In this situation it appears that Britain faces a double task of great difficulty. One task is to avoid Churchill's 'harsh, clammy, clumsy, tyrannical hand' by avoiding Communism. But it is no contribution to offer as the alternative to Marxism a political philosophy which, when analysed realistically, is found to be a defence of the interests of a few successful businessmen. Britain, it seems, needs Socialism as its Labour Party has built it with some very efficient Conservative help. Indeed, many other nations appear to need it or something very like it.

What, then, is this Socialism? In attempting to define it I have been helped by some conversations with Socialists who are well aware that this is a real question – and by some British literature from Anthony Crosland's *The Future of Socialism* (1956) to Stuart Holland's *The Challenge of Socialism* (1975), in the international context provided by George Lichtheim's *Short History of Socialism* (1970).

Socialism puts the interests of all above the interests of the few. That very simple moral definition would probably be the heart of the matter for a great many Christians and others who would accept Socialism today. So defined, Socialism reflects a revulsion against the sacrifice of people to money-making, and against a privileged minority 'getting on' while most of their fellow-citizens are left frustrated. This revulsion has, for example, brought about the end of an educational system which in Britain left most children with the feeling that they were failures from the age of eleven, doomed to second-rate 'secondary modern' schools and to unrewarding and unfulfilling jobs. The acceptance of comprehensive education in Britain during the 1960s and 1970s probably shows more clearly than any other change what British 'Socialism' is all about – but also emphasizes how wide is the meaning of 'Socialism' at this level, since comprehensive education has been accepted in the USA since the 1920s.

Socialism takes power from landlords. There is widespread agreement – in theory, if not in Latin American or Indian practice – about the necessity of 'land reform', to give control of agricultural land back to the farmers and peasants on whom it depends. There is widespread admiration for the dramatic increases in food production that have been achieved by people working for their own family-like group rather than for a landlord (whether in a Chinese commune or in an Israeli kibbutz). But the same case often applies to urban land. A thousand million extra people are expected to arrive in the cities of the Third World in the period 1975-85 by birth or as refugees from rural poverty. Developments which could mean health instead of disease, decent homes instead of shacks, jobs instead of marginality, dignity instead of squalor, are desperately urgent – but have been thwarted because the cities do not control the land on which they are built. Even in Britain, where the cities are paradises compared with Calcutta or Bombay or Jakarta or Manila or Buenos Aires or Rio, the public control of urban land is an urgent priority. Much has been done by planning laws, but even so fortunes far in excess of their service to the community have been made by urban developers skilled or lucky enough to secure the agreement of the planning authorities – one of the ugly and unacceptable faces of capitalism as this was on display in the early 1970s. It is not surprising that, all round the world, the community is demanding and getting a larger share in the harvest of food and profit from rural or urban land.

Socialism gives the State control of key services and industries. In countries at an early stage of industrialization it is usually impossible to build a solid basis safe from foreign control unless the State issues the commands and supplies the capital. Soviet Russia has impressed the world by transforming itself from virtual feudalism under the Tsars to its present industrial strength. Amazingly, Russia defeated the highly industrialized Germany and rebuilt itself after its wartime devastation. While it is possible to speculate that American businessmen could have run the show better, Communism naturally gets the credit. Many countries taking the same road to industrialization now share the belief that the State must set the pace. In the Third World the position is often complicated by the need to rely on foreigners for capital, management, technical skill and marketing, but the nationalization of the key industries – of oil in Iran, for example – is regarded as a great step towards real nationhood, escaping the invisible shackles of neo-colonialism. In Britain nationalization has so far been used not to create fresh wealth but to run key industries which would have had an even more uncertain future, and would have been troubled by even more strikes, if left in private hands. The nationalized industries in Britain produce a tenth of the gross domestic product. A few unfortunate industries have provided battlegrounds between nationalizers and denationalizers, but a large element of State ownership is generally accepted. No one is going to return electricity or gas or the nuclear power stations or the BBC or the coal mines or the steel works to private ownership. Some industries have been left to die; an example is the manufacture of motor cycles. But public money has been pumped into other industries, and accountability to the State has inevitably been part of the price; an example is the manufacture of motor cars.

Socialism means that the State can supply much of the stimulus and capital needed for economic development. Imitating Soviet Russia's five-year plans, many countries (including France under fairly Right-wing regimes) have dedicated themselves to the National Plan. In countries unable to reach that measure of agreement – for example, in Britain after the collapse of George Brown's plan of 1965 – there is emphasis on a more piecemeal system of planning agreements between the State and the major industries, and in particular the banking system is subjected to close government control or pressure. After such stimulus from the government all the forces of the nation can be mobilized, or so it is hoped – from the computers in government offices to the workers on the shop floor who now know it is patriotic to fulfil their 'work norms'. And one of the aids which the State can supply is capital – in small amounts to meet emergencies, or to the extent regarded as 'Socialism' under Communist regimes.

Socialism means that the State, not a handful of big companies, dominates the economy. Under Marxism central planning is as complete as the economy's complexity will permit, given the shortcomings of the bureaucracy. But all non-Communist states take for granted an extent of economic regulation that would have astonished the nineteenth century. The contented prosperity of the non-Communist industrial nations, including Britain, in the 1950s and 1960s rested largely on the application of the economics associated chiefly with J. M. Keynes. He was a Liberal not a Socialist, and the faded Liberal leader Lloyd George was his first convert among the major statesmen – but he advocated massive intervention by the State in order to rectify the trade cycle (boom-slump-boom) which otherwise would have made capitalism unacceptable. In the era of Keynesian economies, the State has pumped public money into projects which would counter unemployment; has adjusted its taxation in order to move consumers' demands up or down; and in general has fussed like a nurse to make sure the economy is neither too cold nor too hot. However, the crusade for full employment has not been the only reason why non-Communist governments have regulated economic life. The State's intervention has been thought essential in the battle to get exports and imports into a healthy relationship; in the fight against industrial diseases and the pollution of the environment; in the defence of the more backward regions and of the scarcer resources; and in many other campaigns. And it is no accident that one instinctively uses military metaphors. In practice these interventionist policies of central planning came to seem practical to governments because they worked during the two world wars. Governments which were driven to these policies then found that they led to victory, contrary to all the warnings of the *laissez faire* economists of the Adam Smith tradition.

The alternative to this dominance by the State is seldom the unregulated but wealth-creating competition of many rivals, of the kind that Adam Smith advocated (*The Wealth of Nations*, 1776). In Britain, for example, two centuries after Adam Smith some forty per cent of the industrial output was being produced by the hundred largest manufacturing enterprises. Such a concentration of economic power in the hands of a few directors of giant companies (many of them operating in many nations) needs to be balanced, and where necessary corrected, by the power of the State and by the international agencies to which the State belongs.

Socialism means that the State can shield the worker, the customer and the environment from the ruthlessness of an uncontrolled industrialism. It is not inevitable that a Socialist state must do this, or that a state whose average citizen has a horror of 'Socialism' cannot do it. (In its legislation to secure humane standards of health and safety in factories, or to ensure a square deal for the customer, or to subject new industrial developments to scrutiny by those primarily interested in conserving nature, the USA has a better record than the USSR.) But it is quite clear that the protection of the worker, the public and the environment involves in practice large-scale interventions by central or local government. It cannot be left to the spontaneous activity of private enterprise. The manager must be commanded by legislation and inspection. Standards of quality and fair description must be regulated so that no competitor has an unfair advantage over others. The polluter must be punished for anti-social behaviour.

Finally, Socialism means that the State provides education, social security, a health service and some of the housing without charging individuals at the market rate. All those whose pay is too low or uncertain to permit adequate saving for these purposes – and they of course are the vast majority – turn to the tax-supported State. The whole process causes a transfer of wealth from the rich to the less well-off (even if, as many studies suggest, the really poor often do not take full advantage of the benefits); and this shift of wealth is widely regarded as desirable. In a Welfare State such as Britain the services provided are so massive that everyone at work has to get used to receiving a large part of the reward in the shape of the 'social wage'. Certainly pockets of private enterprise can remain: private education, private pension schemes, private charities, private medicine, private housing (this last being more than a pocket). But it serves the interests of the majority if there is large-scale activity by the State in these areas so crucial to private happiness.

These features of Socialism seem to be permanent fixtures in many countries. In Britain, for example, the establishment of Socialism is shown in the facts that fully a quarter of the manpower is employed by central or local government or by the nationalized industries; and almost forty per cent of the gross domestic product passes through the State's hands in taxes or social security contributions.

However, the definition I have given of Socialism would seem to many ardent Socialists to be an evasion of the issue, which is: do we need a more thoroughgoing Socialism based on a far more extensive ownership of the economy by the State as suggested by Clause 4 of the Labour Party's constitution – and if so, do we have any good reason not to call it Marxism? For the most impressive fact about Socialism, as defined and put into practice by Marxists, is that it has transformed two of the world's most important nations. And its offer is to achieve the same miracle for Britain and the rest of the world.

2 The Appeal of Marxism

For many years there had been talk of modernization in Russia and China. But what was modernization to be? It was not enough for an elite to adopt the West's technology and general sophistication. What could change the attitudes of the people?

The traditional religious sources of inspiration proved inadequate when tested. There was some talk of religion being in the vanguard of progress, but in the villages religion usually meant a deadly inertia, the exaltation of the ancestors, a helpless guilt and a despair about humanity's potential, the recommendation of magic instead of thought and work, an escapist mysticism. A moral power was needed which would hold the people's allegiance like a religious faith in its heyday, but which would encourage a new spirit of self-confidence, excitement about the present, innovation, scientific thinking and self-sacrificing toil. Marxism supplied that dynamic motivation, at first within revolutionary cadres but at length in a great nation's official philosophy.

That semi-religious achievement springs from the family likeness between Marxism and Christianity – a resemblance which has often been pointed out, perhaps most perceptively by Nicholas Berdyaev who lived through the Revolution of 1917. Marxism can be more loyal than is conventional Christianity to the roots which both traditions share in the prophetic religion of Ancient Israel. In China, for example, the Maoists have been incomparably more effective than the missionaries in arousing large numbers of people to 'fight self'.

Christians have been among those backing Social Democratic movements such as the Labour Party in Britain. The two most outstanding figures of post-1914 Protestant theology, Karl Barth and Paul Tillich, differed about many things but both were convinced Socialists – in their younger days, very actively so. The greatest American theologian yet to appear with a social message, Reinhold Niebuhr, was a lifelong Socialist. So was William Temple, the greatest Archbishop of Canterbury in the twentieth century – with many lesser Britons assembled in Stephen Mayor's *The Churches and the Labour Movement* (1967). And many Christians have gone further and have accepted Marxism as either tolerable or desirable.

In *Discretion and Valour* (1975) Trevor Beeson studied the response of the Churches of Eastern Europe to their Communist governments. For all the conflicts and tensions, the main response has been the acceptance of 'Socialism' meaning

Marxism as the inevitable ordering of society for all the conceivable future. Outside the Communist countries there has still been much sympathy among Christians, as Peter Hebblethwaite recorded in *The Christian–Marxist Dialogue and Beyond* (1977). From admirers there has even been a response to Maoism summed up in Dr Joseph Needham's verdict: 'I think China is the only truly Christian country in the world in the present day, in spite of its absolute rejection of all religion' (*Anticipation*, WCC, 1973).

In Latin America the identification of many of the most dedicated of the clergy to a 'Socialist' or frankly Communist answer to the people's misery has been striking. It was articulated at the 1968 Bishops' Conference at Medellín, Colombia, and at the 1972 'Christians for Socialism' conference in Santiago, Chile. Some priests and preachers have openly sided with Communist guerrillas, the most famous among them being Camilo Torres, killed in 1966, whose theme was: 'The Catholic who is not a revolutionary is living in mortal sin'. This 'liberation theology' has been summed up by (for example) José Miguez Bonino of Buenos Aires in his two books, *Revolutionary Theology Comes of Age* and *Christians and Marxists* (1975-76). And it has burst out of Latin America – as may be seen in Roman Catholic writings such as *The Militant Gospel* by Alfredo Fierro of Madrid (1977) or in many of the publications of the World Council of Churches. A movement of thought so influential in the Christian world deserves a sympathetic exposition, which I now offer.

Marxism offers a life-changing union of theory and practice. Of course many nominal Marxists, like many nominal Christians merely conform to the conventional creed. But how much more Marxism, like Christianity, is in its own view! It is nothing less than a philosophy of history, and it can give to any individual who previously felt isolated and ineffective the sense of belonging to a great and ultimately invincible mission which moves across the centuries and the continents to claim a total allegiance. Joining this movement means conversion, the authentic commitment of one's total personality and transformation of one's total behaviour; for a Communist, like a religious believer, is known by his fruits. Communism, like Christianity, denounces the hypocrisy of clinging to selfish privileges while professing to serve the people. Although it calls its philosophy 'materialism' it is contemptuous of material comforts because there is a higher call to be answered. The militant Communist, like the Christian enthusiast, gives a low rating to the bourgeois way of life if that means no more than individualism and acquisitiveness. But how can such a conversion to a noble cause come about? Not by the speculation which may lead to the apprehension, real or supposed, of timeless, metaphysical truths. Not by the contemplation of one's inner self, or of nature at large, which may lead to one or other of the varieties of mysticism. One is converted to Communism, as one is converted to Christianity, by saying yes to an actual challenge, by joining a living community, by filling one's mind with the examples of heroes and martyrs, by dedicating oneself to specific tasks and a definite lifestyle, by giving oneself humbly to one's fellow-members and to one's neighbours in need.

Marxism breathes a passion for justice. In practice it has often been a cloak for monstrous injustice, but that is also true about the religions, including Christianity. Karl Marx was descended from a line of Jewish rabbis and was profoundly influenced by the semi-Christian philosopher, Hegel. Particularly in his early years he was motivated by a humanism with a religious depth and thrust – as the publication of his pre-1844 manuscripts revealed in the 1930s. This was the moral force which carried him through a life of detailed labours and frequent disappointments; and still that force has its impact on his followers. The *Communist Manifesto* is a document in the history of prophetic religion in so far as it declares that Marx sides, and calls on mankind to side, with all the oppressed against all the exploiters. Here the Communist prophet who was an atheist drew on the tradition bequeathed to him with his Jewish blood – the tradition of belief in a God who loves justice and hates robbery. In the Hebrew scriptures the test of a ruler is much the same as it is in the Marxist ideal. Jeremiah 22: 16 declares:

> Your father gave the poor a fair trial,
> and all went well with him.
> That is what it means to know the Lord.

In the teaching of Jesus, not only the good ruler but everyone who is righteous is found feeding the hungry, giving a drink to the thirsty, welcoming the stranger, clothing the naked, visiting the sick and the imprisoned (Matthew 25:31-44), for it is the mission of Jesus to proclaim liberty to the captives, sight to the blind and freedom to the oppressed (Luke 4:18), to give good news to the poor (Luke 7:22). And according to James (5:4), an early Christian who may have been the brother of Jesus, the rich get the news that their riches have rotted away and 'the cries of those who gather in your crops have reached the ears of God, the Lord Almighty'. As the Kingdom of God comes, the hungry are filled and the rich sent away empty-handed (Luke 1:53). Marx's collaborator, Engels, himself recognized the affinity of such New Testament passages with his own burning indignation at the condition of the working class in Victorian England.

Marxism also breathes a passion for the future. In practice it can degenerate into the propaganda of a Communist Establishment, to which the response of most of the young is cynical. But in looking forward to the Messianic age of glory, and in his determination to change the inglorious world of the present, Karl Marx should certainly be reckoned among the major prophets of Israel. Marx dreamed of a society where there would be no division into classes and no stunting specialization at work; where there would be no need of the police or the State; where there would be such plenty that each could be given according to his needs. Comparing this Utopia with the Communist societies of the twentieth century, we may laugh or weep. But history shows that in order to be hopeful a people needs some such dream; and the dream must be about Utopia, if only to measure the distance between the dream and the reality. In this way the Utopian dream – called by Raymond Aaron 'the opium of the intellectuals' – actually gets history moving again. It is no more 'opium' than the Christian religion is. Certainly Christians will not wish to mock such optimism. A central trend in recent theology has been the rediscovery of the 'eschatological' or forward-looking element present almost everywhere in the Bible. Christianity, no less than Marxism, is in search of a Kingdom. It has its gaze fixed on 'new heavens and a new earth, where righteousness will be at home' (2 Peter 3:13). Their central act, the Eucharist or Holy Communion, has been to perceptive Christians a foretaste of the final banquet in this Kingdom of God.

Marxism calls for a disciplined participation in the peoples' struggle for liberation. Historically Marxism has, like Christianity, insisted on adherence to scriptures and dogmas, and has backed up this fundamentalism with the punishment of an Inquisition. In history both creeds have also pronounced their blessings on tyrannies. But for Marxists as for Christians, 'discipline' can have a nobler meaning. It can refer to discipleship – to the obligation of membership in a community that works for the arrival of the future. The duty of each Marxist comrade, like the duty of each Christian brother or sister according to the Sermon on the Mount, is to live as if the glorious future were already here; to live so that, in relation to that future, one's actions are contributions not contradictions. The discipline of the mind can mean nothing more sinister than the need to take very seriously the scriptures written in the most creative years of this movement to which one belongs – so that, wrestling with the words written long ago, one discovers a truth which is not available on a casual reading of the newspaper. While many Christians have been bullies and crooks, other have been self-disciplined 'martyrs' or 'witnesses' to truth in their living and dying – and exactly the same is true of Marxists.

The Long March of the Chinese Communists under Mao has often been classed with the Exodus under Moses, and the Maoist regeneration of China has been compared with the work of the Christian Church at its best. 'Remember what you were, my brothers,' wrote Paul to some dockland Christians. 'Few of you were wise or powerful or of high social standing. God purposely chose . . . what the world looks down on and despises, and thinks is nothing' (1 Corinthians 1:26-28). 'You are the chosen race,' reads the first letter of Peter, 'the King's priests, the holy nation, chosen to proclaim the wonderful acts of God, who called you out of darkness into his own marvellous light' (2:9). Marxism can achieve something of the same electric excitement in its summons to the workers and the peasants – and something of the same effect in its power to make militants. The most essential revolution has been one of attitudes, so that people who for generations had regarded themselves as not masters of their own fates, as not the equals of their social betters, even as not fully human, awoke to their own inalienable dignity and realized their own potential power. Intellectuals who have joined this uprising of the submerged have often spoken and written like the apostles of a religion.

Such is Marxism as many today believe.

3 The Reality of Marxism

Why, then, am I not a Marxist? And why do I hope that the future of Socialism in my country will not be Marxist? It is because I consider Marxism to be the twentieth-century Antichrist. When using that traditional Christian term I do not forget what I have just written about the spiritual splendour of much of Marxism. The term Antichrist when properly used refers to the biblical pictures of 'false Messiahs and false prophets' who will 'perform miracles and wonders in order to deceive even God's chosen people, if possible' (Mark 13:22); the 'Wicked One' who will 'sit down in God's Temple and claim to be God' (2 Thessalonians 2:4); the 'dragon, that ancient serpent, that is the Devil or Satan' who 'will go out to deceive the nations, scattered over the whole world' (Revelation 20: 1-10). Antichrist is Christlike and Antichrist is very successful. Accepting the deceit of 'Antichrist' is, however, the way to the death of the spirit of man.

Even the word 'liberation' can be used deceitfully. Of course it, too, is splendid, and I have often used it as a twentieth-century way of saying 'salvation'. Many have shared the nineteenth-century liberal vision of history as the story of liberty; and if one works on the word 'free' in the Christian Bible one gains some idea of freedom's religious dimensions. But 'liberation' as the key idea immediately suggests the defeat and destruction of enemies. It certainly does so in the Exodus tradition of Ancient Israel, to which religiously-minded Marxists have so often appealed. When celebrating their own liberation, the Israelites had no inhibitions about rejoicing over the fate of the plague-smitten, robbed and drowned Egyptians. In this sinister tradition, for more than a century modern Marxists have been uninhibited in wanting liberation for themselves – and powerlessness, imprisonment and death for their many enemies.

Corrupting the noblest dream, Marxism seems to show more than the corruption which goes with human nature anywhere. Its corruption is the pus and the stench of total power, sought deliberately.

It is highly tempting to believe that a favourite movement can use total power with impunity to bring in Utopia or the Messianic Kingdom. History, however, shows repeatedly that the actual consequence of such power is submission to the demonic forces of arrogance and fear. The tyrant becomes drunk with his own righteousness and infallibility. He believes his own propaganda. There seem to be no limits to what he can manipulate with the totalitarian apparatus of force and terror. But he pays for this power by becoming the victim of irrational obsessions about national or personal enemies; and many innocent people suffer terribly. This is the message of the novels of Boris Pasternak and Alexander Solzhenitsyn – novels which, springing from the depths of the Christian tradition of Russia, are the truest voices of the prophetic protest in our time.

Marx himself, who would protest that he was no Marxist, was a scholar who derided censorship and the police. Lenin called for a 'new economic policy' to give freedom to the peasants and for a 'true cultural revolution' to put the factories under the direct control of their workers. His rival Trotsky went further in advocating the transfer of power to the people.

Khrushchev in 1956 seemed to be remembering some of these ideals when he denounced Stalinism. Ten years later Mao led a 'cultural revolution' against his own bureaucrats. In Yugoslavia, and even in those Eastern European countries which have remained under Russian control, there have been many concessions to the peasants, the workers, the local managers and the small businessmen. In the West, where Marxism has remained largely theoretical, it has been the day of the New Left. In Western Europe the Communists loudly proclaim their independence of Moscow. Marxist-minded members of Social Democratic movements such as the British Labour Party sincerely declare their hatred of tyranny and show by their idealism that their own position is in fact much closer to anarchy. Yet despite all this liberal clothing of Marxism, whenever Marxism has gained power it has shown its insistence on total power. This has turned out to be the road to the Party which tolerates no rivals, to the police force which is politically motivated, to the immense 'new class' of bureaucrats, to the small Politburo making the decisions at the top because it knows what the people want better than they know it themselves.

What Lenin founded was in fact State Socialism on a gigantic scale, and it is not surprising that the next ruler of Russia defended the people by sending some thirteen millions of them to their deaths. These included Trotsky; although the Trotskyite element in international Marxism has been frankly anti-State it has been equally frank in rejecting reliance on non-violent persuasion. In practice the Trotskyites have been thugs as much as the Stalinists, with different opportunities. What Mao founded was in fact a giant state without concentration camps but with a ruthlessly systematic, and more effective, programme of indoctrination and thought-control; and when he died the army and the bureaucracy were ready to move back into control. Even under the most admired Communist regimes – such as Cuba, where in 1516 Sir Thomas More located the original Utopia – it has always been found necessary to send critics to prison. And even the most idealistic and liberal Communists have often suffered fates which were warnings.

NOT MARXISM BUT EUROPE

Thus in France Roger Garaudy, the author of *The Alternative Future* (1975) and other excitingly attractive books, began taking both democracy and Christianity seriously – and was expelled from the French Communist Party. History supplies no example of a Marxist 'liberation' producing liberty, or of a powerful Marxist group being tolerant. The persecution of religious believers in a Marxist state is a symptom of a wider and deeper contempt for freedom.

In many countries Marxists can offer the consolation of freedom from foreign exploitation (unless the foreigners are Marxists) and, above all, freedom from hunger. This is often a persuasive consolation. When a peasant sees his children starving, he does not worry too much about what freedom of speech they will enjoy as adults. But to a country such as Britain, which at least laid the foundations of economic freedom, freedom of speech accompanying freedom of thought is considered precious and worth defending. Nor is a country such as Britain wholly uncertain about how the liberty of the individual is to be defended.

For more than seven hundred years electors have sent representatives of the people to the House of Commons, latterly with the secret ballot and the vote for both men and women at the age of eighteen. And increasingly since Anglo-Saxon times the theory has been honoured that all are equal under the law – latterly with laws of universal application, with trial by jury in the more important cases, with non-political judges, and with an effective right of appeal to the law against the executive. In many parts of the world such structures of personal freedom have never been known; or if they have been briefly established by some liberal regime, they have been abandoned as luxuries when a stronger regime promised order and food. But the British people have, on the whole, no wish to throw away their heritage. That is why in Britain most people do not feel amused or easy when it is reported that Marxist students have shouted down a visiting speaker; or that Marxists have gained power in a trade union because most of that union's members did not bother to vote; or that Marxists have led a strike in order to enforce their own policies in 'advance' of democratically agreed decisions; or that Marxists have argued that Parliament and the law do not represent the 'real' will of the people. To the majority of the British people, such incidents are steps towards George Orwell's 1984, straws in a wind that blows from Siberia.

This is not a scare about 'Reds under the bed'. Ridicule is properly aimed at reactionaries who wish to pretend that all social progress is a Communist conspiracy. But it is not ridiculous to remember how Marxists have achieved power in real history. The theory of Karl Marx was that the triumph of Communism was the inevitable result of industrialism. The workers, who would constitute the majority, would arise to make the Revolution. In fact Marxism has never been given power over an industrial nation by the votes of a majority in a free general election. (Allende did not win the presidency of Chile by a majority; no other Marxist regime has ever been voted into office.) Nor has Marxism ever been given power by the action of the workers of an industrial nation. (The failure of the Spartacist rising in Berlin in 1919 was decisive.) Marxism's present hopes in Britain do not rest on the majority of the British people voting Marxist. They rest on Marxism having sufficient influence in the Labour Party, which may win sufficient seats in the House of Commons; or on Marxism being imposed on the nation by sufficient strikes or other 'direct action'. And such hopes of gaining power without first gaining the hearts of the majority are in a sinister harmony with Marxism's actual record.

Marxism first achieved power in the chaos caused by the defeat of the Tsar's armies at the hands of the Kaiser's. In Russia before 1914 it had seemed likely that Socialism would one day prevail in a fairly mild form. The Bolsheviks did not rise to rule post-war Russia at the head of an inflexible proletariat; the industrial workers' numbers in 1917 were not large enough to be decisive, and in any case their ambitions were to own the factories with their own local Soviets, not to hand them back to managers installed by the Bolsheviks from the centre. Even the peasants, to whom the Bolsheviks had to appeal in theory, were unwilling to toil for the new State or its 'collectives'; the grain to feed the towns, and the land on which it was grown, had to be extracted from them by force. Lenin and his fellow-Bolsheviks rose to the top because they were the professionals and had been since the 1890s. This was the group that best knew what it wanted, how to comprise without forgetting this for a moment, and how to eliminate rivals.

Marxism won its next triumph when it was transformed into Maoism, exalting the peasants and fiercely nationalist. Even this success would not have been possible had not the ruling party in China, the Russian-supported Kuomintang, first allied with the Communists and then forced them out of the cities into the countryside; had not the Kuomintang then become so corrupt and inefficient that it was incapable of ruling that vast nation; had not China been thrown into chaos by the Japanese invasion; and had not the Chinese Communists been able to draw some help from Stalin's Russia, although less than they wanted. It is true that Maoism, because of these roots in the world of the peasants, has always placed great emphasis on equality while Russian Communism had built up a new elitist society. But it seems clear that Maoism murdered one, two or three million 'class enemies' in the 1950s – and has been marked throughout the 1960s and 1970s by vicious struggles for power among the comrades in Peking. It also seems clear that Maoism's appeal to the toiling masses of the world has been substantially less than might be expected because that appeal could not be separated in practice from the nationalist ambitions of Chinese foreign policy.

The only empires remaining in the world of the 1970s are Communist – for Eastern Europe is kept in subjection by the Red Army and the economic apparatus of COMECON, and one hundred and forty million non-Chinese and non-Russians have seen Central Asia, Mongolia, Tibet, the Caucasus, the Ukraine and the Baltic States absorbed by military might into the nations which in theory carry the banner of the toiling masses' liberation. To say that is not to pretend that the peoples of these lands would have been happy to continue toiling indefinitely for the benefit of landlords or monks. But it is indisputable that power was used under the Red Flag – most brutally in the Chinese invasion of Tibet and in the Russian intervention to crush popular movements in Eastern Europe: East Germany in 1952, Hungary in 1956, Czechoslovakia in 1968.

Elsewhere Communist regimes are not the result of Russian or Chinese conquests – but only in mythology are they solely the result of popular uprisings. In Cuba, the world's most popular Communist government has depended on special circumstances the specially inefficient Battista dictatorship; the specially humiliating and debilitating dependence on the United States – to win popular acceptance of its decision to depend instead on subsidies and supervision from the Soviet Union. In South-East Asia and Southern Africa the success of Communism is due substantially (although not completely) to the Russian or Chinese arms supplied to those who were liberating their native soil from the French, Belgians, Americans, Portuguese or Rhodesians.

Despite its ruthless intolerance Marxism has not succeeded in preserving a monolithic uniformity. Marx himself was tormented by various heretics, and since his death the succession has continued – the German revisionists, Trotsky, Tito, Mao, the advocates of a more human face in Eastern Europe, the New Left in the West. This history of the survival of heretics has naturally been used by some Communists to give the reassurance that a great variety would still exist in a world gone Marxist. But it is not easy to be completely reassured. As a matter of fact, Trotsky was murdered by Stalin's agents; Tito survived because the Red Army did not dare to invade; war did not break out between Russia and China because neither side saw any hope of victory; Moscow's concessions of freedom to European Communists were conspicuously reluctant. It seems still to be the natural tendency of Communist power to crush unless checked by some other power – and those liable to be crushed are understandably nervous.

We ought to ask why Latin America outside Cuba has not accepted Communism. It is possible to point to Yankee bribes and marines, to the apathy of the ignorant and undernourished peasants, to the brutality of the police, or to the capacity of the armed forces to install their candidates in presidential palaces.

But that is not the whole answer. We have to ask why Che Guevara met those blank expressions on the faces in the Bolivian villages and why within ten years of his death there was no substantial body of rural guerrillas still in the field. We have to ask why in the cities the workers do not stage more general strikes, and why those whose skills are necessary to run the economy do not insist on a Marxist answer to the economy's problems. It would seem that the evils of the present system are thought preferable to the evils which would follow a Communist take-over. Economic growth is thought to be possible under a capitalism tempered by Socialism (rightly, according to the statistics); and the North American connection, both economic and cultural, is thought to bring benefits to Latin America on balance. If these were not the prevailing attitudes, Latin America would be Marxist today from the Mexican border to Cape Horn.

We ought also to ask why India, whose villages are often so close to famine and whose cities are often so close to hell, has not turned to Marxism, although Russia has poured in aid and publicity to support Indian Communists and China is allied with its own rival Communist Party. It would seem that India did not win independence in order to be aligned under Moscow; that the memory of its border fighting with China in 1962 has never faded; that it rejects authoritarianism of every kind (as the fall of Mrs Gandhi showed); and that it sees its all-pervasive Hinduism as an essential part of its future. It insists on being India.

4 A Marxist Britain?

Karl Marx derived from the grim realities of industrialism in the England of Charles Dickens, and from the even bleaker theories of David Ricardo and other economists, the conviction that the process must end in collapse. Prices must rise; wages must fall; markets must contract unless artificially enlarged by imperialism; unemployment must grow with the improvement of the machines. A larger population must sink lower and lower into misery – not only the workers but also the smaller businessmen deprived of their livelihood by the giants of 'monopoly capitalism'. The struggle between the classes must intensify. Yet to Marx and the Marxists the end is certain, and many are the denunciations of those who urge compromise. In *The Coming British Revolution* (1972) Tariq Ali endorsed Trotsky's *Where is Britain Going?* (1925). 'Throughout the whole history of the British Labour Movement,' Trotsky wrote, 'is to be found the pressure of the bourgeoisie on the proletariat by means of radicals, intelligentsia, drawing-room and church socialists, Owenites, who reject the class struggle, put forward the principle of social solidarity, preach co-operation with the bourgeoisie, curb, enfeeble and politically debase the proletariat.'

But the course of events has falsified Marx's predictions about the future of capitalist industrialism. In the world's most advanced industrial nation the falsification is so striking that American Marxists scarcely know what to say now about economics. In the USA employees (admittedly there has been an appalling problem of unemployment) have found slimming, not starvation, the problem. The middle classes have bulged and trade unionists, so far from taking from the works of Marx with them into their automobiles, have refused to belong to the same international organizations as Communists. In booming Japan, the Communist Party is only a little less embarrassed by the evident contradiction of Marx's gloom. In Western Europe, the electoral fortunes of the Communists have varied with the nations' economic prosperity. The austere 1940s kept Communist votes substantial in Italy and France, and the recession of the 1970s has brought about a recovery on the far Left. But most electors have not forgotten the achievements of private enterprise in the 1950s and 1960s, setting records which seem likely to be beaten in the 1980s. What Harold Macmillan said in 1957 was, if crude, accurate. 'Let's be frank about it; most of our people have never had it so good. Go round the country, go to the industrial towns, go to the farms, and you will see a state of prosperity such as we have never had in my lifetime – nor indeed ever in the history of the country.'

It is not easy to prove that Communism would have done better. To be sure, Communism controls inflation – by shooting inflators. And Communism puts capital into heavy industry – by giving no opportunity for any other option. But the economies of the EEC's Communist neighbours are not models of a general efficiency; West Germany does not have to build a wall to keep its citizens from fleeing to the East. As capitalism has prospered it has been changed (although 'reformism' has always been a dirty word to Marxists). Effective control has largely passed from owners, whether individuals or shareholders, to managers. The motivations of managers are many and complex – ambition for higher salaries and benefits, pride in increasing output and sales, rivalry with competitors, satisfaction in earning the respect of colleagues – but it is clear that few managers take a delight in grinding the faces of the poor. On the contrary, many managers have given earnest attention to the problems of industrial relations in order to keep the work force continuously and co-operatively at work: a whole new managerial skill in consultation has been exercised. And many managers have alarmed many governments by their readiness to raise wages – and so, it is feared, to stoke up inflation – rather than run any risk of a strike or of unpopularity within the firm. The result is a stage of capitalism where it is estimated that in British industry (for example) the proportion of salaries and wages to dividends is about 50:1. And even if their personal interests might be served by conflicts with the workers, it is clear that the managers and their political mouthpieces would still be shrewd enough to acknowledge the general advantage to capitalism of a high level of purchasing power in the lower middle and working classes. A concession to a worker is an opening to a market. All these signs of health in capitalism have persuaded many that it is truer to the facts of economic history to abandon the Marxist analysis and to talk instead about the 'managerial revolution' and the 'end of ideology', about the 'affluent worker' with the outstretched hand replacing the clenched fist; about the dictatorship of the advertiser and the end of the workers' alienation in the supermarket.

Such talk has recently died down in Britain, as the economic recession of the 1970s has uncovered memories of the 1929-34 slump. Even under affluence these memories had never been buried very deep. So Marxists have again won a hearing for their argument that an insurmountable crisis must be created by the 'contradictions' within capitalism. But it remains improbable that the long-term trends of the British economy are set according to these Marxist predictions.

The British working class must, it seems, choose between hoping that a modified, partly Socialist, capitalism can be made to work in the interests of all, and trusting Communism to deliver the goods; there is no third choice. And to choose 'Social Capitalism' is to make a choice which most working people seem to feel is plain common sense. They follow their own economic interests, as the Marxists urge. The General Elections of the 1970s have given no hint that the British people are in anything like a revolutionary frame of mind. On the contrary, the British have seemed well aware that their prosperity doubled in the years 1945-75, and would have increased still further had their productivity grown faster (it, too, doubled).

So the peoples of many countries including Britain can reasonably conclude that they do not need to entrust power to Marxists in order to achieve their goals. What is needed is less dramatic. These peoples need to be more efficient in paying their way to these self-chosen goals.

The trouble is that the non-Marxist road is so expensive. It involves a very high level of public expenditure in order to achieve the Socialist goals which genuinely attract a free people; and this public expenditure must be financed by taxing, or borrowing from, people with money. But it also involves a very high level of private expenditure, for under the mixed economy people with large or small amounts of money to contribute require substantial incentives in order to work, invest and lend. In the absence of the Marxist stick, the capitalist carrot must be displayed; and so the creation of incentives – wages, salaries, dividends and interest rates – imposes a test of 'Social Capitalism' which is not necessary under the police states of real-life Marxism. That is the problem. But if the answer is given by a people determined to earn the benefits of 'Social Capitalism' by its own efforts, that answer would seem to have a moral content – which implies that efficiency supporting justice and freedom is no less moral than are justice and freedom themselves. The background to this argument has been presented by three non-Marxist Christians, the British John Sleeman in *Economic Crisis: A Christian Perspective* (1976), the American J. P. Wogaman in *Christians and the Great Economic Debate* (1977) and the British Owen Nankivell in *All Good Gifts* (1978).

However, the loss of confidence during the 1970s – apparent in the United States despite that vast country's fabulous resources – has specially afflicted some European peoples, among them most notably the Italians and the British. The British have real economic problems but often exaggerate them, speaking as if all their standards have slipped so far since the Victorian Age that it is only fair that they should be beaten in international competitions, whether in exports or in sport. Without attempting to answer the unanswerable question 'Was the world of Charles Dickens better – more moral or more efficient – than Britain towards the end of the twentieth century?' It is possible to point to certain facts. The average annual rate of economic growth at the height of Britain's Victorian prosperity was no higher than the rate which brought such dismay to the 1970s. The proportion of national output that has been exported recently by the legendary West Germans is no higher that the proportion exported by the British; the proportion exported by the Japanese or French is less; the proportion exported by the Americans is approximately half. The economic decline of Britain is not absolute. Its citizens in the 1970s are, on average, four times more prosperous than their counterparts in the 1870s. The decline is a decline in relation to industrial competitors who have developed since Victorian days. In the period 1950-75, Britain lost half its share of world trade. It prospers – but others prosper more.

The most dangerous feature of growth which is slow in relation to other rich nations is that it may persuade the British (or the Italians) that their whole economic system has failed, and with it the value-system of their society. The loss of self-confidence so often noticed in Britain or Italy is an ominous reminder that Marxism has not won its victims by giving sensible advice about how to run an economy. It has powered the whole life of a society previously lacking in unity and confident purpose. It has been something 'more important than the price of potatoes,' as Allende said in Chile. Marxism can therefore appeal to a nation where there has been a collapse of self-confidence rather than a collapse of the economy.

If Britain is to avoid going Marxist in the long run, it seems necessary for it to achieve a very solid strengthening both of its economy and of its self-confidence, involving nothing less than a new identity in the world of nations. That is of course a colossal task, and it is a thought-provoking fact that outside Western Europe so little success has come to the kind of Socialism that Britain has voted for – the kind that emphatically accepts the freedom of a parliamentary opposition to oppose its policies, and the freedom of a large private sector in the economy to make money as it decides. Success has not come to this liberal Socialism because there has been so little conviction that an economy operated on these principles could be adequately successful. The option has not seemed real. However, it does now seem to be another fact that, as part of the movement in history far wider than Britain, for Britain now this option *is* possible: and the country's main problem may be how to believe its good luck.

At precisely the time when the economy so clearly needs to be reconstructed on a more competitive basis appealing to a larger market, and when a new role, a new drama and a new theatre have so clearly become essential to cure the national sense of nostalgia and fear, the gift of North Sea oil gives Britain one more economic chance – and the emergence of the United States of Europe invites it to one more creative adventure in keeping with its ancient tradition of freedom.

5 What Europe Means

Although it is likely that in the perspective of history the entire second half of the twentieth century will be seen as the time of the birth of the USE, those of us who live in this period know how painful the birth has been for Britain. In 1940 there really was talk to the effect that the island was safer now that it stood alone and could not be let down by Continental allies. Churchill's 'Europe Arise!' speeches after the war are likely to be remembered as prophetic visions; but Churchill the politician was never a practical European. The Churchillian vision of Europe at Zürich in 1946 or the Hague in 1948 was an encouragement to foreigners to clear up the mess in their countries; it was not a serious proposal that Britain should join in the work of renewing Europe. Of course future generations will lament the blindness of British statesmen and public opinion, but they ought not to imagine that British membership of 'Europe' was psychologically possible in the 1940s and 1950s. Churchill saw as far as anyone could reasonably expect when he envisaged Britain and the Commonwealth, along with the United States and (he hoped) the Soviet Union, as 'friends and sponsors of the new Europe'. They were to be the godparents at this christening, or perhaps they were to smoke cigars in the churchyard. They had no intention of stripping off to get into the font with the baby.

When the foundations of European unity were laid by the 1950 Schuman Plan to pool French and German coal and steel production, it was immediately pronounced to be inconceivable that Britain could accept foreign control of its pits and foundries. All through the talk about the European Defence Community, active before the French killed it off in 1954, Ernest Bevin spoke for Britain. 'Europe is not enough,' he told the House of Commons; 'it is not big enough, it is not strong enough, and it is not able to stand by itself. It is this great conception of an Atlantic Community that we want to build up.' In 1956 both

Harold Macmillan and Roy Jenkins told the House that the further idea of a European customs union to include Britain 'is out' (Macmillan), 'manifestly impossible' (Jenkins, who twenty-one years later advocated a single currency for the EEC). Britain refused without hesitation to take part in the European co-ordination of nuclear power, Euratom, or to get involved in drafting the Treaty of Rome (1957). The island identified itself instead with Norway, Denmark, Austria, Switzerland, Sweden and Portugal, in the so-called European Free Trade Area. At length in 1961 the Macmillan government applied for membership of the EEC – but public opinion polls showed that the majority of the British people were against or didn't know, while Hugh Gaitskell, the Leader of the Labour Party, voiced concern over the loss of a 'thousand years' of independence. Even Conservative statesmen who had become keen on the EEC always had to stress that it must be adjusted to meet Britain's terms; that it must not take precedence over the Commonwealth; that it must not damage Britain's special relationship with the USA; that there must be no commitment to any political union. In January 1963 President de Gaulle was surely wise to proclaim an icy veto on an application so lukewarm.

The election of a dedicated European, Edward Heath, to the leadership of the Conservative Party in 1965 was followed by the decision of the Labour Prime Minister, Harold Wilson, and his colleagues to reopen the negotiations. The July 1966 financial crisis had persuaded most of the experts that Britain could not be sufficiently prosperous outside the EEC to warm itself from the white heat of the technological revolution. But both the Conservatives and Labour were deeply split on this issue, and it was generally taken for granted that a popular referendum was out of the question, not only because it would damage the sovereignty of the Westminster Parliament but also because it would fail to deliver a yes to Europe.

When de Gaulle slapped down his second veto on the Wilson government's application, and Wilson himself was turned out of office in 1970, the Labour Party's coolness to Europe surfaced like an iceberg in a frank anti-Europeanism. Eventually, in 1971, Edward Heath persuaded the House of Commons on a free vote to accept the EEC's terms for British membership. But Labour still reckoned a commitment to 'renegotiate' to be more vote-winning than any commitment to abide by the 1971 decision, and it could not be said that the UK was fully and finally 'in' the EEC until after the referendum of 1975, following minor concessions by the EEC. And even then, how European was the heart of Britain? Public opinion polls soon suggested that any enthusiasm had died right down. EEC membership had not sheltered British housewives from the world-wide rise in food prices and EEC subsidies had not compensated British manufacturers for the rigours of competition in the new market.

The moral of this tale is surely that membership of the EEC was always going to be far more problematic than its advocates admitted. But it does not follow that the leaders of British industry, who were almost unanimously Europeans in the long debate, did not know their business; or that the British people were totally lacking in common sense when in 1975 they gave overwhelming (67.2 per cent) support to their EEC membership. At the end of the 1970s, Britain still seems to have at least a sporting chance of prospering within Europe. The key question seems to be whether Britain wants it. In the days of empire-building and industrialization obstacles in Britain's chosen path tended not to stay there for very long. But does Britain want to make a success of the new Europe? Has its imagination been aroused by the European adventure?

The EEC is, in Professor Hallstein's famous phrase, 'in politics'. Superficially it looks like a business arrangement monitored by a labyrinthine bureaucracy, the news it makes is news of business deals or disputes, and any talk of political or even economic union – of federation or of some looser structure – tends to be talk of problems. But basically the EEC has always said that it serves its peoples' total welfare by creating a strong, stable and impregnable material base for its peoples' values. And these values are precious. The EEC contains less than seven per cent of the world's present population – but perhaps rather more than seven per cent of its civilization. An inheritance which cannot be reduced to statistics is the essential

Europe, to be sustained by the new economic organization. The preamble to the 248 articles of the Treaty of Rome hinted clearly enough at this dimension when it recited that the signatories had 'decided to ensure the economic and social progress of their countries by common action in eliminating the barriers which divide Europe, directing their efforts to the essential purpose of constantly improving the living and working conditions of their peoples.'

It was no accident that although the toughest negotiations took place in Paris the treaty was signed in Rome. The European mind has always been haunted by Rome. When Charlemagne had been crowned Emperor in Rome on Christmas Day 800 the conscious desire to return to the unity of a splendid past revived amid barbarism, and the Holy Roman Empire lasted as a reminder of that dream until 1806, even if the Emperor was often in practice little more than the most dignified of the German princes. These were the memories that pleased those who signed the treaty on 27 March 1957. But the founders of the EEC were perfectly right to concentrate on their economic tasks, for the weakness of its own economy was the reason why the original Roman Empire collapsed. The Romans were eventually ruined by the ease with which they conquered and defended their world by hiring legions, and ran it by making slaves. In almost every field they left the technology of peace as primitive as they found it, and they never mastered economics. The Treaty of Rome was an attempt to put the European civilization on a more solid foundation – the co-operation of free men in the creation of an industry both more efficient and more humane.

No single nation of a size to be seen within twentieth-century Europe is able to sustain by itself all the research and experimentation which are essential to technological advance. No one European nation provides a market large enough to sustain the scale of production that is most economic in many areas of an ever more and more sophisticated industry. Every nation stands to benefit in the long run from the mobility of capital and labour. Finally, if the Europeans will not get together to arrange these things for themselves giant American firms stand ready to do the job for them. Such arguments for the EEC as a single modern market of 260 or more million have been made familiar to all the publics of its member-states. What is not so generally acknowledged is that this new community is also an effort to respond to deep-seated public fears about industrialism itself, whether national or continental.

Despite the attractions of its products industrialism can still seem a monster to the civilized mind – slipping beyond any national government's control, turning a countryside into hideous and thoroughly inhuman cities, irreparably damaging the Earth. One of the great purposes of the EEC has therefore been to stabilize the industrial foundation by obtaining the people's consent to it. It has been recognized from the start that this will require efforts on the same scale as the problems – to improve human relations and fulfilment in industry; to raise the standards of health and safety at work; to spread the benefits of industry to disadvantaged regions and groups; and to protect the whole delicate web of human life from the ravages of the Frankenstein shambling out of the industrial laboratory. The EEC has made the greatest impact on daily life during its first twenty years by standardizing weights, measures and technical specifications. In what remains of the twentieth century it is likely to make a much more deeply transforming impact by insisting on a 'social policy' based on 'consensus' as the control of industrial and commercial progress. That possibility of Europe with a human face was the central theme of Lord Kennet's study of *The Futures of Europe* (1976).

It is often said that the EEC has no values apart from economic efficiency with a touch of humanity in order to appease democracy. 'The Common Market has nothing to do with religion'. With those words a Conservative Central Office pamphlet once sought to reassure British electors that the Treaty of Rome was not a sell-out to the Papacy. If that were the case people such as Christians would have to treat it as their predecessors treated the Roman Empire; they could pray for its welfare without thinking that it has much to do with the City of God. But in 1967 the British Council of Churches (for example) could issue an elaborate report on *Christians and the Common Market*, and in subsequent years books, periodicals, study centres (in Brussels and Strasbourg) and conferences (in which I have been glad to participate) have explored the significance of the EEC to Christians. A history such as R. C. Mowat's *Creating the European Community* (1973) brings out the importance of the fact that the most prominent statesmen involved in its formation – Schuman, Adenauer, de Gasperi – were passionately convinced Roman Catholics who had been through the tough school of resistance to Hitler and Mussolini. Schuman, at any rate, was in his private life a saint. In 1945 France, Germany and Italy were all so widely ruined, morally as well as politically, that the new democratic politics depended directly and heavily on inspiration from the explicitly Christian tradition and on practical support from the Churches.

Such mixtures of religion and politics are reminders that the history of Europe is the Christian sequel to the Roman Empire. It was the thesis of (for example) Hilaire Belloc that 'Europe was the Faith and the Faith was Europe' over many creative centuries; and the scholarly comment on that phrase points out exceptions rather than denying the general rule. However great the tensions were between the officers of the Church and those who pioneered new movements, the general principle holds that Christianity was the spiritual basis of medieval Europe, as much as Communism is today the spiritual basis of Russia or China or Cuba. The feudal system of mutual obligations as a network covering the countryside, the conventions of chivalry that did something to tame war, the justice administered by barons and kings, the guilds and parliaments with their gropings towards democracy, the monasteries and the improvement of agriculture, the cathedrals and the consecration of art, the towns and the growth of craftsmanship and trade, the universities and the beginnings of science – all these slow and complex developments took place in a setting provided by those who with a more single-minded zeal had planted the Church's faith and organization all over Europe. At a level which is far more difficult for the historian to describe, the faith which presented the resurrection of Jesus as one of its central images spread an ultimate confidence about the human condition and by this must have done something to make the Europeans such an energetic civilization. The image of Jesus as Judge must have done something for the European conscience which (at least occasionally) checked this energy, and the image of him as a child with his Virgin Mother may have done more.

The Christianity that built Europe out of the ruins of the Roman Empire was itself a richly diverse religion, from the Celtic abbots in Ireland to the Byzantine emperors in the New Rome, from St Francis among the poorest to some of the Popes among the war-lords. But the arrogance of Roman power and the sharpness of Roman law were inherited to such a large extent that the Faith was institutionalized and regimented in ways which Europe's own conscience came to reject. So the medieval unity disintegrated and new Europes arose – the Protestant Europe of Luther and Calvin, Bach and Handel, with all its stress on the individual's direct access to God under the guidance of the Bible-based preacher; the new Catholic Europe of Ignatius Loyola and Francis of Sales, El Greco and Rubens, with a new emotionalism and heroism; eventually the Liberal Christian Europe with its blessing on everyday morality, hard work, scholarship and science. All these Europes created literature, architecture, music and lifestyles which are still important realities for millions. Their diversity meant that any idea of a single 'Christian Republic' (as it was termed in the famous grand design of the Duc de Sully for European unity in 1638) was now visionary.

Even this variety was not enough for the European conscience, however. The scientific movement arising in the seventeenth century demanded the freedom to pursue truth and efficiency without any interference by religion. The Enlightenment of the eighteenth century included a rejection of the whole claim of Christian preachers to proclaim a social order and a social morality which Europe must obey. The intellectual revolutions associated with the genius of Darwin, Marx and Freud led to a widespread disbelief in the traditional Christian picture of human life. Then the cultures of other continents began reaching Europe's heart and mind, and finally there was the whole modern insistence on honest self-expression without regard to religious or other conventions. So by the twentieth century there was a widespread desire to end 'Christendom', meaning by that the imposition on Europe by the clergy of an authoritarian creed – and implying the union of the baptized nations against the surrounding infidels. The new European spirit attending the birth of the EEC was pluralist and tolerant, eagerly open to truths and movements later and wider than Christendom.

But once any comparison is made with a Communist area or with an area steeped in a non-Christian religion, it is seen that Western Europe is not thoroughly secular. It abides by convictions which can be called Christian and which were, as a matter of history, taught to Europe mainly by Christians. These are the basic beliefs that life has a meaning; that history has a progressive pattern; that within that pattern every human person is very precious; that the State exists to serve that person; that freedom is necessary for the person's fulfilment; that interpersonal love rather than force ought to, and will, prevail ultimately. Such convictions inspired the 'European Convention for the Protection of Human Rights and Fundamental Freedoms' signed in Rome in 1950. So while the new Europe has not been an attempt to perpetuate the old Christendom, its symbolic institutions such as the European Court of Justice and the European Parliament express a philosophy which is, at the least, not anti-Christian. So do the everyday conversations of the Europeans.

The EEC can thus be described without too much sentimentality as an attempt made by peoples who have shared Christianity for a thousand years to assert spiritual values which Christians will recognize – although nowadays Christians do not have the monopoly in them. It is an effort to give, in the age of science and industry, a solid basis to the old dream of the European nations submitting themselves to the European idea. This was Gladstone's dream in the nineteenth century, when he spoke of 'the Concert of the Powers' adhering to the 'public law of Europe' and so constituting 'the highest and most authentic organ of modern Christian civilization'.

For many centuries Europe was surrounded by the power of

Islam. This was a military power, and the Arabs or the Turks could strike terror deep into Europe (Poitiers in 732, Vienna as recently as 1683). But the main reason why Islam was feared was that it seemed the more confident civilization, far more united, disciplined and efficient. Gradually Europe strengthened its civilization on the base of an economy which became much stronger than Islam. And Europe flourished. In the twentieth and twenty-first centuries it is the task of Europe to repeat this recovery, but this time when surrounded by the armies, totalitarian philosophy and rigidly planned production of Communism. Perhaps only the impact of Communism will eventually form the EEC into the USE, as Islam helped the medieval Europeans to reach such unity as they did attain. Certainly without this harsh challenge the idea of a United States of Europe (which goes back at least to Victor Hugo in 1849) seems likely to remain a dream – a dream supported by solid arguments for economic integration, only to be defeated by the emotional realities of nationalism. The new challenge does not call for a new crusade, but it does seem to demand the pondering of what Robert Schuman wrote in *Pour L'Europe* (1963): 'Democracy owes its existence to Christianity. It was born on the day when man was called to realize in his temporal life the dignity of the human being, in the freedom of each person, in respect for the rights of each and by the practice of fraternal love for all. Never before Christ had such ideas been formulated ... The working out of this vast programme of an expanding democracy in the Christian sense of the word finds its flowering in the making of Europe.'

6 What Europe Offers

The new Europe is in a position to renew old nations willing to join themselves to its promise. The influence of the EEC seems to be the main hope that one day East Germany, Poland, Czechoslovakia, Yugoslavia, Rumania and Bulgaria will be drawn back into the mainstream of the European Christian civilization, whether or not the degree of Socialism that their peoples choose will make it right to call those nations still Marxist. Already many of their young people rather sadly listen to the radio coming from the West and wear clothes as Western as possible. Some of them, it seems, go to church to make the same point. And already in the 1970s the attraction of the EEC has been a chief cause of the restoration of democracy in Greece, Spain and Portugal. But Britain, which in the 1940s was the hope of Europe, is now among the nations which need hope. The end of the British Empire and of the First Industrial Revolution must mean that Britain needs a new economic basis not dependent on raw materials or markets provided by subservient colonies or on labour provided by servile workers.

The historical comparison that has forced itself upon the British in the 1970s – for example, in the Hudson Institute's report, *Britain in 1980* – has been with the Spanish Empire three centuries ago. Spain had discovered and conquered a new world under a monarchy of towering prestige, celebrated by a rich Church. It was flooded with silver and the other products of its colonies, and culturally the empire produced a golden century. But the Spanish Empire had no solid economic base and its glamour was an active discouragement to the hard work of modernization in agriculture or industry. In the end what was left was a memory – and inflation. In the post-imperial 1970s the British fear that unless a new economic basis is found, the nation is liable to disintegrate in mutual recriminations and class war. And no suggestion able to convince the experts has ever been made that this new economic basis can be found outside the EEC. On the contrary, every theme in the experts' usual recommendations – reliance on up-to-date technology, the fully economic use of manpower, a large, stable and guaranteed market – is found embodied in practice in the EEC. It seems reasonable to conclude that Britain ought to throw itself into the economic life of the new Europe with gratitude for the offer of a reprieve from the fate of imperial Spain. It will still be a battle (unemployment is a problem throughout the EEC in the 1970s) – but the battle will not be hopeless.

Britain has particularly good reasons for welcoming the

EEC's efforts to make industrialism democratically acceptable by humanizing it.

The brutal reality is that Britain has suffered much, and is still suffering, from having made the mistakes along with the pioneering advances in the world's first industrialization. British cities still contain areas which are dreadful museums of nineteenth-century exploitation, and other areas which are monuments to the twentieth-century habit of rehousing statistics while forgetting the needs of living people. Equally desolating has been the damage done by the Industrial Revolution to human relations at work. Of course the French, the Italians and to a lesser extent the Germans have similar problems resulting from their own history, and the institutions of the EEC are far from perfect. But in the EEC the proper standards of a responsible use of raw materials are becoming clearer – and are gradually being enforced. The incentives and the penalties needed to fight pollution are being strengthened. The class war is being pacified by the growing psychology and legislation of the 'concerted effort' as managers and workers alike see themselves as partners all responsible for the key decisions and all entitled to handsome rewards. Such a revolution in attitudes, backed by all the moral authority and financial power which the European Community wields or could wield, seems likely to bring to the British people in their everyday lives a happiness far greater than any which they knew in the days of empire and early industrialization.

It is no small matter that this new hope is offered to Britain by a community which trancends nationalism. In the 1970s the dangers of nationalism are, or ought to be, thoroughly familiar to the British. For it is very clear that Britain needs to overcome its own national pride in past conquests in order that it may take a legitimate pride in the achievements of a new age; and it needs to throw away a threadbare sense of superiority to foreigners in order that it may work alongside them and share their success. One luxury which the impoverished islanders certainly cannot afford is a nostalgic patriotism about a land of glory but no hope. How, then, can the British break out of the trap of their past? The move into Europe seems to be the only possible escape.

In particular Europe seems to be the only long-term answer to the problems of nationalism *within* the British nation. The Scottish, Welsh and Irish problems tend to seem a bore and an embarrassment in Westminster, but they are the legacies of English colonialism within the British Isles and they will not go away merely because the English are indifferent.

The grievances are great. To call only one witness: Professor H. J. Hanham, who was not a Scot, wrote in his *Scottish Nationalism* (1969) that 'the ordinary Scot has been prepared to accept that his more enterprising fellows will emigrate as a matter of course and that Scotland will become a pensioner dependent on England'. To cite only one fact: all through the 1950s and 1960s unemployment in Scotland (where eighty per cent of the population is reckoned to be working class) was double the English average. It was inevitable that once oil was found off Scotland's shores it powered this resentment; and that many of the Welsh should seize the opportunity to voice their grievances. It was also inevitable that the Scottish and Welsh Churches should share many of these nationalist sentiments. In 1946 the General Assembly of the Church of Scotland agreed on 'the necessity for a greater measure of devolution by Parliament of legislative and administrative power in Scottish affairs'. Yet it has never been practical politics simply to tear up the 1707 Act of Union between Scotland and England, any more than the Tudors' incorporation of Wales into the administrative structure of England could be easily dismantled. The disadvantages of complete independence would not only be economic. In his book *The British: Their Identity and Their Religion* (1976) Daniel Jenkins commented powerfully on the cultural and spiritual disaster of introversion in a little nation. There are, after all, only five million people in Scotland and three million in Wales and half the population of the UK lives within 125 miles of London. The long-term answer to a complex problem seems to be a looser association of the English, the Scots and the Welsh within a United Kingdom but also within a 'Europe of the regions'. For the United States of Europe, if it is to rest on popular consent, will have to recognize effectively that there are important units of human self-identification in tension with the present political capitals; and these units will have to recognize their own basic similarity and their own common need of each other.

So far only token violence against the English has been offered in the name of modern Scottish or Welsh nationalism. But in Ireland relations with the English have been sour, and often bloody, since Henry II landed in 1171. In Northern Ireland the violence which exploded in August 1969 has made the labels 'Catholic' and 'Protestant' notoriously identical with hatred and murder. The claims for compensation for personal injuries have covered the equivalent of one person in every sixty and hundreds of millions of pounds have been paid in partial compensation for wrecked homes and workplaces. The horror of it has been felt around the world, and (as many statements and brave personal actions show) has deeply troubled the consciences of the Irish Churches. The nearest this tragic country got to peace after the collapse of the political initiatives of 1973 was the Church Leaders' Peace Campaign in the winter of 1974-75, and when that effort failed the best sign of hope was the Women's Peace Movement, led mainly by courageous Christians. But politicians and churchpeople alike have seemed powerless before the primitive strength of the tribalism which has been thinly disguised as religious sectarianism; and if one thing has been clear, it has been that no British government can impose peace. The fact that all the Irish have since 1973 belonged to the EEC appears to offer the only context in which the presently insoluble problems of Northern Ireland will die – instead of its citizens. By offering some guarantee of security and the possibility of prosperity to all the Irish without exception, and by establishing strong common institutions while it is still impossible to build them on Irish soil, the new Europe offers Ireland peace. It is, in its own way, an offer as moving as the achievement of peace between the French and the Germans.

All this was in our minds when on New Year's Day 1973 we put the national flags of the EEC on permanent display in Westminster Abbey near the grave of the Unknown Warrior. His body had been brought from Flanders to lie among

England's most famous dead – and beneath monuments recalling many battles which had conquered and defended the British Empire. Now we saw that the warrior had sacrificed his life in order to teach the Europeans how mad their quarrels were. It was his death, and the deaths of millions whom he represented, that had made it necessary and possible for Europe's flags to be brought together in a unity marked by freedom and hope.

Part Five

NOT DOGMA BUT RESPONSE

1 A Response to Life

On Whitsunday 1961 Dag Hammarskjöld made an entry in his private spiritual diary, published after his death as *Markings* (1964). In it he looked back on his years of service to the Swedish government and as Secretary General of the United Nations. 'I don't know Who – or What – put the question, I don't know when it was put. I don't even remember answering. But at some moment I did answer *Yes* to Someone – or Something – and from that hour I was certain that existence is meaningful and that therefore my life, in self-surrender, had a goal'.

Such words introduce the religion that is needed in the last years of the twentieth century. But how remote they are from the arrogant dogmatism which has almost ruined Christianity, Hammarskjöld's ancestral religion!

Disaster overtook Christianity in the periods when the Church was outwardly most successful. None of these spiritual disasters – or the social triumphs which caused them – could have been foreseen by Jesus or his apostles. When it filled the spiritual vacuum left by the incredibility of the official religion of the Roman Empire, Christianity took over many of the functions of that religion. It was itself now the bearer of the imperial prestige, power and law. The Popes governed Rome; the bishops became the local guardians of law and order, or civil servants at the new royal courts; the priests blessed the ordering of society and preached submission to it; emperors and kings were anointed and crowned; the churches became the throne rooms of an invisible emperor.

It was not a total catastrophe. The conversion of the Emperor Constantine produced over many centuries the European civilization which I have just been praising. But one disastrous aspect of the complex fact of Christendom was that Roman methods of law-definition and law-enforcement were applied to religion. It was as suitable as feeding a baby with a bayonet.

The mysteries of religious belief had been, it was thought, clarified by philosophical theologians trained in the metaphysics of the Greek school, Neoplatonism. In successive Councils of the Church the bishops had met to decide which of these theologians had defined the mystery of Christ correctly (or least incorrectly). In themselves many of those definitions were intellectually courageous attempts by clever thinkers to respond to the Christian message in terms of the philosophy then dominant. What made the orthodoxy enacted at these councils spiritually disastrous was that it was gradually enforced by methods which would have aroused abhorrence in the first Christians. The official Church decreed that outside the ranks of those who believed this precisely formulated creed there could be no salvation. By 'no salvation' was often meant the everlasting torture of hell. In order to deter heretics from this fate, the rulers of the time were encouraged to penalize, imprison and kill those who dissented from the Church's orthodoxy. The first heretic was executed by Christians little more than three hundred and fifty years after the crucifixion of Christ. And the world at large has never forgotten how, by these steps, the Way of the Cross led to the Inquisition.

But the end of the Middle Ages in Western Europe around Rome, and the end of the Byzantine Empire in Eastern Europe around Constantinople, did not mean the end of Christian dogmatism. New dogmatic systems arose, equally remote from the spirit of the New Testament.

From the fifteenth to the nineteenth centuries AD intensely personal emotions were poured into religion. At its best this was an age of saints, heroes and heroines of charity, and visionary preachers. But the 'revival of religion' was also marked by morbidity, hysteria, superstition and fanaticism, insisted on as the only 'true religion'. In the Roman Catholic Church this was the age of the Counter-Reformation, which identified Christianity with an emotionally intense religious system: the infallible Pope, the dominant priest, the rigid doctrine, the moral code, the physically miraculous Mass, the Virgin Mother who was exempt from the ordinary lot of women. In the Protestant world it was the age of the Reformation, which protested against the Papal dogmas by substituting others. In order to be saved from everlasting damnation the Protestant believer had to admit a total guilt and claim the forgiveness open to those who accepted Christ's death as the sacrifice which had appeased and satisfied God's wrath. He then had to accept a moral code which if anything was more severe than that of the Roman Catholic Church, and had to accept the Bible – or, at the very least, those sections of it most dear to Protestant preachers – as the infallible Word of God, a Papacy on paper.

These rival creeds, Catholic and Protestant, were pitted against each other, as in the Thirty Years' War which devastated Central Europe in the seventeenth century. They were often also pitted together against scientific research or political liberalism – for example, in the Protestant and Catholic Fundamentalists' long battle against Darwin. From the Pope in the Vatican to the preacher in the village pulpit, it was the deliberate intention of many of these Christians to wage a crusade against reason and freedom, for the sake of the dogmatism which they believed to be the only safeguard for their own favoured brand of intense religious emotion.

I have no need to enter here into the details of ecclesiastical history. The literature fills libraries but the essential tragedy was related by two English journalists who in successive years published books for their fellow-laymen: Paul Johnson with his *History of Christianity* (1976) and Bamber Gascoigne with his *The Christians* (1977). What I want to stress is that when a twentieth-century layman looks at the record of Christianity, this dogmatism is what he is most likely to notice. And if he does identify Christianity with that spirit – as so many Christians of the past would have urged him to do – he is likely to conclude that this religion is greatly inferior to other movements of thought about which he will have some knowledge. It is inferior to the scientific movement, which has so humbly and so patiently studied the phenomena of nature from the largest to the tiniest; and which has made progress by the frequency with which it has revised its opinions. It is inferior to the methods used by modern students and helpers of society, when they attempt to get at the facts as scientifically as possible and to reach the people as sympathetically as possible. Christianity, it seems, shares not only the enthusiasm but also the persecuting arrogance of Marxism. The case was put with anger in, for example, Joachim Kahl's *The Misery of Christianity* (translated into English in 1971).

Inevitably the dogmatism of the Christian Church has won many dramatic successes in weak hearts and credulous minds – especially when the local ruler has reinforced his authority by imprisonment or the stake or when employment, success in trade or the tenancy of a cottage has depended on conforming to a churchgoing 'respectability'. But it was equally inevitable that such a religion should fail to satisfy the deepest religious instincts and the highest moral aspirations.

The dogmatism of Latin Catholicism and Eastern Orthodoxy, although entrenched in Europe, was not admired by the Arabs. It had split Christianity into Churches which excommunicated each other and it had obscured the One whom the Arabs hungered to worship instead of local idols. So the Prophet of Islam, although he still gave a special status to Jews and Christians, founded his own religion for those who would be obedient (*muslim*) to Allah. That religion has beyond question provided for many millions through thirteen centuries an encouragement to frequent prayer and a clean life. And the vast empire of Islam, although won by conquest, certainly found acceptance among many non-Arab peoples who were grateful that it displayed a civilized tolerance (by the standards of that time). In comparison European Christendom appeared crude, spiritually as well as materially, as it displayed the cross on the shields of those whose crusade consisted of murder, rape and loot.

But the history of Islam did not consist entirely of the Koran's vision of the Creator or the mystical devotion of the Sufis. It consisted also of a fanatical dogmatism and legalism based on the Koran as a document dictated word by word by God (or the angel) and on a later tradition also demanding obedience. Such a religion has been more thoroughly Fundamentalist than Christianity, and like Christianity it has split into sects absorbed in questions about authority. It has been a creed well armed and not reluctant to use its arms in the holy war; and it has been in no position to show Christianity how to avoid a spiritually corrupting entanglement with political forces. Kenneth Cragg, who over twenty years has written a series of books on Islam showing an intimate knowledge and profound respect, rightly sees that the current challenge is to Muslims as well as to Christians – as in his *The Christian and Other Religion* (1977).

I have already noted the comparison that can be made between the medieval challenge of Islam and the challenge of Marxism to the European tradition today. But I have also stated my conviction that Marxism, for all its appeal, fails to satisfy because it is ultimately irreligious and cruelly inhuman. In this situation, it is not surprising that many members of a civilization which was in the past Christian (at least in name) have turned for the enlightenment so obviously needed beyond the Soviet Union, and even beyond Red China, to the ancient religions of the East. For clearly these are not dogmatic in the way that Christianity or Islam has been. Although the Brahmin in India and the monks in Buddhist countries have exercised great power, neither Hinduism nor Buddhism has ever been organized like Christianity – presumably because neither has inherited the legacy of the Caesars and the legions. (A contrast can be drawn between Ashoka the wise Buddhist ruler of India and the thugs who were called Christian emperors in Europe.) Neither Hinduism nor Buddhism has ever been as theological as Christianity despite a wealth of story-telling and spiritual meditation – presumably because it has never taken over Greek philosophy. Today both Hinduism and Buddhism appeal to many not brought up in their traditions because they offer peace of mind through meditation techniques which do not depend on any dogmas – for example, Yoga or Zen.

But it is still possible to ask whether Eastern religion is a realistic replacement for the discredited dogmatism of Christianity.

One well-known problem is that 'Hinduism' is not a religion like Christianity, with scriptures and a tradition which can be understood and applied (more or less) anywhere. It is simply the name given by European visitors to the religious life of India – a mixture as varied as Indian life itself, with the charming myth of the Lord Krishna romping with the milkmaids alongside the terrifying image of Kali the goddess of destruction. India has produced the purest philosophy, refined by aristocratic scholars and soaring above the illusions of the world; it has also produced the naïve superstition of the temple. The scene is wide, from the brotherhood of all mankind associated with honoured names such as Aurobindo and Rhadakrishnan to the caste system which has ground down the poor; from the non-violence of Gandhi to his own favourite scripture, the *Bhagavad Gita*, which is an exhortation to a warrior to perform his duty in a civil war. All these many faces of Hinduism are at home in India, and there are many books and other influences which present them outside India. But it has proved extremely difficult to pack and label Hinduism for export. Essentially, does it have so many gods that the truth about them is not a question worth asking? Or is it finally monotheism, and if so which of the gods is the supreme manifestation of God? Is its essence the devotion of the *Bhakti* tradition or the 'non-dualism' of the *Advaita* tradition – the worship of the transcendent God, or a mystical apprehension of every self and all nature as divine? And is India, for all its glories, really able to provide the light which will guide a civilization based on science and industry? In *Hindu and Christian in Vrindaban* a German monk, Klaus Klostermaier, has provided a tenderly beautiful account of a long stay in a Hindu holy place, watching and listening (1969). He came away deeply impressed, but still feeling that there was room for something more.

Another trouble about this proposal to replace Christianity with Eastern wisdom is that while 'Buddhism' is certainly available for export it, too, is notoriously difficult to define in Western terms. Zen Buddhism, while rightly admired for its virtues, is difficult to state as a creed in a way that does not seem simply nonsense. Is *Mahayana*, the Northern School which has produced a luxuriant mythology around many Buddhas or Bodhisattvas, a legitimate development – or must Buddhism be more loyal to Gotama the Buddha of history, who regarded the existence or non-existence of gods as a matter of indifference?

And if one is to be enlightened by the *dharma* of the Buddha, must one agree that the basic human problem is how to avoid reincarnation? What unites Buddhists and may be called the essence of their Noble Way is the belief that existence is *samsara* (impermanence) and *dukkha* (suffering). Therefore the wise person seeks to escape from this unsatisfactory, futile and painful existence, and from future rebirths, into *Nirvana*, where no thing and no person survives. Is this really the response most needed in the rich countries of a scientific civilization – or in poorer countries which could now seize their opportunity to escape from idleness, squalor, hunger and disease? This question was put in the context of a great love for Buddhists by a Japanese scholar, Kosuke Koyama, who wrote *Waterbuffalo Theology* in Bangkok and Singapore (1974).

I have criticized my own Christian inheritance rather sharply and I humbly acknowledge the holy lives and the great truths to be found in the Muslim, Hindu and Buddhist traditions. I believe that Christianity needs to be enriched by these lives and truths – as many Christian scholars are now teaching, by saying that Christ is to be found in them. My only point is that made by T. S. Eliot, who deliberated on whether to embrace Buddhism when he was turning to religion after the waste land of his early manhood. He remained always grateful to the Buddhists and fascinated by their inner peace; but he decided that since he belonged to the West it was impossible for him to feed his soul mainly from Eastern sources. So he sought and found Buddhist elements in Christianity; and celebrated them in his *Four Quartets*.

For these reasons I remain convinced that the science-based industrial civilization of Europe and North America, if it is to make a religious response, must make it within its own tradition – which means coming to terms with Christianity. But this need not be, and should not be, a response which in any way loses the sense of a sacred obligation to speak the truth although the mystery which surrounds human life is beyond speech. I recall some other profoundly true words of Dag Hammarskjöld: 'God does not die on the day when we cease to believe in a personal deity, but we die on the day when our lives cease to be illumined by the steady radiance, renewed daily, of a wonder, the source of which is beyond all reason.'

Can one with integrity say more than Hammarskjöld's 'Someone or Something'? I want now to make an experiment which is in accordance with the Jewish and Christian tradition of finding the presence of God in the changing facts of history. I want to ask: when the pressure of 'Someone or Something' arouses a religious response, is that pressure felt more precisely by considering the pressures which come to us in a public and matter-of-fact way with the time in which we live? Is God to be found revealed within the world we know?

If the story of the universe as it is told to us by science is a revelation of the real Creator, it exposes us as no previous generation has been exposed to God's mind-boggling creativity. From one fireball of matter-energy, he made a universe which light takes at least thirty thousand million years to cross. For all we know he has made other universes. He has never rested from his creativity for we know that the galaxies are all the time exploding to form new stars and planets and rushing towards any frontiers there may be in space. He has never ceased to be interested in novelty, since we know that the evolution of life on this planet, already unstoppable for some 3,500 million teeming years, is all the time adding new species to the five hundred million or so already created. The scientific picture may be seen as a new portrait of a Creator head-over-heels in love with matter, with flesh and with life. But the revelation of the universe by science also exposes us to a heart-chilling fact. Everything in this whole universe will die as surely as we ourselves will die. So the new portrait of the Creator has its dark background filled in. We begin to see, as no previous generation has seen, the full contrast between this Creator and Life-giver who alone is immortal and the creation which, from the flower in the field to the Sun in the sky, is entirely destined to decay and perish.

We are able to respond because for the time being we are alive, with bodies and brains which work marvellously. It is possible that this life which we share with so many other species on this planet is unique in all the universe. At any rate, the sheer marvel of its existence and of its evolutionary progress must stagger us. That in itself is a religious response. The response is, however, sharpened if we see in this story signs of the almost incredible patience of 'Someone or Something'. We glimpse – in modern science as in the old religion of the cross – the Creator's willingness to let progress depend on the stumblings and gropings of the few or the one; and the Creator's acceptance of defeats and losses. We are bewildered by the method of evolution which, we now know, the Creator has chosen – if there is a Creator. We cannot fit it into our ethics or aesthetics. The wonder overwhelms us. But at least we can feel the pressure on us of a creativity which loves and trusts life's freedom; and we cannot believe that the appropriate response is for us to reject life or to distrust freedom or to lose hope.

We cannot know what the purpose behind this creativity is. The joy which the Creator takes in a universe so vast and so intricate is beyond our understanding – although perhaps we may sometimes get near to it in music. We do not even know what use is to be made of our own personalities when the bodies and brains on which they have depended have ceased to live. But our response to what we see and know is that a development so huge cannot be entirely without point or purpose. We begin to see, too, that the 'Someone or Something' behind and within it all cannot be incapable of bringing this purpose to completion. So far as our existence in our little day is concerned, the pressure on us is to co-operate with what we glimpse of that purpose.

Just now the experiment of making man, so far the brainiest of all the creatures, is at a particularly critical stage. The pressure is on us to respond to this crisis not by withdrawing into a private denial of life but by throwing ourselves into work useful to the future – whether or not our work lies, as Dag Hammarskjöld's did, in leadership.

If the 'Someone or Something' we know in the pressure of religious experience on us is the Creator of all, then whenever we try to act responsibly and justly we are in deepest reality responding to that pressure. We are responding to God if we try to build or maintain that system of social justice which is often called Socialism. We are also responding to God when we defend the freedom of man – and, in particular, man's freedom to worship his Creator according to his conscience – against the system of tyranny so deceptively attractive as Marxism. And when the events of our time seem to produce new political units which are more effective than the old units in pursuing justice with freedom, we respond to God by renewing our politics.

Thus the alternative to Christian dogmatism need not be a vague sentimentality or the acceptance of a religion which, however glorious, is likely to baffle those who approach it from within a heritage deeply influenced by Christianity. The alternative to dogmatism can be a response within the Christian tradition to the 'Something or Someone' – a response made a bit clearer by meditating on the knowledge and the news of the twentieth century. Offering this response, we can understand what Hammarskjöld wrote: 'I was certain that existence is meaningful and that therefore my life, in self-surrender, had a goal'. When he died in a plane crash in Africa he was about to translate into Swedish Martin Buber's classic of modern Judaism, *I and Thou*; and he had in his pocket a copy of *The Imitation of Christ* by the medieval saint, Thomas à Kempis.

2 The God above Idols

Many false gods have been smashed in our century. The ground already covered in this book has been full of their fragments.

The revelation of the real universe by modern science, although incomplete, has destroyed for ever the picture of God as a watchmaker who has left the whole machine ticking smoothly for our convenience. The physical insignificance of our planet in the real universe, the lateness of the emergence of human life, the element of chance so prominent in the process of evolution, the frequency of disaster – all these facts and others have made the old cosy image of God incredible. The description of mankind's contemporary crisis by economics and sociology has also shattered the idea of inevitable progress all over the Earth – a progress over which God was believed to preside like a benevolent (if useless) grandfather in the sky. It is now known to be possible for man to annihilate his civilization by nuclear weapons, to exhaust the physical resources on which civilization depends, to pollute the soil, water and air, to bring his cities to a halt by his own lack of self-restraint, and to wipe out the majority of his own race by famines and plagues. If man is *not* to do these things, then he must transform his own psychology. And the idol which before 1914 was displayed to the whole world with the expectation that the world would fall down and worship – the idol of the God who was the close friend of his talkative salesman, the white-skinned capitalist – has fallen in our time into the smallest fragments of all. As our century nears its end the basic problem of the white man, particularly of the middle-class white man, is how to recover self-respect. The idea that he has a specially close relationship with God is now completely abandoned. Support is given instead to the suggestion that he has a specially close relationship with the devil.

All that is often said. But it needs to be remembered that other idols have also come crashing down in our age. The theory that the creation of the universe and the evolution of life on this planet can be attributed entirely and exclusively to the random joining together of physical and chemical elements and of genes is so all-embracing that it amounts to a religious theory. Indeed, it attributes success to these random unions on such a scale that it amounts to the idolatry of Chance. Viewing the astounding panorama to which we ourselves belong, we always find ourselves wanting to be grateful to 'Someone or Something' and here, like the gamblers at Monte Carlo, we are invited to be grateful to Chance. But many in the twentieth century have refused to worship that idol, because they have found it incredible that Chance alone should have created a universe so much more substantial than the fortunes of Monte Carlo (or Las Vegas), a universe so amazingly large, fertile, orderly, beautiful and glorious. The brain of *Homo sapiens* himself, when invited to pay this comprehensive tribute to Chance, hesitates because of its own intricate splendour. Can it be merely a happening that we are here to see and to wonder? So man still asks. Yet it is equally hard for man nowadays to worship himself.

Man's own ability to master his fate is hard to believe when the problems are so many and so terrifying. For many in our time it seems much more reasonable to believe that man is doomed unless a power greater than himself creates in him a radically different nature, so that rich and poor nations can be rescued from the fates towards which they now drift. But whether or not this hope is believed to lie within the bounds of possibility – whether or not the God who cares for man is dead – the idolatry of Superman is over. We have only to look in the mirror.

The false god of Marxism, although it has attracted many admirable people, has not been able to survive what has taken place in the countries where it has been enthroned. New rulers arose in Russia to replace Stalin, and new rulers in China to replace Mao – but they have not been able to restore the dream that the establishment of Communism would mean the total liberation of man. In practice Communism has secured some continuing appeal by identifying itself with nationalism; and nationalism has been a fascinating idol in the twentieth century. But Europeans have learned what is the cost of worshipping that idol: nationalism demanded human sacrifices and the burning of Europe. It does not seem too much to hope that in other continents the lesson is being learned at a smaller price. The United Nations – which, to be sure, has not joined the idol class – is an organization which has the merit of pointing in the direction of sanity and survival.

Where in the world is the God worthy of worship? A reality which is no idol has been found by man looking inwards. This exploration of 'inner space' is, indeed, far more important than the space travel which has yielded some scientific knowledge and some fun, but which is almost entirely irrelevant to the real crisis.

The neglect of religious meditation by the science-based civilization has been the main cause of this society's spiritual starvation, and the official religious bodies have done surprisingly little to teach it. But all over the world people have quietly gone on seeking this spiritual reality within themselves, cleaning away the dirt that hides it, calming themselves after all the stresses and fears that contemporary life brings, and so unlocking treasure which they had half-glimpsed. This is no place, and I am no man, to describe religious meditation, but there are many books available which do the job: books which record outstanding achievements in this spiritual life, and books which give specimens of the discoveries made. Here I mention only two books, both by Roman Catholic priests who have gone to live and learn in non-Christian environments. *Return to the Centre* (1976) by Bede Griffiths, an English Benedictine monk, came out of the experience of a Christian community in India following the customs of a Hindu *ashram*. *Silent Music: The Science of Meditation* (1974) by William Johnston, an Irish Jesuit, was written after years of study and practice among the Zen Buddhists of Tokyo.

What is found by such meditation? Its practitioners in every culture and religion are always united by certain characteristics. They are deeply peaceful, because they have by these means grown out of the immaturity of self-conscious and fretful anxiety. They have accepted themselves, because they have found within themselves – perhaps buried deep within – selves worth loving. And they are compassionate to those around them, because they recognize similar selves in their neighbours, even in the most sensual or hostile. These are among the marks of holiness in any place and at any time; and here is the spiritual salt of the Earth. But it is another mark which the saints of every religion all have in common. That is the conviction that their life's meaning is to discover, to adore and to be reunited with a reality more ultimate than themselves. This conviction distinguishes them from those who use meditation merely in order to increase their self-knowledge and self-control – those for whom meditation is no more than a shampoo without soap or a massage without hands.

In their descriptions of the ultimate reality, those who have gone far in the self-discipline of meditation often differ. It is a great disappointment to those of us who follow. This may be because they find different realities within themselves; or it may be because in the attempt to describe what lies beyond words or understanding they have to rely on images and phrases which are sacred in the cultures around them – and these cultures are very different. For whatever reason, there are at least two major traditions in mysticism. One is pantheism or monism. It worships all that is, including the purged self – for that self can be merged indistinguishably in the ultimate reality. The other is theism, the mysticism of the God-fearers. It denies the divinity of all that is, insisting on the 'infinite qualitative difference' between the Creator and the creation. The Creator alone is worthy of worship. But at the same time, the created universe and all life in it are seen as at least potentially good, and the worshipper hopes to be united (but not completely merged) with God in eternal life. Among the innumerable books discussing mysticism, the best historical introduction known to me is Ninian Smart's *The Religious Experience of Mankind* (1969). Professor Smart was an adviser in the making of an instructive and moving series of BBC television programmes on the world's faiths and wrote a book based on that series: *Background to the Long Search* (1977).

I do not claim that the twentieth century has succeeded in solving these mysteries when all previous ages have failed. Indeed, I believe that man can never 'solve' such mysteries in the sense that he can solve so many of the puzzles presented by the creation. But I can record my feeling that it has become a little easier to worship a God above idols in our time because of the reflections of some great minds and souls belonging to our time. Among them has been the German-American philosopher-theologian, Paul Tillich. The biographies of Tillich that have appeared since his death in 1965 have dwelt on his very human weaknesses, anxieties and confusions, partly arising from his exile from Hitler's Germany in mid-career. But they have also helped us to understand the permanent value of his insights into the God who is real when the false gods have come crashing down. Tillich spoke about penetrating 'to the boundaries of our being, where the mystery of life appears'. This characteristic phrase was picked up to provide the title of a collection of his sermons and an autobiographical sketch: *The Boundaries of Our Being* (1973). That book is perhaps the easiest introduction to his thought. Here I can only give a few of my own simple conclusions.

The real God is the ultimate reality and he is worshipped whenever man is concerned with this reality 'in spirit and in truth'. It is truer to say that he is 'Necessary Being' whose life is in all life, than it is to say that he is one object among others. It is truer to say that he is the transcendent One, to whom all creatures turn, than it is to say that he is one person among others. So whenever people sense through meditation that there is this Being on whom all existence depends, or that there is this One behind the 'multiplicity of the phenomena', they are beginning to affirm the reality of God, whether or not they would be happy to say 'yes' to the colloquial question: 'Do you believe in a personal God?' They are saying with the psalmist: 'When you take away their breath, they die' (104:29). But to leave it there is to leave it vague. Religion is not only concern for this ultimate reality. Religion is joy that this reality has shone into our lives. The acknowledgement of the light that streams from God is fundamentally what heals the distress and conflicts at the deep levels of our personality – and it is fundamentally what reconciles us to the world where, without this light and healing, we feel absurd and condemned, lonely and afraid. So we can say that whenever people experience such joy of a new unity, God is known. And we can especially rejoice that God uses things we can touch and see people who share our flesh to make himself known. As he discloses himself to us, God in some sense looks like a thing and acts like a person. That is why we can pray to him.

Talk about such a God is necessary because he is now known in this joy. But it is also impossible, because he is never known perfectly. As Ian Ramsey put it in his *Religious Language* (1957), to talk about God is to use 'models' which are only models, not complete reproductions of the reality; and every model should be accompanied by a 'qualifier' – a word, or at least a mental note, which reminds us that it refers to Being, the One. Words which make this qualification include 'holy', 'eternal', and 'infinite'. To call him 'Holy Father' is to remember that although God's strong love is, we think, fatherlike, he is not literally our father and there are many things to be said about human fathers which are not true about him. To call him 'him' is no more than to use a picture of God as a man – a picture which certainly needs qualifying.

Our choice of what to say about God depends on the force of the experience which makes us speak. Conceivably every thing or person ever in existence, or any event, could show God. A mountain, a crocodile, a cow, a wild flower, a sunset, a storm, a battle, a plague, a murderer, an idiot, a general, a philosopher, a prophet or a crucified criminal could disclose him. Many sincerely religious people have felt unable to decide which item or event in nature or history is the supreme manifestation of the divine; these are the pantheists (for whom God is everything). Others have felt unable to say that any story about God has unique value; these are the polytheists (believers in many gods). But others have felt grasped and held by some particular experiences in which they have found God more fully than anywhere else and they have felt compelled to interpret all other experiences in this light. These are the theists, who worship One God.

The question then is which human experiences have the most value. The answer which many give is: the experience of being loved. Those who give this answer, even though they are not Jews, can appreciate what it has felt like for Jews to celebrate being saved from destruction by their loving God. But the Hebrew scriptures teach that the God who reveals his saving love is not revealed completely:

> The God of Israel, who saves his people,
> is a God who conceals himself

(Isaiah 45:5)

The first letter of John declared in the New Testament that the best description of God after the coming of Christ is: 'God is love'. But to call God 'love' is only to compare his greater reality with human love – which John teaches when he goes on to say that 'this is what love is: it is that he loved us' and 'no one has ever seen God' (4:7-12). If any reader wishes to explore this theological approach further, I can only say that I have found the work of John Macquarrie illuminating, for example his *Thinking about God* (1975). That Professor Macquarrie is well aware of the twentieth century may be gathered from his book on secular and religious *Existentialism* (1972). The best summary of recent thought on the subject known to me is Keith Ward's *The Concept of God* (1974).

There are, we may conclude, two features of man's relationship with God that rescue it from idolatry. The first is the sense of mystery. The word 'God' is itself a word in a particular human language, used to point to a mystery. This mystery can never be fully described, for it is the mystery of the unlimited and inexhaustible 'Being' present in all that exists. The cry of devotion is: 'Blessed be God, only and divinely like himself!' The idea of God as a watchmaker suiting his human customers, or as a grandfather applauding the inevitable progress of his superbly clever grandchildren or as the close friend of the white capitalists, was idolatrous and deserved its twentieth-century fate. Religion when true to its own deepest instincts was never identified with such false gods. But the modern worship of Chance, or of Superman, or of the Communist Party, or of the nation State, has been an even more idolatrous activity, an even more unworthy and disastrous exercise of the religious instinct of man. At its heart, our century may have been an education out of such idolatries.

The second feature of man's relationship with God that rescues it from idolatry is that it is always worship before it is talk. In the distinction made famous by the Jewish philosopher who died in 1965, Martin Buber, religion is not the relation of 'I' to 'it'; it is the relation of 'I' to 'you'. It is not like ploughing a field or chopping down a tree or playing chess (although corrupt religion has often seemed like that, and magic has always been that manipulation of the world for selfish purposes). It is much more like a marriage. The God above idols is the God who is addressed with awe in the religious activities which have continued beneath the surface of the twentieth century: seeking, waiting, listening, wondering, confession, thanksgiving, praise, petition, contemplation.

But such a relationship with God is not easy to achieve. In practice we need a teacher.

3 The Christ above Doctrine

Christians in the twentieth century have had to face a challenge, sharper now than during many previous centuries, that their own worship of Christ may itself be an idolatry. There are passages in the New Testament, and in the prayers and hymns still used in churches, which say that Jesus Christ made the Earth and the universe. Particularly memorable are the poems which dwell on the contrast between Christ's divine, creative status and the helplessness of his hands in the manger where he was born or on the cross where he died. This tradition that in Christ, and Christ alone, God was enfleshed or 'incarnate' is now under heavy fire.

To the Jews, the Christians' worship of Christ has always seemed blasphemous. Muslims have always echoed their Prophet's condemnation of it. Almost all Hindus are happier with the idea of the incarnation of God; in Indian mythology Vishnu is generally believed to have had at least ten incarnations (*Avatara*) so far. But all Hindus reject as arrogant the claim that the incarnation of God in Christ was unique. Many Buddhists have accepted the idea that 'the Buddha nature', fully enlightened, has been, or has remained, incarnate in a man of outstanding wisdom and compassion. But all Buddhists share the Hindu dislike of the traditional Christian claim as arrogant, adding that as Christians have defined 'God' the claim is to them unintelligible. This challenge from the great non-Christian religions has been pressed home by immigrants and visitors appearing in the nominally Christian countries –

and by the resurgence of these religions in their homelands. But probably the challenge from within the nominally Christian countries, whose thought is now scientifically-based, has been even more disquieting for Christians. It is certainly a simpler challenge. It simply says that it is meaningless to assert that one member of the species *Homo sapiens* 'made' the universe described by science – and made it before being born. And it explains the rise of Christian claims to that effect by comparing them with the myths of the Hindus.

Some Christian theologians in England responded to these challenges in a book of essays published in 1977 under the title *The Myth of God Incarnate*. The editor of that volume, John Hick, has put forward the suggestion that Christianity must now undergo a revolution comparable with the Copernican revolution in astronomy (*God and the Universe of Faiths*, 1973). Before Copernicus, many people thought of the Earth as the centre of the universe; after Copernicus, the Earth was known to be one of a number of planets in orbit around the Sun. In some such way, Professor Hick suggested, the twentieth-century challenges to Christianity must be met by admitting that this religion is one among a number in orbit around God. This is the background of his advocacy of the abandonment of the 'myth' that God was incarnate in Christ.

Such challenges certainly deserve the best efforts of Christians in making a careful and honest reply. The first step in such a reply is, surely, to consider with care what has been the orthodox doctrine about Christ. It was never the intention behind that doctrine to abandon the Jewish insistence on One God. Among the very earliest words to have survived in the literature of Christianity are these, addressed to ex-pagans: 'You turned away from idols to God, to serve the true and living God' (1 Thessalonians 1:9). Always the method of combining this monotheism with teaching about the divinity of Christ was more subtle than its critics acknowledge.

It is fair to study not only the prayers and hymns of the Christian centuries but also their considered theology. For this purpose we may turn to an article on 'Incarnation' contributed by its editor, Karl Rahner, the most distinguished Roman

Catholic theologian of his day, to the German work translated as *Encyclopaedia of Theology* (1975).

The article is peppered with technical terms and with references to heresies which have been condemned – but it is also of some general interest because it is a superb summary of what Father Rahner calls the 'valid' formula decreed by the Council of Chalcedon in 451 and of what he calls 'the actual official teaching of the Church' today. The reader who is patient for a few moments will find himself rewarded. 'By the hypostatic union the eternal (and therefore pre-existent) Word (*Logos*), the Son of the Father as the second person of the Trinity, has united as his nature with his person in a true, substantial and definitive union a human nature created in time with a body and spiritual soul from the Virgin Mary, his true mother. The effecting of this union is common to the three divine persons, but the union of the human nature is with the Word alone. Even after the union the unmixed distinction between his divine and his human nature is not affected'.

Father Rahner then summarizes the orthodox definition of the divine nature of Christ. He is 'true God; the consubstantial Son of the Father, his Word, God from God, begotten not made, the only-begotten; a person of the Trinity; creator of all things, eternal, incapable of suffering; because he is true and consubstantial Son, he is not (in addition) an adopted son like us.' But he adds this about Christ's human nature: 'He has a true body capable (before his resurrection) of suffering, not an apparent body or a heavenly one. This was united to the person of the Word (*Logos*) from his conception and has a rational spiritual soul in its essential form ... Jesus Christ is, therefore, consubstantial with us, a son of Adam, born of a mother in true human fashion, related to us by blood, our brother. We must acknowledge the real free created will, energy and operation of the man Jesus Christ, a will distinct from the divine Word (*Logos*) but fully in harmony with it. In his activity he stood truly God-fearing, under God's rule.'

The many subtleties of this summary of the orthodox doctrine show how far it is from being an unconsidered fairy story concluding with the naïve statement that Jesus is God.

Yet many Christians – and Father Rahner has repeatedly shown that he is himself among them – think that merely repeating this orthodoxy is not enough in this century.

One of the challenges is what Christians say about Christ should make sense as an interpretation of their experience – for how can anyone know anything except as a result of experience? Many Christians today find it hard to talk with confidence about the heavenly life of the three 'persons' of the Trinity. Many find it impossible to speak about the two 'natures' and the two 'wills' of Jesus Christ, one nature being of the same substance as God the Father. Many think that it goes beyond his fellow-men's experience of him to say that Christ possessed an 'infallible knowledge appropriate to his mission including the vision of God from the beginning' (as Rahner goes on to say). Even the word 'perfect', applied to Christ in the past by many devout souls who would not have used the technical terms of theology, would not be used so easily today – because, as Jesus is himself recorded as saying, 'there is only One who is good' (Matthew 19:17).

Probably the most important hesitation which many Christians have concerning the traditional orthodoxy of the Church is, however, to do with the practical purpose of the incarnation of the second person of the Trinity. The whole elaborate Christology worked out in the past was thought to be necessary because it safeguarded the practical salvation of man. The second person of the Trinity 'united as his nature with his person in a true, substantial and definitive union a human nature created in time with a body and spiritual soul' in order to save man from hell. If human nature had not been thus assumed into the divine life, it could not have been saved: that was a theme very frequent in the teaching of the Fathers of the Church. And the Fathers did not hesitate to say that those not saved would end up in hell. But many Christians today would hesitate here – as, for example, the Anglican scholar Maurice Wiles did in his *The Remaking of Christian Doctrine* (1973). They find it very difficult to believe that man's salvation has depended on an incarnation which very few men today are able to understand. And they find it very difficult to believe that the millions who have never heard of this incarnation – the great majority of the human race in history – could have been consigned to hell by the God whose best name is Love. So here they tend to accept the protest of non-Christians against Christianity's exclusive claims.

But there is still another way in which many Christians today accept criticisms of their religion. For they themselves reject much that has passed for Christianity in moral attitudes and practical action.

They utterly reject the antisemitism that has been encouraged by many Christian preachers with their sweeping attacks on 'the Jews' as 'God's murderers' – a tradition, both Catholic and Protestant, which was partly to blame for the other Germans' acceptance of the Nazis' murder of six million Jews. For many centuries official Christianity accepted slavery and members of the Church including bishops and monasteries owned slaves or serfs. It was not until the nineteenth century that the British withdrew from the slave trade or freed the slaves in their colonies, the United States resolved to remain united without slavery, and serfs in Holy Russia were legally liberated. The general attitude of better-off Christians towards the poor was also harsh until the humanitarian movements of the nineteenth and twentieth centuries – movements which were often led by people in revolt against official Christianity. The recognition of the equal human rights of women, and the protection of children as fully personal, generally had to wait until the modern period. The protection of animals from cruelty and the conservation of nature against man-made pollution and exhaustion are also causes which were little stressed by Christians until recent years. The pacifist protest against all war was little heard until modern times; official Christianity blessed 'just' wars, and it was indeed rare for Christianity's spokesmen within any nation to condemn any war undertaken by that nation as unjust. The protest against colonialism was also little heard; indeed, official Christianity eloquently consecrated empire-building right from the time when the Papacy divided America, Africa and Asia between the Spanish and the Portuguese. In short, the whole movement of the conscience which in our time has seen that the rich must restrain themselves, and that the poor must liberate themselves, finds only doubtful backing from the moral teaching associated with the establishment of Christ's religion in Christendom.

Almost all Christians who take their religion with a moral seriousness would now say that the blessing of Jesus Christ rests on such a programme as the Universal Declaration of Human Rights adopted (at least in theory) by the United Nations in 1948. If they believe this, they seem bound to add that in the centuries when human rights (plus animal 'rights' and the 'rights' of nature) were trampled underfoot, Jesus Christ was in practice the mascot of ruthless oppressors, although he was at the same time worshipped as 'God from God'.

But does it follow that Jesus Christ should no longer be regarded as utterly unique among those who have claimed to reveal God to men and to save men from their sins?

Every man, woman or child is unique. But Jesus of Nazareth is portrayed in all the evidence which we possess of his life as being solitary in his claims and achievements. To say this is not to be dogmatic, but to be true to history – and the history need not be that which has been written by Christians. Non-Christian scholars have extensively studied the life of Jesus in the twentieth century and many books are available to give the results of their researches and reflections, among them *Jesus the Jew* by the Jewish historian Geza Vermes (1973) and *Jesus* by the agnostic historian Michael Grant (1977).

The facts that are universally agreed upon ought at once to alert us to the appearance of a very strange phenomenon. Jesus was crucified by the Romans, and before this had been in conflict with the religious leaders of his own Jewish people. Since the Romans were not interested in the religious disputes of their subjects, it is clear that Jesus was thought to be an enemy of the State. And since the Jewish leaders were bound by a very exacting religious law and code of piety, it is clear that he was thought to be a heretic. To give these impressions, his message must have been revolutionary – more so than the teaching of the great liberal rabbi of his century, the honoured Hillel. Certainly it produced a revolution in the lives of his followers, who within thirty years of his death could be found writing to each other in letters which have survived about a new life 'in Christ'. Plainly Jesus was not just an admired preacher of religious and moral platitudes.

He was original partly in the simplicity of his message, which reduced many complex situations to the stark relationship between God and the individual. He was also original in his power as a story-teller, using homely incidents to make his unlearned hearers think deeply. And he was original in the quality of his personal influence – attracting some to abandon homes and jobs in order to follow him, including women and even prostitutes in his circle of friends without incurring charges of immorality, and healing many by awakening their faith (a healing which could include the cure of some physical diseases). But above all he was original in his message and in the life which illustrated it so clearly. He had all the reverence for God characteristic of the Hebrew or Jewish saints but he prayed to God as *Abba*, the equivalent in his language of the English 'Daddy'. He was humble before God and even accepted his very painful death as part of God's will for him, but it was his strong belief that through him God was acting as he had never acted before, to set up his 'Kingdom' or government. It was an idea familiar to his Jewish hearers, but it usually had a nationalist and military flavour which never appeared in the teaching of Jesus. For Jesus, the essence of God's Kingdom was that God's will would be obeyed on Earth as in eternity. Meanwhile, before the Kingdom came fully, Jesus admitted sinners into its joy by forgiving their sins without any hesitation or qualification. They had only to ask. The morality which he taught was not a code. So far as we know, he never wrote a book or formulated a programme. Nor was his morality adjusted in order to apply principles to situations in a practical manner. So far as we know he never compromised or qualified. His morality depended entirely on his conviction that God's Kingdom was coming. He commanded his hearers to make a complete self-surrender, and to reach a perfect holiness and love, simply in order that they might belong to this kingdom. The moral teaching which some of his followers collected as the Sermon on the Mount (Matthew 5-7) was amazing, authoritative, unforgettable – and deliberately incomplete.

He was a man of his time. Presumably he was olive-complexioned and black-haired. His education had been in a devout Jewish home and in the school attached to the synagogue at Nazareth. The only way in which he had supplemented it was by watching, listening and praying as he wandered around the villages, fields and lakeside of Galilee. So far as we know, he talked with few Gentiles. His teaching as it has come down to us is soaked in the images and phrases of his Jewish tradition. In particular his pictures of the coming Kingdom of God were derived from scriptures and the daily life of his own people, and he almost certainly shared the hope, which we know to have been very common in the Palestine of this generation, that this kingdom would come very soon. Yet he was more than a man of his time. This was shown when his followers did not think his message discredited even when the promised kingdom failed to materialize. In *Jesus Christ and Mythology*, Rudolf Bultmann explained why Jesus, like other ardent souls in his time, expected the end of the world to occur in the immediate future: 'The majesty of God and the inescapability of his judgement, were felt with such an intensity that it seemed that the world was at an end, and that the hour of crisis was present.'

His message and life with their impact gained in power when Jesus had been tortured to death. Whatever we make of the stories that his tomb was found empty and that he appeared to some of his followers alive, we can see that something happened after the crucifixion. Something changed these followers into the Christians whose joy, courage and love were to prove so infectious as their message spread so rapidly around the Eastern Mediterranean. And we can see that the fascination of Jesus has drawn and held many millions over nineteen centuries. He has seemed to them their contemporary.

Nowhere in non-Christian religion or in the secular world is there a figure really like the Jesus who is known to history. To list the revealers and saviours is in the end to admit that he remains solitary. If we speak of the Copernican revolution now needed in Christianity's estimate of itself, it must be with the remembrance that the planets in orbit round the Sun are very different, only the Earth being able to support life. It would not be true that only faith in Christ supports life with God; clearly God is known and worshipped by many non-Christians and mankind would be spiritually impoverished if the emphasis of the Jews on a community's life under God, of the Muslims on the austere holiness of God, of the Hindus on the richness of religious experience, or of the Buddhists on the importance of silent meditation were to disappear (which it shows no signs of doing). But it does seem true to say that faith in God through Christ supports a unique way of life.

What, then, does Jesus reveal? And whom does he save? And who is he for us today? These are questions which many Christians in our time have faced, knowing that new thoughts must be hammered out and (more important) new lives lived out in response. The literature is vast. I select from it *On Being a Christian* by the Roman Catholic theologian, Hans Küng (translated into English in 1977), and *God as Spirit* by an Anglican, G. W. H. Lampe (1977). And I briefly give my own conclusions, which (not by accident) use biblical quotations.

The light which comes from God is certainly not confined to the historical Jesus of Nazareth or to the Christ of the Christian creed. There is always, everywhere, 'the light that comes into the world and shines on all mankind' (John 1:9). But Jesus makes the fatherly love of the Creator clear – as it certainly is *not* clear throughout nature and history – by putting it into his stories, his healings and above all his life, so that it is the best verdict on his life to say that in it the Light or Word of God 'became a human being' (John 1:14). In this one human life the initiative which the Creator has taken through such immense tracts of space and time is shown to Christians in such a way as to arouse in them that loving worship which, if given to any other than God, is idolatry: 'my Lord and my God!' (John 20:28). It also rightly leaves them convinced that this revelation of God's fatherly love is unique in all mankind's religion – so that in this sense it is true to say that 'no one goes to the Father' except by way of Jesus who is 'the way, the truth, and the life' (John 14:6).

Jesus saves those who accept him; he saves from separation or alienation from God. 'We know,' says the first letter of John in the New Testament, 'that we have left death and come over into life' (3:14). Christians are clearly not exempt from acute depression, tormented bewilderment or squalid sin – but they know a reality which, when trusted, gradually proves stronger than these other elements in the human situation. Christians are not the only members of the human race to be loved by God or to be rescued by him from the separation which, if left as it is or has been, must end in complete or 'everlasting' death – but Christians know that they have been rescued. Therefore they want others to share this liberation.

At the very beginning, some of his followers (we are told) informed Jesus that people were saying that he was John the Baptist risen from the dead; or Elijah come back; or one of the prophets. Jesus pressed them, 'What about you? Who do you say I am?' (Mark 8:27-29). The story points to the obligation which rests on every Christian to make a response authentically his own, even if the title used in tribute is unsatisfactory. In the story Peter used the title 'Messiah', which usually meant the victorious King of the Jews. In the gospels the most frequent title is 'Son of Man', which usually referred to the myth of a glorious figure appearing at the end of history (for example, Daniel 7:13-14). The image of Jesus as a pop musician deserted by his fans, made world-famous in *Jesus Christ Superstar* – or the image of him as a clown who makes people happy, used with such effect in another musical, *Godspell* – is no more distant from the facts of history than were those earliest titles with their suggestions of a military or miraculous conquest of the world. All that can be said is not enough. Yet something must be said after an experience which is overwhelming.

When Christians meet Jesus they meet God's love embodied. That they can experience; about that they must talk. So to speak, they meet the heavenly Father running to sinners – running in judgement, mercy, peace, joy and something not unlike suffering; but running to reach men through the life of a brother-man. To call this Jew of the first century AD the 'humanity of God' (in Karl Barth's twentieth-century phrase) or 'the Son' or 'the Word' of the Father (in the New Testament) is not a dogma based on mythology or metaphysical philosophy. It is the result of an experience which shines also in some other words of the New Testament. 'See how much the Father loved us!' (1 John 3-1). 'This message is Christ, who is the power of God and the wisdom of God' (1 Corinthians 1:24). 'We are ruled by the love of Christ... When anyone is joined to Christ he is a new being; the old is gone, the new is come... Our message is that God was making all mankind his friends through Christ' (2 Corinthians 5:14-19). 'Nothing in all creation will ever be able to separate us from the love of God which is ours through Christ Jesus our Lord' (Romans 8:39). 'He reflects the brightness of God's glory and is the exact likeness of God's own being' (Hebrews 1:3). 'We saw his glory, full of grace and truth' (John 1:14).

Such a Christ can be met in the records about him. In the twentieth century as in previous ages, people have become Christians by reading the gospels. But in practice Christ is most often met as his character is reflected in Christians.

4 The Church above Decline

The steep decline in the number of churchgoers during this century is a familiar fact in many countries which still claim to be in some sense Christian. In the Church of England to which I belong, the numbers receiving Holy Communion at Easter, when adjusted in relation to the total population in the period 1900-70, halved. Naturally many explanations of such a decline have been canvassed.

Is the main cause to be found in the divisions of the Churches? Perhaps; but churchgoers do not display enthusiasm about ending those divisions and non-churchgoers do not seem to be very interested in them. Is the main cause the error made by those

Churches which have rejected the Pope's authority? Perhaps; but the statistics of churchgoing in Italy, including Rome, are not reassuring. Is the main cause a departure from the traditions preserved in the Eastern Orthodox Church? Perhaps; but not many could be found to say that the Communists' criticism of the Russian Orthodox Church was in no way deserved. Is the decline due to the Churches' isolation? Perhaps; but some of the most heavily secularized countries in the world are Sweden, Denmark and England, where National Churches are still officially 'established' by the State. Is the cause a lack of theology? Perhaps; but in the country that has exported theology with the most success many Germans feel that they can get along without sermons. Is the cause too much conservatism? Perhaps; but some of the Churches which have been the quickest to embrace passing fashions have been left with the most pathetic emptiness. The basic reasons for the decline in churchgoing must be found elsewhere.

People, it seems, have often tended to think of churches as shops. Nowadays these shops apparently do not sell anything necessary, although supporting them as clubs may be the hobby of a minority. When asked why they have withdrawn their support people may give answers which, on the surface, conflict with each other. What goes on in churches is too old-fashioned or else not stable enough; too showy or else not interesting enough; too intellectual or else not intelligent enough; too political or else not relevant enough. Or people may produce relatively trivial reasons for absenting themselves: the distance, the hymns, the heating and so forth. Fundamentally, however, all the 'reasons' given add up to the one clear conviction: there is no longer any important positive reason to go to church.

Not very detailed analysis of contemporary trends is needed to see why. Whether or not these people have consciously rejected traditional beliefs about God or Christ, they see little need to affirm those beliefs in what they take to be religious exercises formalized in the remote past. But other factors seem to be equally or more important. People no longer need the Church to provide charity, medicine or education. In most countries the State has taken over most of this field, and charities not controlled by the Church fill in the gaps in the social services. People no longer depend on the Church for entertainment. Television has taken over, supplemented by a richer provision for hobbies. And people no longer need the Church to act as a rallying point in the neighbourhood, or to give them information or advice about what is going on nationally or to provide a sphere where they can express themselves.

Evidence that the decline of churchgoing has been mainly due to the feeling that the Churches are like shops without anything essential to sell is provided by many historical and sociological studies as well as by personal observation. And this conclusion about the decline is confirmed by the reasons which are generally given for churchgoing in countries where the habit persists on a large scale. In the USA at the beginning of the 1970s surveys reported that almost seventy per cent of the population claimed to be in the habit of attending a religious service at least once in every four weeks. The popularity of churchgoing in Ireland (South and North), Spain, Poland or Greece is almost as dramatic. The main cause of this phenomenon does not seem to be the greater readiness of the Americans, the Irish, the Spaniards, the Poles and the Greeks to lead holy lives in peace and love. Many churchgoers in these countries give reasons which are somewhat less spiritual. They say that it is part of the way of life, implying that the Churches offer the Americans, the Irish, the Spaniards, the Poles or the Greeks a means of identifying themselves. To go to church is to say that this person or family is not un-American; is not Protestant or Catholic (whichever this particular Irishman may not wish to be), is not Arab (for the function of Catholicism as linking Spain with Europe rather than Morocco has persisted); is not Communist (for the flourishing Catholic Church in Poland is the only institution left to preserve the continuity of the nation's life); or is not Turkish (for the Orthodox Church in Greece and Cyprus has taken the lead in those peoples' anti-colonial struggles).

Where no similar reasons remain to persuade large numbers of people to make the effort to go to church, the effort is not made. It therefore seems clear that in these still nominally

Christian countries the popularity of churchgoing has depended on factors which are analysed better by sociologists than by students of mysticism.

It is also plain that the Christian Church in traditionally Islamic, Hindu, Buddhist, Confucian, Taoist, Shinto or pagan countries has been profoundly affected by the political fact of the end of the colonial era as well as by the religious fact of the recovery of non-Christian creeds. The past identification of Christianity and colonialism should not be over-simplified if historical truth is to be respected. Stephen Neill's *History of Christian Missions* (1964) emphasizes how often Christian missionaries were regarded by Western traders or colonists as embarrassing nuisances – and how strongly religious, rather than political, were the expressed motives of the missionaries and of those who supported them. The Churches and other Christian bodies have had a long record of concern for 'native' rights and the medical and educational work which they sponsored at great expense has been almost universally admired. The Churches gave increasing scope to 'native' leadership before the colonial powers realized that their time was running out. However, although the true story is more complex than anti-colonialist emotion admits, basically the expansion of Christianity into North and South America, Africa, Asia and Australasia was a part of the commercial and colonial expansion of Europe's peoples who were nominally Christian; and the technical and military superiority of the European civilization did much to persuade the missionaries, particularly in the nineteenth century, that the non-Christian religions would surrender fairly quickly and leave room for Christianity 'as the waters cover the sea'.

There was not an identity between Christianity and colonialism, but there was an alliance with practical consequences. Many missionaries kept power over church life in their own hands, not trusting the 'natives', and their converts depended on them for many daily purposes. A factor making for dependence was that often converts had to withdraw from their own societies in order to form specifically Christian villages, 'mission compounds' or other groups. In many places, too, the missionaries knew that when in trouble they could rely on the protection of the colonial powers – most notoriously in China after the 'unequal treaties', or in the French conquest of Indo-China.

The ending of colonialism brought about the expulsion of all missionaries from China; restrictions on their work in many other countries; the almost complete transfer of ecclesiastical power to 'nationals' of the new nations. The development of these nations also often meant that the importance of the Christian Church in charity, medicine and education diminished. But above all Christianity was branded as the 'white man's religion'. The new nationalism took a pride in the traditional religion of the area and ceaselessly stressed the moral and other failings of the Christians who had taken part in the colonial exploitation. In the triumphantly anti-colonial 1950s and 1960s some Christians were killed – in China, Kenya, the Congo, Uganda and elsewhere. But remarkably little violent retribution was taken. The rejection was usually silent. The Christians were not joined by the flood of baptized converts previously expected. By the 1970s the Christians constituted less than three per cent of the population of Asia.

Such has been the decline or stagnation in the worldly fortunes of the Christian Church during the twentieth century. Yet in this same period it has become clear that there is a Church that is above decline. It is a Church in two parts. The first and larger part consists of those who, with greater or less earnestness, seek to worship the 'God above idols' through the 'Christ above doctrine' – but without frequent churchgoing.

In most of the countries which still claim to be Christian in some sense, the organization of religion now plays a far less significant role than in the days of accepted dogmatism – for the essence of this form of Christianity is the individual's own response to God through his or her own understanding of Christ. The response is made chiefly in the individual's own mind and in the natural setting of home, work and neighbourhood. It depends remarkably little on what clergymen say. Even in the USA, religion is popular on the understanding that it, too, supports the dominant philosophy of individualism within a tolerant democracy – and the constitution provides that no law or act of the State may favour any religious body. Even in Ireland, Spain, Poland or Greece the power of the bishops and priests is more limited than it used to be; the individual believer may use contraceptives, for example.

Some theologians have called this new form of Christianity the 'latent' or 'anonymous' Church, but such adjectives scarcely do justice to the size of the phenomenon. It seems better to speak of the 'dispersed' Church – as the majority of Jews are dispersed in the Diaspora outside Israel. For surveys suggest that in most of the countries with a Christian heritage the bulk of the population would now reckon itself to belong to this Church. Although they are not regular churchgoers, they are also not convinced atheists. They like, rather than dislike, having their conduct called 'Christian'. Although they probably employ the words when swearing, they are made uncomfortable if people are seriously rude about 'God' and 'Christ'. They like the currency to be adorned with 'In God We Trust' (in the USA) or 'Defender of the Faith' (in the UK). The cross is often worn in personal jewellery. When they watch television or listen to the radio they do not usually switch off or get indignant when the subject is religious. They are interested to read some religious news or articles in their papers or magazines, and some of them buy religious books. They want their children to get acquainted with the Bible. They like to have their children baptized, their marriages blessed, and their dead buried according to the rites of the Church – partly, no doubt, because the old habits have not completely died out but also in order to assert a serious wish to see their lives at these turning-points in a Christian context. The fact that many of them have themselves been baptized in infancy has not become completely meaningless.

What does such a dispersed Church look like? In 1970 a study of *Religion in Britain and Northern Ireland* was published by the Independent Television Authority. It had been conducted by Opinion Research Centre with the advice of Michael Argyle, author (with B. Beit-Hallahmi) of *The Social Psychology of Religion* (1975). It suggested that eighty-one per cent of Britons would consider it 'very' or 'quite' important that theirs was a

Christian country; fifty-eight per cent would themselves claim to be 'very' or 'fairly' religious; and only six per cent would say 'I am certain there is no God'. Those who believed in God were divided between those who thought of 'a person' (thirty-seven per cent) and those who thought of 'some kind of impersonal power' (forty-two per cent).

The numbers of those who are sympathetically interested in religion, but not prepared to identify themselves completely with the traditional Churches, seem to be large in Russia and Eastern Europe, although naturally public opinion is never polled. A veneration for Jesus and a respect for Christianity, without a willingness to be baptized, are agreed by observers to be widespread in Muslim countries (where Jesus is presented as a prophet by the Koran), in India (where it is perfectly compatible with Hinduism to worship Jesus as *an* incarnation of God), and in some other non-Christian lands.

People who are happy to remain within the Churches usually underestimate the influence of such attitudes. Those who are determined to secularize these countries completely, or to preserve their ancient religions intact, do not make this mistake.

In fact the nominally Christian countries, because they are not willing to reject Christianity, do adhere to many values taught by Jesus – and assert those values against the presentation of Christ by the Churches in the past. These societies obviously fall far short of moral perfection when judged by the highest standards of Christianity; if they were nearer to those standards, there would not be such room for doubt whether they will achieve the self-restraint necessary to their future as rich societies in the post-modern world. But both the American and the European peoples have given practical evidence of their wish to preserve values which they would describe as 'Christian' against Communism. They have also been willing to pay massive taxes in order to equip their states to practise compassion for life's unfortunates. In their personal attitudes they rate love and kindness very highly.

The interest taken in Jesus outside the nominally Christian countries and outside the circle of churchgoers is in many cases profound. Visitors to the Soviet Union agree that after sixty years of atheist pressure in the schools, the press and public life, many Russians still remain interested in the religious dimension which Christ personifies. The Russian press shows that anti-religious propaganda has to be kept up all the time. Christians dare not evangelize openly, preachers have to be cautious, theologians are not published – yet many Russians ponder the Christian content of the novels of Dostoevsky and Tolstoy, whom not even the Soviet authorities have been prepared to ban. M. M. Thomas, a Christian scholar, has made a detailed study of *The Acknowledged Christ of the Indian Renaissance* (1969), telling the story of the transforming impact of Jesus on Hindus including Gandhi. Apparently a similar book could be written about the reinterpretation of Islam by Muslims who have been influenced by Christianity. In Japan, although the baptized membership of the Christian churches is small the interest taken in Jesus and in Christian spirituality is large. There is every prospect that, as memories of the colonial era and the European or American wars fade, the willingness of many non-Christians to take the teaching of Jesus seriously will grow.

If that is the size of the phenomenon of the dispersed Church in the twentieth century, it is necessary to ask whether it was condemned in advance by the teaching of Jesus; and the answer that has been generally given – even by leaders and scholars closely identified with the organization of the Churches – has been that the historical Jesus addressed an audience wider than the small number he called to 'follow'.

Usually in the story of the gospels there was a crowd in the background. They received the healing and listened to the teaching; and when Jesus taught them it was not about joining an organized Church. The message of Jesus was the message of the Kingdom of God. We are told that once, when he had been moved by a Roman officer's trust in his power to heal, he exclaimed: 'many will come from the East and the West and sit down with Abraham, Isaac and Jacob at the feast of the Kingdom of God!' (Matthew 8:11). After the crucifixion of Jesus the distinction between 'the Church' and 'the world' was drawn far more sharply. Yet it is striking that John's gospel, where the separation between the Church and the world was profound and in places bitter, preserved the wider hope. Successive sentences of this gospel declared that 'now is the time for this world to be judged' and that 'when I am lifted up from the earth, I will draw everyone to me (12:31, 32).

But this dispersed Church whose members are 'not far from the Kingdom of God' (Mark 12:34) is not the only part of the Church that seems to be above decline, even under the challenges of the twentieth century. There remains the Church that assembles Sunday by Sunday.

In the countries which still claim to be Christian, the Churches have managed to maintain a position which is stronger than might be expected after the decline in popular churchgoing and the secularization of public life. They enjoy privileges under the tax laws with public consent; in a few countries such as West Germany they are still rich because the State collects a 'church tax' from all citizens who do not opt out. The clergy are generally not unpopular. Statements by the Churches' leading spokesmen are reported, usually with sympathy. Church buildings are valued as architecture by many who do not use them and are attended by numbers which are usually still noticeable. Those who attend make real sacrifices of money as well as of time. These Churches are served by clergy who come forward for the work although in almost all cases they could earn considerably more from other jobs. Even in countries where the decline has been so steep that reports of American churchgoing arouse disbelief, the Churches have shown a remarkable ability to retain the devotion of the faithful few – and to make rather more think that they ought to go to church. In Britain, for example (where the religious situation was well described in David Perman's *Change and the Churches*, 1977), more people go to church than go to football matches. But of course the most flourishing church life is transatlantic, for reasons set out in Robert Hendy's *History of the Churches in the United States and Canada* (1976).

In Russia and China, the Communists have produced more martyrs for the Christian Church than did the Caesars. But it is clear that some Christians remain willing to face the risk of official displeasure (at least) by meeting with each other for worship. In Russia the figures run into millions and those churches which are allowed by the State to remain open are usually crowded on a Sunday. In China, where the Christian Church was small even before the Communist Liberation, the present reality includes only a few small groups meeting informally; but they meet. The 'blood of the martyrs' remains, as Tertullian said in the Roman Empire, 'seed'. Careful records are kept of the information about religion under Communism which reaches the West at Keston College in Kent, whose Director is Michael Bourdeaux, the author of *Opium of the People* (revised in 1977).

In lands shaped by non-Christian faiths, what is surprising is that everywhere in the anti-colonial climate the Churches have managed to keep their roots in the soil and have usually even achieved some modest growth. In Indonesia the expansion has been rapid, as it has been in many areas of Africa south of the Sahara. A book such as *African Christianity* by Adrian Hastings (1976) is a history of vitality. The baptism of converts increases the African Churches by at least three per cent per annum, with a similar increase due to the birth rate. The growth of the membership of the Evangelical Churches in Latin America from two hundred thousand in 1945 to some ten million in 1975 should probably also be understood as essentially evangelism among pagans, although most of the converts have been nominally Roman Catholics. In his study of *The Coming of the Third Church* (translated into English in 1976), Walbert Bühlmann gave reasons for projecting a growth of the number of Christians in the Third World (Asia, Africa, Oceania and Latin America) during the twentieth century as a growth from sixty-seven million in 1900 to well over a thousand million in 2000 while the growth in North America and Europe would be from 392 million to just short of eight hundred million.

Certain characteristics are found in common among most of those who have entered the last quarter of the twentieth century still adhering to what may be called the 'assembled' Church. These characteristics they recognize in each other, finding a unity of spirit that increasingly transcends their inherited divisions and their geographical separation.

They assemble for religious purposes – a fact often forgotten by those who are interested in them chiefly as potential recruits for political or social movements. Their motives are much the same as can be found in the evidence about the devout members of the Churches in previous periods. In some of them the religious instinct which is common to all, or almost all, of mankind is so highly developed that it is as necessary for them to worship God as to eat food. These are people who are fed spiritually by the traditional words of Christian worship and who find strength in the company of others who share the same love of the depths of the tradition. Some such Christians of our time are linked personally with the many centres of prayer, and of a specifically prayer-based fellowship, that have survived or been built; others get what they need from their local churches.

Others who assemble in local churches, and who occasionally visit other Christian centres, would never be described as advanced in the Christian life. In fact many churchgoers are people who might be classified by psychiatrists and social workers as 'dependent' or 'immature' or 'inadequate'. They are lonely, or weak-willed, or depressed by a psychological illness, or wounded by a blow in life such as a physical disability or bereavement. It is safe to say that every Christian congregation in the world contains some such members, as well as those who are holy or are becoming holy. What the weak and the strong have in common is a sense of their need of the Church's regular worship and assembled activity; and according to the Church's own scriptures and other statements, the weak are particularly welcome.

Although these people do not go to church in order to undertake a political activity, they think of themselves as a world-wide minority that has an allegiance which at least competes with their normal allegiances to their own class, race and nation.

It is not very surprising that the Christian congregations of our time often show themselves to be prejudiced and conservative. Naturally they prefer their cosy habits of life and thought. But it is noteworthy that they are quite often capable of overcoming their prejudices because they recognize the obligations imposed on them by their religion which to them is dear. For their own neighbourhood they may sponsor a youth club although the youth may shock their own respectability; or they may patiently visit old people in their homes although the old may have nothing to contribute except their characters. A congregation which lives in a comfortable suburb of a rich city may be moved by the example of Albert Schweitzer and his pioneering hospital in the African jungle or Mother Teresa and her home for the dying destitutes of Calcutta. Or a white congregation may recognize a Negro spiritual leader such as Martin Luther King, with his dream of the freedom of all God's children. Or solid patriots may be impressed by the heroism of Dietrich Bonhoeffer, the brilliant German theologian hanged by the Nazis, or of Archbishop Luwum, murdered by the tyrant of Uganda. When the members of these congregations are persuaded that it is their duty to take action in support of movements of the conscience sweeping through the contemporary world, their support is likely to be practical, long-lived and self-sacrificing. That must be the reason why so many charities and social work agencies regard these congregations as useful recruiting grounds.

The different Churches accept different styles of leadership and different methods of decision-making. Although the comparison of these styles and methods has absorbed much attention in the Ecumenical Movement ever since the Faith and Order Conference at Lausanne in 1927, few agreements have been accepted by the Churches to merge their organizations. These questions remain important to churchgoers since power is at stake and it, too, could be power to do good. But half a century of debate has left the impression that, while some mergers can be expected to go forward, many of the Churches will have to agree to differ. Already a movement has grown widely to encourage their members to recognize each other, to co-operate closely and to share worship, even the service of Holy Communion itself, before any more complete reunion. (The progress made in Britain by this movement was described by John Huxtable in *A New Hope for Christian Unity*, 1977.) And already an equally vigorous movement has stressed that the professional clergy of the Church matter far less than used to be thought. More use is being made of unpaid clergy, but above all the Churches are returning to the pattern evident in the New Testament, where Christianity is largely a lay movement with no buildings and few employees. (The thinking in Britain in this direction was summed up by Michael Harper in *Let My People Grow*, 1977.)

The worship offered in these congregations is very varied, and any attempt to impose uniformity is an attempt to impoverish the worship; fortunately, such attempts are in the long run self-defeating. But two features of Christian worship are increasingly common in the assembled Church.

The first is the centrality of the act in which the death and victory of Jesus are remembered and (in a dramatic rather than physical sense) re-enacted. When the words of Jesus are repeated over bread and wine, and when the bread and wine are shared by the assembled Church, worship is offered which is stronger than any hymn-singing, sermon or television programme. Since the Second World War this Eucharist, Mass or Holy Communion has become the corporate act of the Church on every Sunday to a degree unknown since the early Christian centuries. The Roman Catholic and Eastern Orthodox Churches have always insisted on this service, but usually in a language unfamiliar to the people and in a style which stressed the dignity of the priest rather than the togetherness of the congregation. The 'liturgical movement' has changed the face of Sunday-by-Sunday Roman Catholicism. At the same time growing numbers of Protestants have valued this service – more than the combination of hymns and preaching which had become their traditional fare. After centuries of controversy Christians in the twentieth century have reached a large measure of agreement about the meaning of this act which they have in common (as in the statement 'One Eucharist' issued by the World Council of Churches in 1975).

Another feature of this century is a movement which in almost all Churches has stressed the need to meet more informally. Sometimes this need has been met by groups meeting quietly in an office or factory, or in a home to which neighbours are invited, for a chat about the problems which people are passing through and for simple Bible study. Others have felt the need to hold sessions for a worship more spontaneous and enthusiastic than has been normally acceptable in the Churches – which have largely shared the inhibitions of the middle classes in modern Western nations. In Latin America the Pentecostal Churches have been by far the fastest growing branches of the Evangelical version of Christianity. In the North American, European and other Churches, the Charismatic Movement has brought Catholics and Protestants together with its joy in experiencing the 'Pentecostal' emphasis on friendship, warmth, clapping, dance, exclamations, ecstatic speech and faith-healing. In Africa the Independent Churches, free from the control or influence of missionaries, multiply. In *Schism and Renewal in Africa* (1968) David Barrett presented a picture of an African Reformation in full flood – with over five thousand distinct organizations numbering some seven millions and expanding, in about a third of all Africa's tribal societies, by at least three hundred thousand new adherents each year. Since then the picture has changed in only one important respect. Some major African Independent Churches have shown a wish to join the World Council of Churches and to have other links with more traditional Christians. The same is true of some major Pentecostal Churches elsewhere.

In such ways the inner life of the assembled Church of the twentieth century rises above the numerical decline in churchgoing. Essentially this Church is the response of those – many or few – who have felt a special need of Christian worship and fellowship, and who have therefore been willing to break (at least on Sunday mornings) with the present customs of their societies. Most members of the assembled Church are not morally superior to the best members of the dispersed Church. What distinguishes them is not their morality but their felt need. It is because of their felt need that they have joined the men and women who, the gospels record, were willing to leave everything behind in order to follow one who fascinated them.

5 The Rock above Nations

Everything in the religious situation points to the necessity of a leadership in Christianity which will state, in deeds as well as in words, the agreement emerging among Christians. Such leadership would be unlikely to bring large numbers of churchgoers back in Europe. Nor could it be expected to melt the hearts of Communist governments, or to expand the Churches beyond the small minority status which they now hold in lands predominantly Muslim, Hindu and Buddhist. But it could express some strengths in the present Christian position.

It could appeal to the consciences of many who regard themselves as Christians, or at any rate as believers in a God not unlike the Christians' God. It could point unmistakably to the urgent tasks which await the people of our time, in rich and poorer countries alike, if the decision of mankind is to be for life rather than death. It could support effectively the social movements which seem to be movements of life, serving the Kingdom of God in our time. It could help powerfully in giving direction and clarity to the spiritual movements which turn in meditation and prayer to the God above idols. It could hold up the great fact of Jesus Christ, historical and contemporary, without concealing the past tragedies in which Christians have betrayed him by their corruptions or hidden him behind their rival dogmatisms. It could encourage the 'dispersed' Church to take its own convictions more seriously and courageously and look with more respect to the 'assembled' Church. It could uphold those who doggedly persist in their support of the Churches by giving them a new vision of their common purpose. It could represent Jesus Christ in the world at the turn of the twentieth and twenty-first centuries after his birth.

It goes without saying that such leadership ought to be as international as possible. Towards the end of the twentieth century nationalism remains a strong emotional force in many places and is a strong ally of some Churches. But as Christian leadership appeals to the most sensitive consciences, it always transcends nationalism. It speaks for a wider loyalty to the Kingdom of God and to the causes which in our time draw people of many nations into common work for man's future. One of the great advantages of the Church in such a period is that it is an international fellowship, chartered by its scriptures as a community where 'there is no longer any distinction between Gentiles and Jews, circumcised and uncircumcised, barbarians, savages, slaves and free men' (Colossians 3:11). Perhaps it is now the largest effective international fellowship in existence. The influence of Christianity as an influence for peace makes it respected far beyond the ranks of those who adhere to its religious beliefs, while those who do worship in its churches find inspiration in the thought that the community offering this worship stretches from the Eskimos to the Maoris from Cape Town to Leningrad, from New York to Calcutta. Whatever may be the roots of the Churches in nations which are still divided from each other clearly the spiritual voice of Christianity has to sound from a position above all nations.

The most obvious claim to supply such international leadership comes from the Papacy, which is already acknowledged in this capacity by perhaps half the Christians in the world. The throne of the Bishop of Rome is surrounded by memories of Peter, whose tomb has been found (almost certainly) beneath St Peter's, and who is known to have been regarded in the first century as the rock on which the Church would be built (Matthew 16:18). As strengthened by Gregory VII and Innocent III the Papacy became the single most constructive force in the rebuilding of Western Europe in the Middle Ages. On the whole it was an influence which supported the spirituality and idealism of Christians, despite notorious vices in the Popes and their courts and despite their having far too large a share in the power politics of the day. The Papacy was a rock of justice to which appeal could be made over the heads of local potentates; a patron of the scholars, the artists and the religious orders of monks, nuns and friars; and an institution preserving at least some of the moral force of Christianity while ranking alongside, if not above, the mightiest rulers of the Earth. When the successful Protestant revolt had finally destroyed the unity of the Middle Ages the Papacy continued to command among Roman Catholics a devotion associated into our own time with phrases such as 'Holy Father' and 'Holy City'. It also continued to inspire true heroism, as in the missionary and educational work of the Jesuit Order. Under Protestant persecutions priests and lay folk were glad to die for it. This religious position of the Papacy was, if anything, strengthened during the period 1860-1960, when it lost secular power outside the tiny Vatican City state but was given centralized power over the whole Roman Catholic Church. More widely Christians and others still regard the Pope as, at least potentially, the most prestigious Christian spokesman in the world. There are few movements which would not be delighted to have the Pope's blessing. Contributors from many Churches expressed their hopes in *A Pope for all Christians?* edited by Peter McCord (1976).

This ancient office has been adorned by some truly distinguished personalities in this century. Leo XIII (Pope 1878-1903) and Pius XII (Pope 1939-58) were aristocrats with many talents entirely consecrated to their duties as they saw them. John XXIII (Pope 1958-63) was a peasant's son who captured the hope and affection of almost all Christians and of many others. The Papacy has also been served with complete dedication by some thousands of Vatican officials and diplomatic envoys.

Despite these unique and vast advantages, however, the Papacy has not been able to unite all Christians and since about 1960 it has not even been able to articulate the consciences of all Roman Catholics. One reason is that the claim to infallibility has not been convincing – as may be seen from books such as *A Question of Conscience* by the Englishman, Charles Davis (1967), *The Roman Catholic Church* by the American, John McKenzie (1969), and *Searching for Truth* by the Australian, Peter Kelly (1978). All three authors are distinguished theologians who have left the priesthood.

The claim was stated in its modern form by the First Vatican Council (1870). The freedom from error at issue is 'that infallibility with which the divine Redeemer willed his Church to be endowed when defining faith and morals'. This freedom belongs to the Pope when he, 'exercising the office of pastor and teacher of all Christians, defines with his supreme apostolic authority a doctrine concerning faith or morals to be held by the universal Church'. 'Such definitions of the Roman Pontiff,' it was decreed in 1870, 'are irreformable of themselves and not from the consent of the Church'. Unfortunately, however, the two most recent Papal pronouncements generally agreed to fall within this class concern the Immaculate Conception (1854) and Assumption of the Virgin Mary (1950). The Popes concerned taught that the mother of Jesus had been born free of the taint of the 'original' sin of Adam (man) and that at the end of her earthly life her body as well as her soul had been assumed into heaven. Many Christians – even the Eastern Orthodox, who generally hold these teachings to be true – have resented the Popes' actions in making such additions to the creed compulsory for all Christians; and many others have strenuously denied their truth, pointing to the lack of historical evidence and to the idolatry, as well as incredibility, implied or risked in the claim that the Virgin Mary was in these two ways exempt from the human lot. Many Roman Catholics seem to have come to regret these dogmatic definitions, or at least their style.

But the storm centre has not been around the Marian dogmas. It has concerned matters more urgent to the layman. Papal infallibility has been at stake only to the extent that a pastor and teacher guaranteed freedom from error on special occasions has in the past been thought worthy of obedience normally. In the eyes of many Christians, including many who remain Roman Catholics, the modern Popes have made two cardinal errors which for the time being discredited their teaching authority.

Pius XII failed to condemn the Nazis' extermination of the Jews in strong enough terms until after Hitler's death; Hitler when he died was still nominally a Roman Catholic and had not been excommunicated. A defence of the Pope's silence is possible – he sheltered some Jews in Rome and won their gratitude; he did not have full details of the extent of the cruelty; he would not have been able to stop the Nazis; he would have risked much for Roman Catholics in Germany and elsewhere. But his timid discretion in the face of such an evil has not spoken well of his claim to be the representative of Jesus Christ. Many Christians, including many Roman Catholics, also deeply regret the condemnation by Pius XII, repeated by Paul VI in *Humanae Vitae* (1968), of 'artificial' methods of birth control. They believe that this condemnation has tied the Papacy to an out-of-date understanding of what is 'natural' and therefore in accordance with God's will. They believe that it puts the Papacy on the wrong side of mankind's current struggle against overpopulation. And they know that it exposes the Papacy – and all bishops and priests who follow its teaching in this matter – to the disobedience of many Roman Catholic married couples. By insisting on this position although the matter is not mentioned in the Bible, the Popes appear to have condemned themselves as incompetent theologians, as teachers without a message for the world's economic crisis, and as pastors unable to understand modern marriage. It is thus the conviction of many who look to Rome for moral leadership that on these two issues a Pope keeps silence when he ought to speak and speaks when he ought to keep silence.

The criticism of the Vatican has extended over a wide field of faith and morals. Many Roman Catholic theologians have joined their Protestant colleagues in free and honest discussion of modern challenges to traditional doctrines (as is shown in, for example, the *Encyclopaedia* quoted on p. 209); but the Vatican by its insensitivity to these questions, and by keeping the appointment of bishops in its own hands, has helped to maintain a gap between the questing theologians and the official Church. Some Roman Catholic theologians have also been pioneers in relating Christianity to the religious traditions and convictions of Africa and Asia. Aylward Shorter's *African Culture and the Christian Church* (1973), for example, was a superbly sensitive and honest presentation of this encounter, as was Raymond Panikkar's *The Unknown Christ of Hinduism* (1964). William Johnston's *The Inner Eye of Love* (1978) began: 'One need be no prophet to predict that Western theology of the next century will address itself primarily to dialogue with the great religions of the East'. But the Vatican has continued to issue some defiantly dogmatic instructions, insisting on the supreme value of the theology of St Thomas Aquinas – a theology which was largely a medieval response to the Ancient Greek philosopher, Aristotle.

A brilliant young Jesuit, Gerald O'Collins, voiced the beliefs of many of his generation in the priesthood when he called his book *Has Dogma a Future?* and answered 'no' (1975). But he had to attempt what he called 'friendly interpretation' of the declaration issued in 1973 by the Sacred Congregation for the Doctrine of the Faith (formerly the Holy Office, of Inquisition fame): 'The objects of Catholic Faith which are called dogmas are and always have been the unalterable norm both for faith and for theological science'. In 1975 this Congregation solemnly 'admonished' Professor Hans Küng for failing to pass this test in his book *Infallible?*

Perhaps of more immediate concern for those not theologically minded has been the sharp refusal of Paul VI (in 1967) even to discuss the question of allowing priests to marry – although it has become the consensus of theologians that clerical celibacy is not essential and it has been widely thought by observers that the insistence on it, dating back to Pope Siricius in 386, is unlikely to survive into the twenty-first century. Even sharper was the Papal reaction to the idea that women might themselves be ordained priests. And many laymen who have not been very interested in the problems of the clergy have taken unfavourable note of the fact that the Vatican has always refused to publish its financial accounts – a secrecy which has been imitated almost everywhere by the dioceses and parishes, and which indicates rather plainly that the clergy do not hold themselves accountable to anyone beneath God.

The Second Vatican Council (1962-65) substantially fulfilled the wish of Pope John, whose idea it was, that it should open a window to the modern world. It refrained from adding any new dogmas to those in existence, rejected the notion that the Church's tradition could be independent of its scriptures, and in general avoided the legal style of doctrine and the military style of discipline. It projected a picture of the Roman Catholic Church as a 'pilgrim people' eager to serve God and man with a fresh energy of love, in a growing unity with other Christians and in friendship with all men of goodwill. It blessed the idea of dialogues with non-Christian religions and with secular men such as Communists. By a rare combination of humility and courage it aroused great expectations, and to some extent the subsequent changes in the Roman Catholic Church have fulfilled them. As priests and people have together celebrated the Mass in their vernacular language, with the altar in the centre and after the simplification of the appearance of the church, much that the Protestant Reformation of the sixteenth century desired has seemed to have come to pass. In parishes and nations the first experiments have also been made in setting up decision-making processes where the key decisions have not all been reserved to the priests and bishops. The bishops have thought of themselves more as a 'college' and less as individuals taking their orders from the Vatican; and an international Synod of Bishops has met in Rome as a somewhat faint echo of the Council. A far greater freedom of speech has been practised.

But the ten years after the Council have also brought much frustration. Many have grown impatient with the immobility of the Vatican and with the paternalism which has remained a mark of much local Roman Catholic life. Recruitment to the priesthood has dropped dramatically and many of the ablest and most active priests have left it. As an Anglican I do not wish to comment further on the agonies of the Roman Catholic Church in transition. I merely recommend, among a number of similar books, *The Runaway Church* by the British ex-Jesuit, Peter Hebblethwaite (1975).

Being myself a priest of the Church of England, I probably ought to make it clear at this stage that I do not believe that the international leadership which the Papacy has so far largely failed to provide is available from any National Church. Nor do I expect it to come from those international fellowships such as the Anglican Communion or the Lutheran World Federation which are in fact heavily dependent on one national culture. ('Anglican' comes from the Latin for 'English' while the inspiration of Lutheranism has come predominantly from Germany and Scandinavia.) Nor do I expect a great deal from the Orthodox Churches' Ecumenical Patriarch (who has been left by history isolated in the largely Muslim Istanbul) – or from the creaking machinery for consultation between the national Orthodox Churches.

The World Council of Churches has filled some of this gap since its formation in 1948. I do not wish to repeat the story of its conferences, or my own tribute to some of them. But as one who is indebted to it in many ways, I feel obliged to add that the WCC is in no position to assume the moral and spiritual leadership of Christianity. The quality of its own leadership has at least competed with the quality to be seen in Rome or in any of the national Churches, but the whole method by which it works means that it is not equipped to take over from the Papacy.

Its staff is small because its budget is small in relation to its tasks, which in theory cover the whole of Christianity and the whole of the world. This staff consists of men and women who are willing to work in an international bureaucracy based on Geneva, and who have in most cases been chosen because they have strong and outspoken views on the relationship between the Churches and the world. In other words, they are not typical churchmen any more than the still heavily Italian staff of the Vatican is typical. It is easy for such a staff – as it is easy for the Vatican – to get out of touch with what the Churches are feeling and doing locally. But periodically the WCC staff is able to convene conferences, necessarily expensive because of the international travel involved. Literature is prepared for these conferences and addresses are given at them, but as a method of studying a question the procedure usually turns out to be unsatisfactory in practice; there is too much of a rush, the difficulties of translation are great, and even more exhausting are the difficulties involved when people meet who speak out of very different cultural backgrounds. A WCC conference is almost always under pressure to get its thinking down on paper, both for the record and for communication to the public, and some of these statements have been valuable summaries of discussions of specific problems. But usually the conference means much more to those taking part than to those who are offered the documents on which it has eventually agreed. These documents are often as full of jargon and rhetoric as are the declarations of the Vatican itself. Although those who have votes at these meetings are delegates of their Churches, the nature of the work means that people likely to find it agreeable tend to get chosen, while others at the meetings are enthusiasts directly recruited by the staff. The general outcome must depend largely on what the staff have prepared.

The topics covered by the WCC have been numerous, and no one who studies its work over the years with any sympathy can doubt the sincerity of the wish of those who have taken part in this work to be of service both to the Churches and to the world. But inevitably certain themes have dominated the WCC's work in so far as this work has made an impact on those not personally involved in it. Two themes in particular have been very widely prominent.

The first may be said to have been dominant in the WCC from the Amsterdam to the Uppsala Assemblies, 1948-68. It was the theme of the Churches' reunion. As defined at the New Delhi Assembly in 1961, the unity for which the Council has worked has involved 'one fully committed fellowship, holding the one apostolic faith, preaching the one Gospel, breaking the one bread, joining in common prayer, and having a common life reaching out in witness and service to all'. It is a fine ideal. The trouble is that despite the agreements of their delegates on these occasions the Churches have seldom shown that this degree of unity is what they actually want, to the point of abandoning their traditional divisions. It may have been the opinion of the majority of Church members (however that category is defined) that the goal defined at New Delhi takes too little account of the diversity of habit and temperament to be realistic. Or it may be that the majority of Church members, while accepting this goal, give it a low priority. At any rate the New Delhi statement has not been treated as a convincing dogma.

Since 1968 the WCC, as if agreeing with those Church members who grew bored with its emphasis on the Churches' reunion, has placed far more stress on the obligation of Christians to take part in the liberation of oppressed peoples. The Council has arranged for grants for humanitarian purposes to be paid to anti-racist organizations (including some lobbying against the restrictions on immigration imposed by a country such as Britain) and liberation movements (including some engaged as guerrillas in an armed struggle against the Portuguese, Rhodesians and South Africans). These grants aroused controversy, as they were intended to do. They were attacked as implying a Christian blessing on violence – an attack which came strangely from some who had been foremost in identifying Christianity with national wars and colonial expansion or with the armed struggle against Nazi Germany. But there was another possible line of criticism. This was to ask whether taking sides with immigrants peacefully campaigning for their numbers to be increased, or with guerrillas killing and burning in order to force a change of government, really was as central to the Christian Gospel as the WCC now believed it to be. Or was it the mirror-image of the mistake made in the past by those who had identified the Gospel with militarism and imperialism?

Whatever may be thought of the stands taken by the WCC on the Churches' reunion and the world's liberation, it would generally be agreed that a body working in this manner does not supply the moral leadership for which so many have looked to the Papacy. It does not possess the historic prestige. It is not adequately staffed. It is not linked sufficiently with the religious activities which in practice absorb most of the Churches' day-to-day concern, and as a sign of this distance from the springs of religion its discussions do not seem to arise firmly enough out of worship. These factors would still handicap the WCC even if the Roman Catholic Church were to change its present 'observer' status to full membership; or if the Russian Orthodox Church, numerically the largest body belonging to it, were to be freed from the necessity to follow its government's political line. It seems clear that in practice only the Papacy itself is likely to provide the necessary centre of inspiration and unity.

It may be significant that in 1977 an international commission of Roman Catholic and Anglican theologians published an agreed statement on 'Authority' envisaging a development in the Papacy acceptable to all or most Christians. In a future of the kind which this report glimpsed, the Pope would assume a very prominent public role as the president and spokesman of the world's bishops and in private would be the chief 'pastor of the pastors'. Except in a very rare emergency when his fellow-bishops could not be consulted, he would presumably avoid making controversial statements. Presumably, too, he would have no power to appoint his fellow-bishops, who would be elected locally. His would be a constitutional throne – somewhat like the present British monarchy, but even further stripped of power since the Pope's field would be religion, where power is finally irrelevant. But to an even greater extent than a British monarch a Pope would have the opportunity to wield a moral and spiritual influence, all the more effective for being personalized. Like a British monarch he would also be the chief figure in a parliamentary system of government, although in the government of the Church the advice of the learned and the spiritually mature, and the conscientious convictions of minorities, would be respected more tenderly than in a political Parliament. Under this Papacy a staff of experts would presumably work in Rome, and around it regional and world conferences would be convened to bring together representatives of the local Churches. Such a Papacy, removed from the storms of theological controversy as well as from the manoeuvres of political power, could enter its most glorious period, fulfilling the commands of Christ to Peter in the gospels – 'when you turn back to me you must strengthen your brothers' (Luke 22:32); 'take care of my lambs, take care of my sheep, take care of my sheep' (John 21:15-17).

At the end of the 1970s such a day seems far distant. But at the beginning of the 1960s no one expected the Second Vatican Council.

6 New Acts of God

What distinguishes the Christian religion from the other faiths of mankind is, at bottom, the bold completeness of its insistence on the unceasing activity of God in the everyday world. Many people who have believed in 'Someone or Something' as the source of the universe have not thought it possible that this ultimate reality, this unmoved mover, could take effective action after the initial act of creation. Others have thought of him or it as taking action only in the world of mythology, or in the private world of mysticism; for them religion has no comment to offer on the world of suffering and change, except perhaps the advice to escape. Creeds as noble as Judaism or Islam have rejoiced in the self-revelation of God in history, but they have not seen God as throwing himself into action to the extent involved in the Christian claim that his love was embodied in the life, death and victory of Jesus. Christians worship the Creator who never ceases to create. In this worship they affirm their acceptance of the message of their scriptures, including (as they claim) the Hebrew scriptures.

'Go to a country that I am going to show you' is the summons to Abraham, as Jews and Christians read Genesis (12:1); and as they read Exodus (3:13-17), they find Moses being told that God will show who he is as he takes action to deliver his people from cruel slavery. The God of the Bible himself leads the people into the Promised Land – and back into it after their exile. One of the prophets (Isaiah 43:18, 19) seems to hear this God saying:

> Do not cling to events of the past
> or dwell on what happened long ago.
>
> Watch for the new thing I am going to do.
> It is happening already – you can see it now!

They waited long for their prophets' promises to come true, but the oldest of the gospels gives as the first public words of Jesus: 'The right time has come and the Kingdom of God is near!' (Mark 1:15). Luke's gospel lists the deeds of Jesus as the fulfilment of the old hopes: 'the blind can see, the lame can walk . . .' (7:22). The fourth gospel offers the explanation: 'My Father is always working, and I too must work' (5:17). And it includes a promise about the work of the followers of Jesus. 'Whoever believes in me will do what I do,' promises the Jesus of John – 'yes, he will do even greater things, because I am going to the Father' (14:12). For the New Testament understands the whole work of Jesus as the supreme act of God – and is sure that any Christian work will reflect this 'to the end of the age' (Matthew 28:20). 'If you remain in me and my words remain in you, then you will ask for anything you wish, and you shall have it. My Father's glory is shown by your bearing much fruit; and in this way you become my disciples' (John 15:7, 8). The conviction that God is at work in the life of the Church is clear in the Acts of the Apostles, as is the conviction that God has never ceased to work in nature, where 'he gives evidence of his existence by the good things he does' (14:17). And the New Testament is full of the faith that this activity of God is going to continue until it reaches its climax. The New Testament pictures its Lord as 'the living one . . . alive for ever and ever' (Revelation 1:18) – and at work until he rides to his final triumph at the head of the 'armies of heaven' (Revelation 19:14). The invitation which the New Testament issues is therefore essentially not an invitation to remember events of the past. It is an invitation to co-operate with the work of God. The work continues until the work is done.

It now appears that the greatest mistake which Christians could commit would be to believe that the activity of God has been exhausted by the creation of the universe as it now is, or by the evolution of man to his present condition, or by the work of the founders of the great religions, or by the work of Jesus, or by Christianity in its first two thousand years. Scientists expect this planet to be inhabitable for another two or three thousand million years at least, unless man first makes it uninhabitable.

The story of agriculture, now only ten thousand years old, is surely going to produce some new developments in that future, as is the six-thousand-year-old story of civilization or the four-hundred-year-old story of science or the two-hundred-year-old story of industry. But the same reasoning suggests, particularly to a Christian, that the story of Christianity is not yet ended. If, as seems to be the case, the physical universe is expanding all the time, if evolution on this planet is always thrusting into new life, and if the human race including the Christian Church has two or three thousand million years of history still to come, it does not seem necessary to believe that the soul of man will be imprisoned for ever in an anxious materialism or in a mummified religion.

New acts of God seem likely to occur in what remains of the twentieth century beyond anything that mankind accomplishes or deserves. In the last resort only this belief makes it reasonable to hope that the peoples now rich and those now poor will rise to the challenges of this period; that the nations will bury their quarrels before their quarrels bury them; and that the Christian Church will be so renewed and reformed that it conveys the light brought by Jesus to the modern and post-modern ages.

INDEX

Aaron, R., 160
African Churches, 227, 231, 236
Aggression, 53-5
Agriculture, 92-4, 129-30, 139-40
Aid to poorer nations, 126, 132
Alienation, 105-6, 120
Amino acids, 42
Anglicanism, 238
Antichrist, 162
Apes, 51, 55
Ardrey, R., 55
Argyle, M., 223
Armaments, 102
Asian Churches, 222, 227
Atheism, 59, 76-7
Attlee, C., 150

Babylon, 67-8
Barbour, I., 58, 60
Barth, K., 57, 218
Beckerman, W., 109
Beeson, T., 112, 157
Bell, D., 124
Belloc, H., 180
Benz, E., 61
Berdyaev, N., 157
Bible, 25-6, 64-74, 142-5, 159-60, 205-6, 212-18, 243-4
Birch, C., 84, 104
Birmingham Conference, 20
Blueprint for Survival, 105
Bolsheviks, 165-6
Bonhoeffer, D., 229
Bonino, J., 158
Bourdeaux, M., 227

Bowden, J., 17
Bowker, J., 60
Brain, 52-3, 202
Britain, 102-3, 108-10, 112-25, 149-56, 169-88, 223-4
British Council of Churches, 16, 90, 179
Bronowski, J., 31-3, 79
Buber, M., 200
Buddhism, 25, 196-7, 208, 216
Bühlmann, W., 227
Bullock Commission, 121-2
Bultmann, R., 17, 58, 215
Buren, P. v., 17
Butler, J., 64-5

Cambridge, 14, 18-19, 34
Camilleri, J., 83
Canterbury, 13-14
Cells, 43-4
Chance, 26, 201-2
Charismatics, 231
China, 89, 92, 98, 101, 131, 139, 156-7, 167, 222, 227
Choice of faith, 74-80
Christendom 19, 191-2
Christian Aid, 16
Christianity and Europe, 180-3
  freedom, 191-3, 212-13
  imperialism, 221-2
  Marxism, 158-61, 195
  other religions, 194-7
  science, 193, 198-9
Christology, 192, 208-18
Chromosomes, 44-5
Churches, 218-31

INDEX

Churchgoing, 218–21, 226
Churchill, W., 150, 175
Cities, 113–14, 139, 152
Clark, Lord, 31, 55–6, 79
Club of Rome, 86–7
Coal, 96
Colonialism, 16, 131, 212–13, 221, 227
Commodity agreements, 126
Communism, see Marxism
Comprehensive schools, 152
Consumerism, 112–13
Continents, 50
Contraception, 99, 236
Copernicus, 70, 209
Cox, H., 17
Cragg, K., 195
Creation, 57–8, 62–73, 80, 198–200
Crimes, 114
Crisis, 143–5
Crosland, A., 151
Cuba, 164, 168
Cupitt, D., 58

Dante, 70, 80
Darwin, C., 33, 46–7, 57, 181, 193
Davis, C., 234
Dawkins, R., 54
DDT, 85, 98
De-development, 104–6
Desmond, A. J., 49
Destructiveness, 54–5
Development, 131–9
Dickens, C., 169, 173
Dinosaurs, 49
Disarmament, 101
Discrimination, 134–5
Dispersed Church, 223–6
Divorce, 117

DNA, 42, 44, 46
Dobzhansky, T., 61
Dogmatism, 192–5, 237
Doom, 83–90

Earth's origins, 37–50
Earthwatch, 100
Education, 134–5, 152, 154
EEC, 130, 175–88
Ehrlich, P., 84
Einstein, A., 32, 34, 37
Eiseley, L., 27
Elements, 35–6
Eliot, T. S., 197
Elites, 135–6, 151–2
Energy, 95–7
Eschatology, 72–5, 142–4
Eucharist, 161, 230
Evolution's meaning, 25–7, 44–8, 57, 75–80, 140–1

Fawcett, T., 59
Fierro, A., 158
Fish supplies, 94
Flew, A., 57
Food supplies, 92–4
France, 89, 95, 153, 170, 173
Freud, S., 85
Friedman, I., 115
Fromm, E., 54

Gaitskell, H., 150, 176
Galbraith, J., 107
Galileo, 70
Gandhi, Mahatma, 135, 196
Gandhi, Mrs, 98, 169
Garaudy, R., 165
Gascoigne, B., 193
Geertz, C., 22–3
Genes, 26, 42, 45–7
George, S., 137

INDEX

Germany, 173, 219
Giddens, A., 125
Gladstone, W., 182
God, 24, 56, 59, 62–78, 142, 196–200, 243–5
Governments in Third World, 136–8
Grant, M., 213
Greece, 184, 220
Green Revolution, 91–2
Griffiths, B., 203
Guevara, C., 19

Hammarskjöld, D., 191, 196–7, 199–200
Hardy, A., 61
Harper, M., 230
Hastings, A., 227
Hayter, T., 132
Heath, E., 176
Hebblethwaite, P., 158, 238
Heilbroner, E., 86
Hick, J., 209, 216
Hill, M., 23
Hinduism, 63, 195–6, 208–9, 216, 223–4
Hirsch, F., 107–8
Hobbies, 116
Holland, S., 151
Holmes, N., 100
House of Commons, 15, 165–6
Housing, 109–10
Hoyle, F., 36, 40, 96
Human rights in Europe, 182
Huxley, A., 85
Huxley, J., 52, 57
Huxtable, J., 229
Hygiene, 98, 134

Ice Ages, 53–4
Idols, 200–8

Ikeda, D., 141
Illich, I., 135
Incarnation, 208–12
India, 92, 93, 98, 132–3, 135, 169
Industrial democracy, 120, 185
Industrialism, 106–10, 169–70, 179, 185
Infallibility, 234–7
Inflation, 115–16
International Monetary Fund, 103, 128
Ireland, 83, 187, 220
Islam, 22, 23, 25, 63, 183, 194–5, 216, 224
Italy, 174, 219

Japan, 120, 173, 225
Jenkins, Daniel, 186
Jenkins, David, 21
Jenkins, Roy, 176
Jesus, 66, 68, 71–4, 142, 160, 208–18, 223–5, 244
Jews, 63, 67, 206, 212, 216
John XXIII, 234
Johnson, D. G., 93
Johnson, P., 193
Johnston, W., 203, 236
Jones, A., 116
Justice, 111

Kahl, J., 194
Kane, M., 112
Kelly, P., 234
Kennet, Lord, 178
Keynes, J. M., 154
King, M. L., 229
Kingdom of God, 160, 214–15
Klostermaier, K., 196
Koran, 63, 194
Koyama, K., 197
Kuhn, T., 60

Küng, H., 216, 237

Labour Party, 150–5, 166
Lamarck, J.-B., 46
Lampe, G. W. H., 216
Latin America, 97, 131–2, 136, 158, 168–9, 227
Lauria, S., 43, 77
Leach, E., 83
Lear, 33
Leisure, 117–18
Lenin, V., 163–4
Liberation, 130–2, 161–2
Liberation theology, 158
Liberty, 111–13, 163
Lichtheim, G., 151
Life's origins, 33, 42–9
Limits to Growth, 83–8, 98
Liturgical movement, 230
Lomé Convention, 130
Lorenz, K., 54
Loss of nerve, 16, 30–2, 83–8
Lucas, J., 120
Lutheranism, 238
Luwum, J., 228

McClelland, W., 122
McCord, P., 234
McKenzie, J., 234
Macmillan, H., 170, 176
Macquarrie, J., 207
Maddox, J., 90
Magic, 56
Malthus, T., 86
Mammals, 50–1
Management, 122, 171
Man's origins, 51–5, 153, 199–200
Mao Tse-tung, 131, 157–8, 161, 164, 167
Marian dogmas, 235

Mark, R., 114
Martin, A., 84–5
Marxism, 27, 149, 154–74, 183
Mayor, S., 157
Mazedier, J. du, 118
Meditation, 203
Mendel, G., 46, 69
Metabolism, 44
Mind, 24, 33
Miracles, 56
Mishan, E. J., 107
Missionaries, 221–3
Mix in economy, 137
Mixed economy, 172–3
Models, 59–60, 205
Molecules, 41–2
Monod, J., 26, 40
Montagu, A., 25
Montefiore, H., 69
Moon, 38
Morality, 57
Morris, D., 113
Morton, J., 58
Motz, L., 79
Mowat, R., 180
Muslim, see Islam
Mutation, 47
Myrdal, G., 136
Myths, 59

Nankivell, O., 173
Nationalization, 153
Nationalism, 102, 185
Neanderthal man, 51, 53, 56
Needham, J., 158
Neill, S., 221
Neo-colonialism, 132
New international economic order, 127–8
New Left, 164
Newton, I., 33, 56

INDEX

Niebuhr, R., 157
Nuclear energy, 87–90, 96–7
Nucleic acids, 42
Nutrition, 133–4

O'Collins, G., 237
Oil, 95–6
Oppenheimer, R., 88
Orthodox Churches, 219, 238
Oxford, 14, 24
Oyster, 45

Packard, V., 104
Panikkar, R., 236
Papacy, 232–42
Paradigms, 59–60
Participation, 117–20
Particles, 34–5
Pasternak, B., 163
Patterson, W., 89
Paul, St, 66, 71, 72, 74
Paul VI, 102, 236–7
Peace, 101–3, 212
Peacocke, A., 48
Pentecostal Churches, 231
Perman, D., 226
Pius XII, 234–6
Planets, 37, 40–1
Planning, 153–4
Poland, 220
Pollution, 85, 99–100, 155
Population, 86–7, 92, 97–8, 106, 125, 142, 236
Port Said, 13, 16
Poverty in world, 16, 124–45
Property-owning, 118
Prophecy, 142–3
Proteins, 42
Protestantism, 192–3
Ptolemy, 70
Purpose in creation, 72–80

Racism, 16, 135, 228–9
Radical theology, 17
Rahner, K., 209–11
Ramsey, I., 24, 205
Ramsey, M., 20
Rawls, J., 111
Reich, C., 105
Religion, 22, 55–63, 141, 157, 205
Reproduction, 43–6
Resources, world's, 83–8, 93–4
Rhodes, F., 48
Ricardo, D., 86
Ritchie-Calder, Lord, 59
Robinson, J., 17
Roman Catholicism, 192–3, 219, 233–8
Rome, Treaty of, 176, 178
Rose, S., 51
Roubiczek, P., 57
Russia, 109, 153, 166–7, 225, 227
Ryle, G., 24

St Margaret's church, 15, 20
St Martin's church, 14
Schuman, R., 179, 183
Schweitzer, A., 229
Science, 32–3, 58–60
Scitovsky, T., 107
SCM, 20
SCM Press, 17
Scotland, 186
Service, 124–5
Sex, 44–5, 113–14
Sheppard, D., 113
Shorter, A., 236
Sleeman, J., 173
Smart, N., 204
Smith, A., 154
Social Capitalism, 172–3
  limits to growth, 107–8

INDEX

Social Capitalism [*contd.*]
  security, 109
Socialism, 151–6, 172–3
Solzhenitsyn, A., 163
South Africa, 16, 135
Spain, 184, 220
Species, 45
Stalin, J., 164
Stevenson, A., 84
Stars, 35–7
Strikes, 118–19
Substitute materials, 84–5
Sun, 37–40, 69–70
Sweden, 95, 119

Taiwan, 98, 133, 140
Tao, 63
Tariq Ali, 170
Taylor, G., 83
Teilhard de Chardin, 61
Television, 102, 117, 125
Temple, W., 157
Teresa, Mother, 229
Thomas, M., 225
Thorpe, W., 79–80
Tillich, P., 204–5
Time in creation, 48
Tinberg, 127
Toffler, A., 90
Tolkien, J., 25
Torres, C., 158
Toynbee, A., 141
Trade unions, 120–1
Transport, 110
Trotsky, L., 163–4, 168, 170

Unemployment, 123–4, 138–9, 185
United Nations, 103, 105–6, 128, 213
Unity of Churches, 229, 239

Universe, 33–7
USA, 93, 105, 107–8, 112, 115, 124, 129–30, 133, 152, 155, 170, 220–3
USE, 149, 175, 183
Utopia, 160, 164

Vatican Councils, 234, 237–8, 242
Vedas, 62
Vermes, G., 213
Vidler, A., 20
Violence, 14–15

Wales, 186
Ward, B., 82–3
Ward, K., 207
Warren, M., 20
Waste, 104
Wegener, A., 50
Weinberg, S., 34, 79
Welfare State, 156
Westermann, C., 67
Westminster, 14–15, 33, 187–8
Whitehead, A., 61
Wiles, M., 211
Wilson, H., 176
Wogaman, J., 173
Women's rights, 135–6
Working hours, 108
World Bank, 16, 132
World Council of Churches, 21, 90, 104, 118, 158, 229, 230, 239–41
Worship, 228–31

Yugoslavia, 120
Young, J. Z., 44
Young, N., 67

Zero growth, 104–10